SDGs

Talking about Global

IBCパブリッシング

カバーデザイン	石浜寿根　*photo:* アフロ
編 集 協 力	株式会社オフィス LEPS
英語編集協力	エド・ジェイコブ
イ ラ ス ト	テッド高橋

はじめに

下の図を見てください。何の形に見えるでしょうか？

どこからどう見ても三角形ですね。では、次の形は何に見えるでしょうか？

これも、誰が何と言おうと長方形ですね。では最後に、これはどうでしょうか？

　三角柱ですね。最初の三角形は三角柱を上から至近距離で見たときの形。2つめの長方形も至近距離で横から見たときの形。3つめは少し離れたところから全体を見たときの形です。このように、1つの視点だけで捉えると見えるものは1つにすぎませんが、広い視野でさまざまな角度から全体を見てみると、実はまったく違った形に見えることがあります。つまり、物事は多角的に見なければ全体像は見えてこないということです。
　本書は、近年、テレビや新聞、企業、学校の教科書などで見聞きするようになったSDGsというグローバルな取り組みを、関連する英語の語彙を学びながら基礎知識や社会問題を理解し、私たちの生活の中で何ができるかを考えるための「初めの一歩」となる本です。SDGsの17のゴールは一見すると私たちに直接関係のないことばかりかのように思えます。しかし、注目するポイントを変えて見てみたり、常識と考えていた思い込みをなくして考えてみたりすると、遠いとこ

ろで繋がっていたり、知らず知らずのうちに関係していたりすることに気づかされます。

　本書はバラエティ豊かな問題に答えながらSDGsについての理解を深めていくものです。関連語彙も豊富に取り上げているので、知識として身につくことができ、気になる世界の問題を英語でより深く理解する手助けとなるでしょう。

　対訳は、日本語に精通しているEd Jacobさんが、読みやすく自然な英文に仕上げてくださいました。本文中に日本語と英語の語句に色がついている箇所がありますが、対訳を読み進めるうえでの目印の役割や日本語に対する自然な英語表現を確認するという役割がありますので、学習のヒントにしてください。

　読み方は自由です。問題を解いて新たな発見をし、ネタとして友だちに話すだけでもいいでしょう。また、解説をじっくり読んで知的レベルをアップさせるのもいいでしょう。そこで少しでも疑問に感じることやより深く知りたいと思うことがあれば、ぜひ自分なりに考えたり調べたりしてみてください。そして、「専門家が言っているから正しい」とか「みんながやっている取り組みだからやったほうがいい」「常識的に考えると正しいはず」とすべてを鵜呑みにすることなく、「この論理は本当に正しいの？」「本当にその問題は“問題”なの？」「別の可能性はないの？」と適切に疑ったり、他の人の立場になって多角的・多面的に考えてみたりすることで、多くの人が気づかない別の新たな側面に気づくかもしれません。考えて調べ、行動し、うまくいかなかったら新たな解決策を探してみる。その一つ一つが自分の生活や未来の世界へときっとつながるはずです。

2022年12月
山口晴代

SDGs とは？

　SDGs（Sustainable Development Goals：持続可能な開発目標）は国連が2015年に打ち出した持続可能な社会の実現をめざす世界共通の目標です。世界には貧困・飢餓問題、環境問題、人権問題などさまざまな問題があり、世界の人口増加にともない地球そのものも限界に直面しています。これまでは、これらの問題を改善できる方法があっても積極的に実行せずに経済社会中心の生活を送ってきました。しかし、地球が悲鳴を上げ始めると、このままでは安心・安全な暮らしを人間が維持していくことは難しくなるのではと気づき始めました。そこで国連サミットで17のゴールと169のターゲットで構成されたSDGsがまとめられ、2030年までに目標を達成することを目指す取り組みが2016年からスタートしました。

　sustainable developmentは、人間の活動が自然環境に影響を及ぼすことなく維持され、長期的に継続していくことです。そして人間の活動を維持していくためには、誰一人取り残さず（Leave No One Behind）に世界のすべての人々が自分の能力を十分に発揮して課題に取り組み、みんなでより良い世界で暮らしていくことも意味しています。

　SDGsはいわばスローガンです。基本的な考えを示し、具体的な行動は私たちひとりひとりに委ねられているのが特徴です。

　SDGsの軸となる17のゴールは以前から社会問題になっていたものばかりです。

1. 貧困をなくそう

2. 飢餓をゼロに

3. すべての人に健康と福祉を

4. 質の高い教育をみんなに

5. ジェンダー平等を実現しよう

6. 安全な水とトイレを世界中に

7. エネルギーをみんなに、そしてクリーンに

8. 働きがいも経済成長も

9. 産業と技術革新の基盤をつくろう

10. 人や国の不平等をなくそう

11. 住み続けられるまちづくりを

12. つくる責任　つかう責任

13. 気候変動に具体的な対策を

14. 海の豊かさを守ろう

15. 陸の豊かさも守ろう

16. 平和と公正をすべての人に

17. パートナーシップで目標を達成しよう

　各ゴールはそれぞれが独立した課題ではなく相互につながり関係しています。例えば、地球温暖化への対策（Goal 13）を行うことで海や陸の問題が改善され（Goal 14, 15）、ひいては貧困や飢餓の減少にもつながります（Goal 1, 2）。質の高い教育がなされれば（Goal 4）、貧困の改善や（Goal 1）、ジェンダーや人・国の不平等の解消（Goal 5, 10）、働きがい・経済成長の解決にも結びつくでしょう（Goal 8）。

　SDGsの構造をよりわかりやすく表したものにThe SDGs Wedding Cake Model（SDGsウェディングケーキモデル）があります。スウェーデンの研究者ヨハン・ロックストローム博士が考案したもので、SDGsのゴールは大きく3つの階層「経済（Economy）」「社会（Society）」「環境（Biosphere）」で構成されています。持続可能な世界を支える基盤は調和の取れた「環境」で、土台がしっかり整うことで私たちの「社会」も成り立ち、安定した生活基盤のもと「経済」が発展・成長していくのです。そして、経済活動を循環させて持続可能な社会を作るためには国や企業、人々のパートナーシップが欠かせないことを、頂点にあるGoal 17が示しています。

The SDGs wedding cake

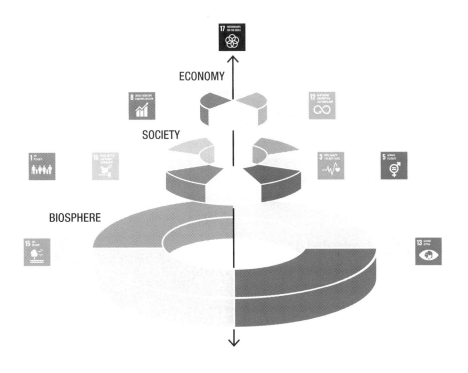

　しかしこのウェディングケーキは理想型であって、現在は下すぼまり（あるいはいびつな形）の不安定なウェディングケーキといえます。元の状態に戻していくには「環境」「社会」「経済」の構造と関連性を理解しながら課題と改善策を考えなくてはなりません。SDGsが目指す豊かで持続可能な社会への期限は2030年となっていますが、年限にとらわれることなくひとりひとりが持続可能な未来のために考え、一歩を踏み出し、つなげていくことが大切でしょう。

CONTENTS

Goal 1

貧困をなくそう
No Poverty

あらゆる場所で、あらゆる形態の貧困を終わらせる。
End poverty in all its forms everywhere.

「貧困」という言葉を聞くと、一日を生きるために必要な食べ物さえも買えないほどの厳しい状態をイメージするのではないでしょうか。確かに、アフリカや東南アジアなどの地域では、こうした「生きていくのが難しい状態の貧困」を抱えている人々がたくさんいます。

一方で日本でも、平均的な生活水準以下で暮らす人々が多くいる現状が社会的問題となっていて、人口の6人に1人（15.4パーセント）、子どもの7人に1人（13.5パーセント）が貧困に苦しんでいます。他人事ではない貧困問題に私たちも目を向けなければなりません。

参照：厚生労働省「令和元年 国民生活基礎調査」

貧困率

「貧困率」を英語で何と言えばよいでしょう。

① poverty percent　　② poverty ratio　　③ poverty rate

　「貧困率」とは、所得が国の平均値の半分に満たない人が全体に占める割合のことです。日本では厚生労働省が3年に1度調査してその変化の割合を公表しています。

　The "poverty rate" is the percentage of the total population whose income is less than half of the national average. In Japan, the Ministry of Health, Labour and Welfare conducts a survey every three years and publishes any changes in the rate.

Point

　「貧困」は英語でpovertyですが、「率」を表す単語が何かは迷うところです。選択肢のpercentもratioもrateもすべて「割合」を表す単語ですが、「貧困率」を表すときには③のrateを使います。rateは、「一定期間に全体から見たときの変化の割合」を示すときに使われる単語です。ほかに、出産率（birth rate）や失業率（unemployment rate）、外国為替相場（foreign exchange rate）などの例があります。

　①のpercentは単位の％（パーセント、百分率）を意味します。例えば、Ten percent of the world's population lives in poverty.（世界の人口の10パーセントが貧困状態に陥っています）のように使います。②のratioは「比」に相当し、「2つの数量や程度を比べたときの割合」を示すときに使われます。男女比（sex ratio）や円周率（ratio of a circle）がイメージしやすいでしょう。

　ちなみに、貧困率が「高い・低い」と言いたいときはhigh/lowを、「増加する・減少する」はincrease/decreaseを使うことを覚えておくと便利です。

Answer　③ poverty rate

人間が生きていくために必要なもの

下の図には、貧困をなくすために必要なものが散らばっています。この中から、生きていくために必要ではないものを選んでください。

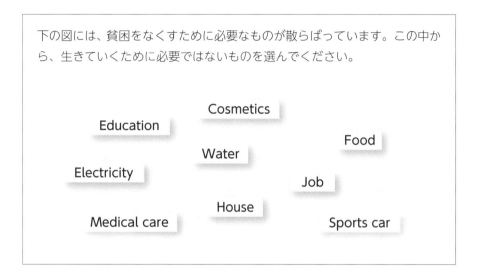

　貧困とは、食べ物、飲み水、仕事、教育、医療、住居、電気・ガスなどのエネルギーなど、生きていくために欠かせないものを手に入れられない状態のことです。化粧品やスポーツカーは、生きていくために絶対必要というわけではないので、この2つが答えです。

　Poverty is the lack of access to things that are essential for survival, such as food, drinking water, jobs, education, medical care, housing and energy, including electricity and gas. Cosmetics and sports cars are not absolutely necessary to survive, so these two are the answer!

Answer　　Cosmetics ／ Sports car

日本の貧困率

ここでは日本で何人に1人が貧困に苦しんでいるか考えてみましょう。①〜
④のうち何番が正解でしょう。

① 6人
② 7人
③ 10人
④ 20人

日本での貧困の基準は、一人暮らしをするときに1カ月にかかる平均金額、約
16.3万円を下回る、10万円以下の生活をしている場合です。このような貧困状態
のことを「相対的貧困」と言います。p. 11にあるように、日本では人口の6人に
1人（15.4パーセント）、子どもの7人に1人（13.5パーセント）が貧困に苦しんで
います。例えば、学校の35人クラスの中だと、5人の子どもが貧困ということです。
相対的貧困は見た目ではわかりにくく実態をつかむのが難しいため見過ごされが
ちですが、子どもの成長を妨げるので、深刻な問題です。

The poverty line in Japan is 100,000 yen per month, which is less than the
average cost of living alone, about 163,000 yen. As shown on page 11, one in
six (15.4 percent) people and one in seven (13.5 percent) children in Japan
suffer from poverty. For example, in a school class of 35 students, 5 children
will be poor. Relative poverty is often overlooked because it is hard to see and
grasping the actual situation is difficult, but it is a serious problem because it
hinders children's growth.

Answer ② 7人

絶対的貧困と相対的貧困

貧困には、根本的に生きていくことが難しい状態を表す「絶対的貧困」と、ある国や地域の平均的な生活水準と比べて貧しい状態を表す「相対的貧困」の２種類があります。次の各文が表す貧困状態は、「絶対的貧困」「相対的貧困」のどちらに当たると思いますか？

① Some families cannot afford food. ◯◯◯◯ are the only ◯◯◯◯◯◯◯◯ for these children. （　　　　）

② Some children ◯◯◯◯◯◯ ◯◯◯◯◯ ◯◯◯ to find something they can sell to get enough money that they can eat that day. （　　　　）

③ Some people live on less than $1.90 a day. （　　　　）

④ Some high school students work part-time to contribute to the household income. （　　　　）

⑤ Some children walk 30 minutes each way to get clean water. （　　　　）

それぞれの選択肢の訳は、以下のとおりです。

① 食費に回す十分なお金がない家庭があり、そこの子どもたちにとっては、学校の給食が唯一の栄養源となっています。

② その日一日に食べるお金を稼ぐために、ゴミ箱のごみをあさり、売れそうなものを見つけている子どもたちがいます。

③ 1日1.9ドル未満で生活をしている人々がいます。

④ 家計を支えるために、毎日アルバイトをしている高校生がいます。

⑤ 片道30分歩いて、きれいな水を調達している子どもたちがいます。

③の例文にあるように、1日1.9ドル未満で生活している人々は「絶対的貧困層」と定義され、英語では the absolute poor と呼ばれています。この、「the＋形容詞（または現在分詞・過去分詞）」の形で「〜層、〜な人々」という関連する集団を表すことができます。例えば、the poor（貧困層）、the rich（富裕層）、the young（若者）などです。通例、複数として扱われます。

Answer
① 相対的貧困
② 絶対的貧困
③ 絶対的貧困
④ 相対的貧困
⑤ 絶対的貧困

世界の絶対的貧困率

世界の約7億人が極度の貧困状態（絶対的貧困）にあると言われています（2017年時点）。これは世界の人口の何パーセントを占めていると思いますか？

① 5パーセント
② 10パーセント
③ 15パーセント
④ 20パーセント

　国連の発表によると、2017年の世界総人口は76億人。うち約7億人が絶対的貧困なので、約10パーセントを占めていることになります。実に、世界の10人に1人が一日2ドル以下でやっと生きている状況です。こうした層は、特に北アフリカを除くアフリカの国々、いわゆるサハラ以南のアフリカに集中していて、この層全体の60パーセントを占めています。

　According to the United Nations, the total world population in 2017 was 7.6 billion. About 700 million people are in absolute poverty, which means that they account for about 10 percent of the population. In fact, one in ten people in the world barely survives on less than $2 a day. This group is particularly concentrated in the part of Africa that excludes Northern Africa, which is known as sub-Saharan Africa, and accounts for 60 percent of the total.

Answer　② 10パーセント

広がる貧富の格差

貧困の原因の一つとされているのが貧富の格差。世界の１パーセントの超富裕層が、世界の富の 40 パーセントを占めています。その１パーセントの中の上位５人の大富豪の名前と、その職業を線で結んでください。

① Elon Musk ・　　　　・ 米マイクロソフト創業者

② Jeff Bezos ・　　　　・ 米投資会社バークシャー・ハサウェイ CEO

③ Bernard Arnault ・　　　　・ 米テスラ・モーターズ CEO

④ Bill Gates ・　　　　・ 仏 LVMH 取締役会長兼 CEO

⑤ Warren Buffett ・　　　　・ 米アマゾン創業者

　この５人は、米経済誌『フォーブス』が発表した2022年版の世界長者番付順に並んでいます。
　１位はイーロン・マスク。テスラ・モーターズは電気自動車ベンチャーです。マスクはほかにも宇宙開発企業スペースＸのCEOやブレイン・マシン・インターフェースを開発する企業ニューラリンクの共同創設者など、多くの肩書きをもっています。総資産はおよそ2,190億米ドル。
　２位はジェフ・ベゾス。世界的に有名なオンラインストアAmazon.comは、創業当初はオンライン書店としてスタートしました。
　３位はベルナール・アルノー。トップ５唯一のフランス人で、クリスチャン・ディオールやルイ・ヴィトンなどの高級ファッションブランドを展開するLVMH

（モエ・ヘネシー・モギビッシュ・ルイ・ヴィトン）グループのCEOです。

　4位はビル・ゲイツ。2020年にマイクロソフト取締役を退任し、夫婦で設立した慈善団体のビル＆メリンダ・ゲイツ財団の活動に力を入れています。

　5位はウォーレン・バフェット。バークシャー・ハサウェイは米国ネブラスカ州にある世界最大の投資持株会社で、バフェットは筆頭株主でもあります。

These five men are listed in the order of the 2022 edition of the Richest People in the World, published by *Forbes* magazine.

Number one is Elon Musk. Tesla Motors is an electric vehicle venture. Musk also holds many other titles, including CEO of the space exploration company SpaceX and is co-founder of Neuralink, a company developing brain-machine interfaces. His total assets are approximately US$219 billion.

In second place is Jeff Bezos. Amazon, the world-famous online store, started out as an online bookstore.

In third place is Bernard Arnault. The only French person in the top five, he is the CEO of the LVMH (Moët Hennessy Mogivish Louis Vuitton) Group, which owns luxury fashion brands, such as Christian Dior and Louis Vuitton.

Number four is Bill Gates, who retired from the Microsoft board in 2020 to focus on the Bill & Melinda Gates Foundation, a charitable organization he and his wife founded.

Fifth on the list is Warren Buffett. Berkshire Hathaway, located in Nebraska, USA, is the world's largest investment holding company, and Buffett is its largest shareholder.

Point

　ここに取り上げた大富豪の名前はさまざまなところで見聞きするので、顔と英語表記は覚えておきたいところです。CEOとはchief executive officerの頭字語で、「最高経営責任者」の意味です。企業のトップに位置する人には必ずと言っていいほど、この肩書きがついています。

Answer

① Elon Musk ＝ 米テスラ・モーターズ CEO

② Jeff Bezos ＝ 米アマゾン創業者

③ Bernard Arnault ＝ 仏 LVMH 取締役会長兼 CEO

④ Bill Gates ＝ 米マイクロソフト創業者

⑤ Warren Buffett ＝ 米投資会社バークシャー・ハサウェイ CEO

社会階級と貧困状態

下のイラストは社会階級と貧困状態をピラミッドで表したものです。それぞれのグループにあてはまる英語を下の語群から選んでください。

・The Middle Class　・Relative Poverty　・The Poor

・Absolute Poverty　・The Rich

　社会には、基本的に富裕層、中流層、貧困層の３つの階層があります。貧困層はさらに２区分に分かれていて、その国の生活水準を下回っている状態のことを相対的貧困、最低限の日常生活もままならない状態のことを絶対的貧困と言います。

　世界の富は、その多くをごく一部の億万長者が占めているとされていて、富の不平等が起こることで貧困が生じると考えられています。また、同じ国・地域の中でも経済格差が起こり、問題になっています。この富の偏りをいかにして再分配していくかが、貧困問題解決の鍵です。

There are basically three different social classes: the rich, the middle class, and the poor. The poor are further divided into two categories: relative poverty, which is below the standard of living in a country, and absolute poverty, which is below the minimum standard of living in a country.

It is believed that most of the world's wealth is held by a small number of billionaires, and that poverty is caused by wealth inequality. Economic disparity also occurs within the same country or region, which has become a problem. How to redistribute this wealth inequality is the key to solving the poverty problem.

Answer

① The Rich
② The Middle Class
③ Relative Poverty
④ Absolute Poverty
⑤ The Poor

貧困問題に関する用語

次の貧困問題に関する単語とその意味を線で結んでください。

① welfare　　　　　　　・　　　　　　　・　失業

② low income　　　　　・　　　　　　　・　低賃金

③ unemployment　　　・　　　　　　　・　生活保護

④ household　　　　　・　　　　　　　・　低収入

⑤ low wage　　　　　・　　　　　　　・　世帯、家庭

Point

　①は livelihood assistance と言うこともできます。②の income「収入」の反意語「支出」は spend です。③の unemployment の接頭辞の un- には、not（否定）の意味と、反対の動作を表す意味（例：unfold（fold「折り畳む」の反対の動作→「開く」）があります。この場合は employment（仕事）がないということなので、「失業」です。④の household は「（血縁の有無にかかわらず）同じ家に住んで、生活を共にする人たち」のことなので、例えば、住み込みのお手伝いさんも household の一員とみなされます。⑤の wage は「日給、週給」など短期に支払われる給与のことです。会社員のように毎月の固定給を表すときには salary を使います。

Answer

① welfare ＝ 生活保護

② low income ＝ 低収入

③ unemployment ＝ 失業

④ household ＝ 世帯、家庭

⑤ low wage ＝ 低賃金

経済格差

次の各説明文に当てはまる言葉を、下の語群から選んでください。

① countries with high levels of industrial activity and where people generally have high incomes
② countries that have less developed industries and whose standard of living, income and economic and industrial development remain generally below average
③ the least developed countries that are at the low end of the poverty scale with the lowest level of development

· developing countries

· developed countries

· the Fourth World

①は「高度の産業活動が活発で、一般に高所得の人々がいる国々」のことで、先進国を説明しています。国連開発計画が発表した2022年の最先進国上位10カ国は、1位ノルウェー、2位アイルランドとスイス、4位アイスランドと香港、6位ドイツ、7位スウェーデン、8位オーストラリアとオランダ、10位デンマークで、日本は19位に入っています。

②は「発達した産業が少なく、生活水準や所得、経済産業の発達が依然としておおむね平均以下の国々」ということなので、開発途上国、発展途上国のことを指します。

③は「貧困線最下部で（産業などの）発達が最低レベルの後発開発途上国」という意味で、第4世界となります。これまでは生活水準の高い国順に第1世界、第2世界、第3世界という3つの世界モデルで区分していましたが、近年では開発途上国の中でもさらに発展が遅れている国々のことを第4世界（後発開発途上国）あるいは「最貧国」と定義しています。エチオピアやスーダン、コンゴなどのサハラ以南のアフリカ地域や、アフガニスタン、ミャンマーやラオス、カンボジア

など47カ国が最貧国として報告されています。

    ＊ちなみに、the Third World や the Fourth World という分類表記は、侮辱的な表現と捉えられることがあるため、知識のみにとどめ、使う場合には注意が必要です。

① describes developed countries, which are "countries with high levels of industrial activity and where people generally have high incomes." The top 10 most developed countries in 2022, according to the United Nations Development Program, are Norway (1st), Ireland and Switzerland (2nd), Iceland and Hong Kong (4th), Germany (6th), Sweden (7th), Australia and the Netherlands (8th), Denmark (10th). Japan is in 19th place.

② refers to developing and underdeveloped countries, since it means "countries that have less developed industries and whose standard of living, income and economic and industrial development remain generally below average."

③ means "the least developed countries that are at the low end of the poverty scale with the lowest level of development," which is the Fourth World. In the past, countries were classified according to a three-world model: First World, Second World and Third World, in descending order of their standard of living. In recent years, however, the Fourth World (least developed countries) or "poorest countries" have been defined as those that are even less developed. The 47 poorest countries include Ethiopia, Sudan, Congo and other sub-Saharan African countries, as well as Afghanistan, Myanmar, Laos and Cambodia.

Answer ▶
① developed countries
② developing countries
③ the fourth world

貧困の連鎖

下の図は「貧困の連鎖」(Poverty Cycle) を表したものです。各空欄に当てはまる語句を、下の語群から選んでみましょう。

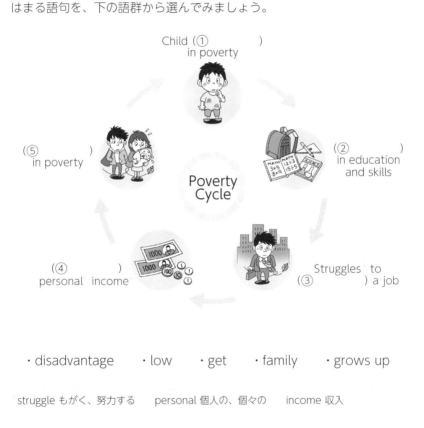

Child (① 　　　　　)
in poverty

(② 　　　　　)
in education
and skills

Struggles to
(③ 　　　　　) a job

(④ 　　　　　)
personal income

(⑤ 　　　　　)
in poverty

Poverty
Cycle

- ・disadvantage　・low　・get　・family　・grows up

struggle もがく、努力する　　personal 個人の、個々の　　income 収入

　貧困は、かならずしもお金がなくて貧しいというだけにとどまりません。図のように、親が貧困だと、その子どもも貧しい中で成長し、貧しいがゆえに十分な教育を受けられずに技術や知識を身につける機会を失うことにつながります。そうなると職業の選択肢が少なくなり、低賃金の不安定な仕事にしか就くことがで

25

きなくなってしまいます。そんな状態で結婚しても、また同じ貧困のサイクルに入ってしまい、なかなか抜け出すことができません。貧困の連鎖を断ち切るためには経済面の支援だけではなく、質の高い教育の支援などさまざまな側面からのアプローチが必要になってきます。

Poverty is not necessarily limited to being poor due to lack of money. As shown in the illustration, when parents are poor, their children also grow up poor, and because they are poor, they do not have access to adequate education, which leads to a loss of opportunities to acquire skills and knowledge. This leads to fewer job options and only low-paid, unstable jobs. Even if they get married in such a situation, they will enter the same cycle of poverty again, and it will be difficult to break out of. In order to break the cycle of poverty, it is necessary to use various approaches to deal with the situation, including support for quality education, in addition to economic support.

Point

選択肢の単語の意味はそれぞれ、disadvantage が「不利」、low が「低い」、get が「得る」、family が「家族」、grow up が「成長する」です。

Answer
① Child (grows up) in poverty
② (Disadvantage) in education and skills
③ Struggles to (get) a job
④ (Low) personal income
⑤ (Family) in poverty

「貧困をなくそう」

── そのために、あなたは何ができると思いますか？

What can you do to "end poverty"?

　国やNGOなどの組織が取る解決策には、貧しい国のインフラ（ガス、水道、電気、道路、路線、公共施設など、日々の生活を支える基盤）などの環境面を整える支援があります。食糧不足を解消させるために、ある程度の期間、食糧を支援するのもいいでしょう。しかし、長期的に見た場合は、その国の人々が自立できるような支援、例えば技術を教えて生産者や労働者の生活を改善したり、教育の質を改善して多くの人に優れた教育の場を提供したり、さらには医療も充実させなければなりません。

　国や地域、国家間の富の格差による貧困には、Goal 10「人や国の不平等をなくそう」にもつながりますが、富裕層や大手企業が得る富を社会貢献に生かす取り組みを考えたり、年金や給付金などで富を再分配したりする必要があります。

　個人でできる小さな取り組みは、お金や物資の寄付やフェアトレード製品を買うことでしょうか。フェアトレードとは、発展途上国で作られた製品について、生産者が適切な収入を得られるように正当な価格を設定して行う取引のことです。製品には、必ず国際フェアトレード認証ラベルがついていて、フェアトレードチョコレートやフェアトレードコーヒー、バッグなどいろいろなものがあります。自分ができることに少しずつ取り組めるといいでしょう。

　Some solutions that countries, NGOs and other organizations utilize include helping poor countries improve aspects of their environment, such as infrastructure (gas, water, electricity, roads, rail lines, utilities and other foundations of daily life). It is also a good idea to provide food aid for a certain period of time in order to alleviate food shortages. However, in the long run, we must provide assistance that will enable the people of the country to become self-reliant, for example, by teaching them about technology to improve the lives of producers and workers, improving the quality of education to provide many people with excellent educational opportunities and even improving medical care.

For poverty caused by wealth disparity among countries, regions and nations, which is also connected to Goal 10, "Eliminate Inequality among People and Nations," we need to consider initiatives to utilize the wealth earned by wealthy people and major corporations to make social contributions, and to redistribute wealth through pensions and benefits.

Small efforts that individuals can make include donating money or goods or buying fair trade products. Fair trade is trade in products made in developing countries at fair prices that allow producers to earn a fair income. These products always bear the international fair trade certification label, and there are various kinds of fair-trade chocolate, fair-trade coffee, bags and so on. It is a good idea to work on what you can do little by little.

Goal 2

飢餓をゼロに
Zero Hunger

飢餓を終わらせ、食糧安全保障および栄養改善を実現し、
持続可能な農業を促進する。

**End hunger, achieve food security and improved nutrition
and promote sustainable agriculture.**

　世界では9人に1人、8.1億人以上の人が飢餓に苦しんでいます。特に体力のない赤ん坊や子どもへの影響は深刻で、5歳未満の子どもの4人に1人（1億5,600万人）は栄養不足で十分に成長できなかったり、飢餓が原因で命が失われたりしています。
　飢餓の原因として、森林伐採、干ばつ・洪水などの自然災害、人口の増加、各地で起こる紛争などが挙げられますが、それだけが原因ではありません。じつは私たちの生活も飢餓に関わっているのです。

参照：国連「世界の食料安全保障と栄養の現状2017」
国連WFP「ハンガーマップ2021」

飢餓に関する用語

飢餓に関する英単語をいくつか紹介します。次の語句とその意味を線で結んでみてください。

① hunger ・ ・ 飢饉、大規模な食糧不足

② food shortage ・ ・ 栄養不良 [失調]

③ famine ・ ・ 飢える

④ malnutrition ・ ・ 飢え、飢餓

⑤ starve ・ ・ 食料 [食糧] 不足、食糧難

Point

①の hunger は、単にお腹が空いた状態から深刻な飢えまで、空腹全般を表す表現です。③の famine は、食べ物がない状況が長期間続くイメージで、hunger より深刻な状態。主に集団や地域の状況について使われます。⑤の starve の名詞形は starvation（飢餓・餓死）で、famine と同じように長期間の飢餓状態を表します。主に個人の状態について使われます。

Answer ① hunger = 飢え、飢餓

② food shortage = 食料 [食糧] 不足、食糧難

③ famine = 飢饉、大規模な食糧不足

④ malnutrition = 栄養不良 [失調]

⑤ starve = 飢える

飢餓を英語で説明

飢餓の意味を説明した文があります。日本語を参考にしながら、空欄に当てはまる単語を下の語群から選んで文を完成してください。

Hunger: (　①　) of food, especially for a long period of
(　②　), that can cause illness or (　③　).

・death
・lack
・time

especially 特に、とりわけ　　period 期間　　cause 引き起こす

Point

　空欄①のlackは「不足」という意味の名詞で、lack of ～（～の不足）という形で使われることが多い語です。空欄②にはtime（時間）が入ります。a period of timeで「（一定の）期間、時間、時期」という意味なので、かたまりで覚えておくといいでしょう。空欄③には、病気や死を引き起こす可能性があるということから、death（死）が入ります。

Answer
① lack
② time
③ death

食品ロス

「食品ロス（フードロス）」を英語で何と言いますか？

① food loss
② food waste
③ food lost

　日本語で言う「食品ロス」あるいは「フードロス」とは、まだ食べられる状態にあるにもかかわらず、何らかの理由で廃棄されてしまう食品のこと。主に、スーパーや飲食店、家庭での「食品廃棄物」のことを指します。

　英語では、生産や製造などの過程で生じる食品廃棄物のことをfood lossと言い、レストランやスーパー、消費者によって捨てられてしまう状態のことをfood wasteと言います。

　例えば、傷がついたり欠けてしまった果物などで、商品としてはなかなか売れないものは、生産者が廃棄してしまいますが、このよう場合はfood lossと見なされます。

同じく、ツナ缶を作るときに取り除かれた魚の骨や皮も食べられない食品廃棄物なので、food lossにカテゴリーされます。一方、賞味期限が切れたコンビニの弁当などは、賞味期限が切れただけでまだ食べられる可能性があるにもかかわらず廃棄されてしまうため、food wasteに当たります。

　世界のさまざまな国で、品質に問題はないが流通させることのできない食品を企業などから集めて、食料を必要とする福祉施設や生活困窮者へ無償提供する「フードバンク（food bank）」という活動が行われています。日本でも2000年以降、フードバンク活動が始まりましたが、食品ロスや貧困問題への認識がまだ不十分なため、なかなか活動が浸透していないのが現実です。

The Japanese term *fūdo rosu* refers to food that is still edible but is discarded for some reason. It mainly refers to "food waste" from supermarkets, restaurants and households.

In English, food waste generated in processes such as production and manufacturing is called "food loss," and when food is thrown away by restaurants, supermarkets, and consumers, it is called "food waste."

For example, when producers discard damaged or bruised fruits that are difficult to sell, it is considered food loss.

Similarly, fish bones and skin removed during the production of canned tuna are inedible food waste and are therefore categorized as food loss. On the other hand, convenience store box lunches past the expiration dates are considered food waste because they are discarded at a later stage.

In various countries around the world, "food banks" collect food that has no quality problems but cannot be distributed and provide it free of charge to welfare facilities and people in need. Food banks first opened in Japan in 2000, but the reality is that they have not become common because there is still insufficient awareness of food loss and poverty issues.

Answer ② food waste

飢餓に苦しむ人の割合

世界では何人に1人が飢餓に苦しんでいると思いますか？

① 2.6人
② 4人
③ 4.6人
④ 9人

　世界では9人に1人、およそ8.2億人が飢餓に苦しんでいます。ちなみに、選択肢②の「4人」という数に関係のある事実として、栄養不良の結果、身体と精神面での十分な発達ができない5歳未満の子どもの割合が「4人に1人」であるということが挙げられます。

　One in nine people in the world, or approximately 820 million people, suffer from hunger. Incidentally, a fact related to the number "4" in option ② is that "one in four" children under the age of 5 are not able to fully develop physically and mentally as a result of malnutrition.

Answer ④ 9人

国連世界食糧計画

国連 WFP（国連世界食糧計画）の正式名称は次のどれでしょうか？

① United National World Food Plan
② United Nations World Food Programming
③ United Nations World Food Programme
④ United National World Food Project

Point

　国連や UN という略語は新聞やニュースでよく見聞きしますが、その正式名称は国際連合です。計画に当たる語として、plan や project もよく使われますが、ここでは programme を使います。この programme のつづりはイギリス式で、アメリカ式の program ではない点に注意しましょう。

　ちなみに、イギリスではコンピュータ関連用語以外は、ほぼこの programme というつづりを使います。現在分詞と過去分詞はそれぞれ programming、programmed と、m を 2 つ重ねてつづります。この点は基本的にアメリカ英語でも同じです。ただし、アメリカでは m が 1 つの programing や programed を使うことも容認されつつあります。

Answer　③ United Nations World Food Programme

森林再生

次の各説明文に当てはまる単語を、下の語群から選んでください。

① The cutting down of trees in a large area, or the destruction* of forests by people

② A forest in a tropical* area that receives* a lot of rain

③ The restoration* or replanting* of a forest that had been reduced* by fire* or cutting

- rain forest
- reforestation
- deforestation

*destruction 破壊   tropical 熱帯の   receive 被る、受ける   restoration 再生
replant 移植   reduce 減少する   fire 火事

Point

　選択肢の意味はそれぞれ、rain forest が「熱帯雨林」、reforestation が「森林再生」、deforestation が「森林伐採」です。

　説明文①は、「広い範囲で木々を伐採したり、人が森林を破壊したりする状態」ということなので、deforestation が当てはまります。説明文②は、「雨量が多い熱帯地域に生育する森林」という意味なので、rain forest が正解です。説明文③は、「火事や伐採によって減少した森林を再生したり移植したりすること」なので、reforestation です。

　選択肢の単語の意味がよくわからなかったり、説明文が十分に理解できなかったりしても、単語の一部がヒントになって答えを導き出すことができます。例えば、reforestation や deforestation の頭についている re- や de- は接頭辞と言い、それ自体に意味があります。re- は「後ろへ、反対に、再び」、de- は「離れて、下に、徹底的

に、反対」などを表します。例えばreforestationは、re（再び）| forest（森林）| ation（すること、するもの）→「再び森林にすること」→「森林再生」ということです。

Answer ① deforestation

② rain forest

③ reforestation

「ハンガーマップ 2021」を見て、下の各文の内容が合っていれば T を、間違っていれば F をつけてください。

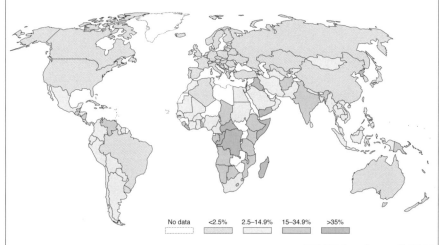

国連WFP「ハンガーマップ」を改編

① In developed countries, such as the United States and Japan, chronic hunger is 5 percent.

アメリカや日本などの先進国では、慢性的な飢餓は 5 パーセントである。　　　（　　　）

② Central Africa and Madagascar are the only countries where more than 35 percent of the population is undernourished.

栄養不足の人口の割合が 35 パーセント以上の国は、中央アフリカとマダガスカルである。　　　（　　　）

③ At the Americas, the Southern Hemisphere tends to have a lower proportion of undernourished people compared with the Northern Hemisphere.

アメリカ大陸において、南半球と北半球では、南半球の方が栄養不足人口の割合が低い傾向にある。　　　（　　　）

　「ハンガーマップ」とは、国連WFPが作成した、世界の飢餓の状況を栄養不足の人口の割合により国ごとに段階分けした世界地図です。現在の傾向が続くと、2030年までに飢餓人口は8億4,000万人に達してしまうと予想されているようです。

　3つの文の中で正しいのは②です。中央アフリカはアフリカ大陸の真ん中あたりに位置し、マダガスカルはアフリカ大陸南東海岸沖に浮かぶ島です。それぞれの国がどこにあるのかわからなくても、栄養不足の人口の割合が35パーセント以上を示す濃いグリーンの国を探していけば、すぐに見つかるでしょう。

　①は、アメリカと日本がうすいグレーで、2.5パーセント以下という一番低い割合に当てはまるため、間違いです。③も、アメリカ大陸において、北半球にはカナダとアメリカ合衆国に加えて中南米も含まれるため、間違いです。中南米の状況を見てみると、15–34.9パーセントの国々がいくつかあり、栄養不足人口の割合がオーストラリア大陸よりも高いことがわかります。

　The Hunger Map is a world map created by the United Nations World Food Programme (WFP) that shows the world's undernourished population in some levels. It appears that if current trends continue, the number of hungry people will reach 840 million by 2030.

　Of the three statements, the correct one is ②. Central Africa is located in the middle of the African continent, and Madagascar is an island off the southeast coast of Africa. Even if you don't know where each of these countries is located, you can easily find them by looking for the dark green countries where 35 percent or more of the population is undernourished.

　① is wrong because the United States and Japan are light gray, which indicates the lowest percentage of 2.5 percent or less. ③ is also wrong because looking at the Americas, the Northern Hemisphere includes Central America in addition to Canada and the United States. If we look at Latin America, we see that the percentage of the population that is undernourished is higher than in Australia since some of the countries in Latin America indicate 15 and 34.9 percent.

Answer　　①F　②T　③F

39

飢餓の原因

下の図には、さまざまな語句が散らばっています。この中から、飢餓の原因と考えられるものを選んでください。

Decent* working environment

Fair trade

Farm crop*

Natural disaster*

Environmental destruction*

Sustainable agriculture

*decent まっとうな、適切な   crop 作物   disaster 災害、天災
destruction 破壊、破滅

　飢餓の原因としてまず思いつくのは、自然災害ではないでしょうか。自然災害には、長い間雨が降らない水不足の状態の干ばつもあれば、大型台風や局地的豪雨などを引き起こす極端な気候変動による洪水もあります。いずれも農作物に深刻な被害を及ぼします。

　森林破壊などの環境破壊もまた、飢餓の原因の一つです。農林水産省によると、2020年の世界の森林面積は約41億ヘクタールあり、世界の陸地面積の31パーセントを占めています。地球は7割が海、3割が陸地なので、地球全体からみると森林はたったの1割なのです。そんなに少ない森林を減少させる要因には、広大な農地や日常生活に必要な燃料を作るための森林伐採や、干ばつ、森林火災などがあります。このような森林破壊による環境の変化で、動植物の生態系が崩れたり、農作物が育ちにくくなったりして、食料不足になり飢えが発生してしまいます。

40

先進国は、これらが原因で飢餓に苦しむ国々に対して、sustainable agriculture（持続可能な農業）を教えたり、公正な貿易やまっとうな労働環境を整えたりすることで、安定した食料生産のしくみを伝えて支援する必要があるでしょう。

The first thing that comes to mind as a cause of hunger is probably natural disasters. Natural disasters include droughts, which are long periods during which there is little rain and a lack of water, and floods resulting from extreme climate change, which cause large typhoons and torrential localized rains. Both can cause serious damage to crops.

Environmental destruction, such as deforestation, is another cause of hunger. According to the Ministry of Agriculture, Forestry and Fisheries, the world's forested area in 2020 was approximately 4.1 billion hectares, accounting for 31 percent of the world's land area. Since 70 percent of the earth is ocean and 30 percent is land, forests account for only 10 percent of the earth's total area. Factors that reduce forest cover include deforestation for the purpose of producing vast tracts of land for agriculture and fuel for daily life, drought and forest fires. These environmental changes caused by deforestation disrupt the ecosystems of plants and animals and make it difficult for crops to grow, resulting in food shortages and hunger.

Developed nations need to support countries suffering from hunger by teaching about sustainable agriculture, fair trade and decent working environment, and by providing a stable food production system.

Answer   Natural disaster ／ Environmental destruction

人口爆発

「人口爆発」を英語で何と言うでしょう？

① population bang
② population pop
③ population explosion

　「人口爆発」は、自然災害や環境破壊と同じく飢餓の原因となる現象です。
　昔から世界の人口の増加は穏やかに進んではいましたが、18世紀半ばから19世紀にかけての産業革命以降、ヨーロッパでは人口が200年間で5倍、アメリカでは10倍に爆発的に増加しています。このことから、産業の発達と経済の成長、医療の進歩による死亡率の低下などが人口の劇的な増加の要因であることは明らかです。
　現在では先進国の人口の増加は穏やかですが、一方で、アフリカや東南アジアでは大幅に増え続けています。理由の一つとして、先進国の企業が発展途上国の人々を安い賃金で労働させるため、発展途上国ではいくら働いても満足な収入が得られず飢餓や貧困が生まれ、働き手を確保するために多くの子どもを産まざるを得ないという状況が挙げられます。
　このまま世界の人口が増え続けると、2055年には100億人を超えるとも言われています。人口爆発の裏側にある問題を理解しつつ、先進国がリードして解決する必要があるでしょう。

　The "population explosion" is a phenomenon that causes hunger as well as natural disasters and environmental destruction.

　Although the world's population once always grew at a moderate rate, since the Industrial Revolution of the mid-18th to 19th centuries, the population has exploded, growing five-fold in Europe and ten-fold in the United States over the last 200 years. It is clear from this that industrial development and economic growth, as well as declining mortality rates due to advances in medicine, were factors in the dramatic increase in population.

Today, population growth in developed countries is moderate, while it continues to increase substantially in Africa and Southeast Asia. One of the reasons is that companies in developed countries force people in developing countries to work for low wages, which creates hunger and poverty in developing countries because they cannot earn a satisfactory income no matter how much they work, and they are forced to have many children in order to maintain the workforce.

If the world's population continues to grow at its current rate, it is estimated that it will exceed 10 billion by 2055. Developed countries will need to understand the problems behind the population explosion while taking the lead in solving them.

Answer   ③ population explosion

食糧自給率

日本の食料自給率は低いことが知られていますが、何パーセントだと思いますか？

① 27 パーセント
② 37 パーセント
③ 47 パーセント

　食料自給率とは、その国の食料供給に対する国内生産の割合を示す指標で、主に、カロリーに着目し、国民1人当たりに供給される熱量に対する国内生産の割合を示しています。農林水産省によると、2020年度のカロリーベース計算の日本の食料自給率は37パーセント。前年度より1パーセント低く、過去最低となっています。日本の食料自給率の低さは、農業従事者の高齢化とともに若い世代の就農者が少ないことや、大雨や日照不足、気温の上昇などの気候変動で農作物が育ちにくくなっていることなどから、どうしても食料の多くを海外からの輸入に頼らざるを得なくなっていることが原因です。

　今後は、世界的に長引いた新型コロナウイルスによる混乱や、ウクライナ紛争などの国際情勢が原因で、海外からの物流が滞ったり、輸入品の値段が高騰したりと、大なり小なり日本も食料危機になる可能性があるかもしれません。

　The food self-sufficiency ratio is an indicator that shows the ratio of domestic production to a country's food supply. It mainly focuses on calories and shows the ratio of domestic production to the amount of heat supplied per capita. According to the Ministry of Agriculture, Forestry and Fisheries, Japan's food self-sufficiency ratio calculated on a calorie basis for the fiscal year 2020 is 37 percent. This is 1 percent lower than the previous year and the lowest ever. Japan's low food self-sufficiency rate is due to aging of the farming population and the small number of young farmers, as well as the results of climate change, such as heavy rainfall, lack of sunlight and rising temperatures, which make it difficult for crops to grow.

In the future, Japan may also face a food crisis, large or small, as a result of the chaos caused by the protracted global outbreak of the COVID-19 virus, the Ukrainian conflict and other international situations that may disrupt distribution from overseas and cause prices of imported goods to skyrocket.

Point

「食料自給率」は英語でfood self-sufficiency ratio と言います。selfには「自己の、それ自体で」といった意味があり、「十分な数、たっぷりあること」などを表す名詞 sufficiency とハイフンでつなげると「自給自足」という意味の単語になります。

Answer　② 37 パーセント

「飢餓をゼロに」

——そのためにあなたは何ができると思いますか？

What can you do to achieve "zero hunger"?

　飢餓には、「突発的な飢餓」と「慢性的な飢餓」があります。突発的な事態が原因で食料不足になると、メディアが大々的に取り上げるため、比較的短期間で支援が集まりやすく、私たちも募金や物資の支援によって一時的に協力することができます。一方で、慢性的な飢餓はあまり表面化せずに問題が深刻化し、飢餓の連鎖が起きてしまいます。慢性的な飢餓の解決には、インフラを整えることが重要ですが、先進国がやみくもに途上国に不足するものを作ったり提供したりするのではなく、途上国の人々が自力で将来にわたって安定した食料生産ができるように、先進国が持続可能な農業技術を伝えたり、公正な貿易の仕組み作りを広めたりするべきでしょう。

　食料の大半を輸入に頼る日本では、食品ロスをなくすために、食べられる分だけを作ったり、スーパーなどでなるべく賞味期限が近いものを選んで買ったりすることができます。また、地元で採れた野菜や果物を食べる「地産地消」を意識したり、国産の商品を選んだりすることもできるでしょう。さらにfood driveという方法もあります。driveには「運転」のほかに、「（募金や選挙などの）活動、運動」という意味があり、food driveは「食べ物を集める運動」のことです。フードドライブは、アメリカで生活困窮者支援の目的で始まったボランティア活動の一つで、家庭で余っている食べ物を学校や職場などに持ち寄って、まとめて福祉施設や団体、フードバンクに寄付する活動です。一つ一つは小さな取り組みですが、それらが日本や世界の未来を支えることは確かです。

　There are two types of hunger, "sudden hunger" and "chronic hunger." When a sudden situation causes food shortages, the media covers it extensively, making it easy to gather support in a relatively short period of time, and we can help temporarily by donating funds and supplies. Chronic hunger, on the other hand, does not surface as often, but the problem becomes more serious and a cycle of hunger occurs. To solve chronic hunger, it is important to build infrastructure. However, developed countries should not blindly create it or automatically provide developing countries with whatever they lack. Rather, they should teach sustainable agricultural technologies and promote fair trade systems so that people in developing countries will be able to produce food stably on their own in the future.

In Japan, which relies on imports for the majority of its food, people can eliminate food loss by cooking only what they can eat, or by selecting and buying items at supermarkets that are as close to their expiration date as possible. We can also be conscious of "local production for local consumption," eating locally grown fruits and vegetables, and choosing domestically produced products. There is also the food drive method. As well as the meaning of "driving a vehicle," the word "drive" can mean "activity or movement (such as fundraising or campaigning)," and a food drive is a "drive" to collect food. Food drives are volunteer activities started in the US to support the needy, in which people bring surplus food from their homes to schools, workplaces, etc., and collectively donate it to welfare facilities, organizations and food banks. Each of these activities is a small effort, but it is certain that they will contribute to the future of Japan and the world.

Goal 3
すべての人に健康と福祉を
Good Health and Well-Being

あらゆる年齢のすべての人々の健康的な生活を確保し、福祉を促進する。

Ensure healthy lives and promote well-being for all at all ages.

　新型コロナウイルス（COVID-19）によるパンデミックの影響で、WHO（世界保健機構）は2022年までに世界中で626万人以上が死亡したと発表しています。しかし、それ以前から、世界では年間およそ500万人もの子どもたちが、さまざまな理由で5歳までに亡くなっています。また、「世界三大感染症」によって、途上国を中心に毎年何百万人もが亡くなっていることを知っているでしょうか。

　一方、日本では、生活習慣病が死因の約6割を占め、心の病などが原因による自殺者が年間約2万人いるといった先進国特有の問題があります。超高齢化社会としての年金や医療費の問題などとともに、異なる側面から健康と福祉を考える必要があるでしょう。

参照：WHO Coronavirus (COVID-19) Dashboard
UNICEF Levels and Trends in Child Mortality 2022

WHO

WHO（世界保健機構）は新聞やニュースでよく見聞きする言葉で、日本語名称は小学校の教科書にも掲載されています。国連の専門機関で、本部はスイスのジュネーブにあります。「人種・宗教・政治信条や経済的・社会的条件によって差別されることなく、すべての人々の健康を増進し保護する目的」で設立されました。加盟国は194カ国で、日本は1951年に加盟しています。

WHOのマークをよく見ると、国連のシンボルマークの上にヘビが絡みつく杖が重なっています。この杖はギリシャ神話に出てくる治療の神・アスクレピオスが持っていたものとされ、ヘビが巻きつく杖が医療・医学の象徴になったようです。このアスクレピオスの杖は世界的に医療・医学の象徴として広まり、日本でも救急車や日本救急救命学会のマークの一部に使われています。また、アスクレピオスの娘で健康の守護神ヒュギエイア（Hygieia）の名前は「衛生学」を表すhygieneの語源とされています。

The World Health Organization (WHO) is a name often seen and heard in newspapers and news reports, and its Japanese name can be found in elementary school textbooks. It is a specialized agency of the United Nations, with its headquarters in Geneva, Switzerland. It was established "to promote and protect the health of all people without discrimination based on race, religion, political beliefs or economic or social conditions." There are 194 member countries, and Japan became a member in 1951.

If you look closely at the WHO symbol, you will see a staff with a snake entwined around it superimposed over the UN symbol. This staff is said to have belonged to Asklepios, the god of healing in Greek mythology, and the staff with snakes coiling around it has become a symbol of medicine and medical science. The staff of Asklepios has spread worldwide as a symbol of medicine and medical treatment, and in Japan it is used as part of the symbol on ambulances and for the Japanese Society for Emergency Life-Saving. The name Hygieia, the daughter of Asklepios and patron goddess of health, is believed to be the origin of the word hygiene, meaning "sanitation."

Answer   ② World Health Organization

世界三大感染症

「世界三大感染症」とは、マラリア、結核と、もう一つは何でしょうか？

① coronavirus (COVID-19)
② AIDS
③ influenza
④ Ebola

　感染症とは、接触や空気、虫や動物などを媒介して体内に侵入したウイルスや細菌、寄生虫などが増殖することで発症する病気を指します。咳や発熱、下痢などの症状が出て、最悪の場合、死に至ることもあります。そんな感染症の中で最も恐れられているのが、蚊によって感染するマラリア、空気感染する結核、そして母子感染や性交渉による感染、血液を介した感染で起こるエイズの3つです。開発途上国では、医療従事者や病院の数が不足し、感染者や死亡者が増えることによって労働力が低下し、社会・経済活動が低迷して貧困につながるという悪循環が起きています。

　AIDSは後天性免疫不全症候群の略称で、HIV（ヒト免疫不全ウイルス）に感染することによって全身性の免疫不全に陥り、さまざまな感染症やがんなどの合併症を発症してしまう病気の総称です。HIVに感染したとしても特定疾患を発症しなければエイズとは診断されません。AIDSはHIV/AIDSの表記で使われることが多いので、覚えておくといいでしょう。

　③は誰もが知るウイルス「インフルエンザ」、④は致死率が90パーセントにものぼる「エボラ出血熱」のことです。

Infectious diseases are illnesses caused by the multiplication of viruses, bacteria or parasites that enter the body through contact, air, insects or animals. Symptoms include cough, fever, diarrhea and in the worst case, death. The three most feared such infectious diseases are malaria, which is transmitted by mosquitoes; tuberculosis, which is airborne; and AIDS, which is transmitted from mother to child, through sexual intercourse and through blood transfusions. In developing countries, there is a vicious cycle: the number of medical personnel and hospitals is inadequate, and the labor force declines as the number of infected people and deaths increases, leading to stagnation of social and economic activities and poverty.

AIDS is an abbreviation for Acquired Immune Deficiency Syndrome, a general term for a disease in which infection with HIV, the human immunodeficiency virus, causes a systemic immune deficiency that leads to various infectious diseases and complications, such as cancer. Even if someone is infected with HIV, they will not be diagnosed with AIDS unless they develop a specific disease. It is worth remembering that AIDS is often used to describe HIV/AIDS.

③ refers to influenza, a virus that everyone knows about, and ④ refers to Ebola virus disease, which has a fatality rate of up to 90 percent.

Answer   ② AIDS

予防接種とワクチン

日本語を参考にしながら、各空欄に当てはまる単語を下の語群から選んで文を完成させてください。

① The (   ) didn't hurt much at first, but now my shoulder is quite sore.
予防接種は初めあまり痛くなかったのですが、今は肩が少し痛いです。

② To enter the country, visitors need to show proof of (   ).
入国の際、訪問者はワクチン予防接種の証明を提示する必要があります。

③ My dog is (   ).
うちのイヌはワクチン接種済みです。

④ I'm suffering from the (   ) side effects.
ワクチン接種後の副反応に悩まされています。

⑤ Masks are not the only way to (   ) the spread of COVID-19.
マスクは新型コロナウイルス拡大を防止する唯一の方法というわけではありません。

⑥ Researchers are testing a new form of flu (   ) that can be given as a spray instead of using a needle.
研究者たちは針を使わないスプレー式の新しいかたちのインフルエンザワクチンを試行しています。

· post-jab   · vaccine   · shot

· vaccination   · vaccinated   · prevent

Point

　①の shot には「予防接種、注射」の意味があり、よく使われます。injection も同様の意味です。「注射を打つ（打ってもらう）」は get a shot と言います。
　②の vaccination は名詞で「ワクチン予防接種」のことです。inoculation という単

語も同じく「予防接種」という意味で、ニュースなどではよく使われるので覚えておくといいでしょう。なお、「〜日」はdate of 〜で表され、date of birth（生年月日）やdate of purchase（購入日）などは記入用紙などでよく見かける表現です。

　③のvaccinatedは動詞vaccinateの過去分詞形です。vaccinateは人に対して「ワクチン接種をする」という意味なので、「ワクチンを受ける」ことを表す場合には、「be動詞＋vaccinated（過去分詞）」の形をとります。inoculatedを使うこともできます。

　④のpost-jabのjabは、shotやvaccinationと同じく「予防接種、注射」のことで、会話でよく使われます。ボクシングの軽いパンチを意味する「ジャブ」は、このjabです。post-は「〜の後の」という意味で、反対はpre-「〜の前の」です。なお、sufferfromで「（病気や身体的問題）を患う、〜に苦しむ」という意味です。

　⑤病気などのまん延を「防ぐ」ことを表すにはpreventを使います。protectにも同じく「防ぐ」という意味がありますが、けがや病気にならないようにあらかじめ「守る、保護する」というニュアンスがあります。例えば、Wash your hands to protect yourself from viruses.（ウイルスから守るために手を洗いなさい）のように使われます。

　⑥の「ワクチン」に当たる英語はvaccineです。昨今の新型コロナワクチン関連の報道文などでは、短縮した形のvaxやvaxxedもよく見かけます。vaccineよりもつづりが短いので使いやすいのでしょう。vax mandateは「ワクチン義務化」、vax rateは「ワクチン接種率」、anti-vax movementは「反ワクチン運動」の意味です。

Answer

① The (shot) didn't hurt much at first, but now my shoulder is quite sore.

② To enter the country, visitors need to show proof of (vaccination).

③ My dog is (vaccinated).

④ I'm suffering from the (post-jab) side effects.

⑤ Masks are not the only way to (prevent) the spread of COVID-19.

⑥ Researchers are testing a new form of flu (vaccine) that can be given as a spray instead of using a needle.

少子化と医療費

次の単語とその意味を線で結んでください。

① pension · · 国民健康保険

② well-being · · 介護

③ social insurance premium · · 福祉

④ National Health Insurance · · 年金

⑤ care · · 社会保険料

　日本の「国民年金制度」は少子高齢化社会によって、年金の給付額がこの先かなり減ってしまい、今の若い人は払った分が戻ってこないと心配しています。しかし社会全体を見た場合、もし年金制度がなければ働き盛りの世代が各自高齢の親を金銭的に支えなくてはなりません。経済が拡大すれば、公的年金に割けるお金も増えるので、公的年金制度を維持しながら経済の規模を大きくしていく必要があります。あわせて、子どもを産みやすく育てやすい環境を国が整え、少子化問題を解決しなければ、根本的な改善にはつながらないでしょう。

　国民健康保険制度は、保険証があれば全国どこの医療機関でも受診でき、一定の割合の自己負担額を支払えば国民が平等に高度医療を受けられる優れた制度です。しかし、少子高齢化によって、高齢者は増える一方、現役世代の人口は減るため、経済成長が鈍化して保険料の収入が減少しています。また、高齢者の寿命が延びればそれだけ医療費も増加するため、国民負担率も増加し、結果として税金と現役世代の保険料を引き上げてカバーしなければならないという問題に直面しています。

It is said that the benefits from the "Japanese National Pension System" will decrease considerably in the future due to the declining birthrate and aging society, and some young people worry that they will never get back the money they paid into the system.

However, looking at society as a whole, if there were no pension system, the working-age population would be forced to financially support their own elderly parents. The economy needs to grow in size while maintaining the public pension system through a mechanism that allows more money to be allocated to the public pension system as the economy expands. In addition, unless the government creates an environment in which it is easy to have and raise children, and solves the problem of declining birthrates, there will be no fundamental improvement in the situation.

The National Health Insurance system is excellent and allows people to receive medical care anywhere in Japan as long as they have an insurance card and pay a certain percentage as a co-payment. However, due to the declining birthrate and aging population, the number of elderly people is increasing while the working-age population is decreasing, resulting in a slowdown in economic growth and a decrease in income from insurance premiums. In addition, as the life expectancy of the elderly increases, so does the cost of medical care, and the national burden rate also increases, resulting in the problem of having to raise taxes and working-age insurance premiums to cover the costs.

Point

①の pension は国や企業などから給付される「年金」のことです。

②の well-being は「福祉」のことで、welfare も同じ意味です。「社会福祉」は social welfare と言います。

③の social insurance premium は「社会保険料」です。social insurance fee にも同じく「保険料」の意味があります。日本の社会保険には、健康保険（health insurance）、厚生年金保険（employees' pension insurance）、介護保険（nursing-care insurance）、雇用保険（employment insurance）、労災保険（workers' compensation insurance）の５種類があります。

④の National Health Insurance は「国民健康保険」のことです。「保険証」は health insurance (ID) card、「後期高齢者医療制度」は Medical Care System for the Elderly Aged 75 and Over と表現されます。

⑤の care には「介護」の意味があります。代わりに nursing も使われます。「～を介護する」は care for ～で、必ず for を伴います。「介護施設」は care facility です。

Answer　　① pension ＝ 年金　② well-being ＝ 福祉
③ social insurance premium ＝ 社会保険料
④ National Health Insurance ＝ 国民健康保険
⑤ care ＝ 介護

世界の主要死因トップ10

下の表は、WHO が発表した 2019 年の世界の主要死因トップ 10 を示した
ものです。空欄に当てはまる語句を下から選んで表を完成させてください。

	Leading Causes of Death	死因
1	Ischemic （ ① ） disease	虚血性心疾患
2	（ ② ）	脳卒中
3	Chronic obstructive pulmonary disease	慢性閉塞性肺疾患（ ③ ）
4	（ ④ ） respiratory infections	下気道感染症
5	Neonatal （ ⑤ ）	新生児固有の状態
6	Trachea, bronchus, （ ⑥ ）	気管・気管支・肺がん
7	（ ⑦ ） and other dementias	アルツハイマー病を含む認知症
8	（ ⑧ ） disease	下痢性疾患
9	（ ⑨ ）	糖尿病
10	（ ⑩ ） disease	腎臓病

- kidney　　・diabetes　　・heart　　・stroke
- conditions　　・COPD　　・diarrheal　　・lower
- lung cancers　　・Alzheimer's disease

　2019年の世界の死亡者数は5,540万人、表の上位10以内の死因が全体の55パー
セントを占めていました。興味深いのは、これらトップ10のうち1、2、3、6、7、
9、10位の7つが非感染性疾患ということです。非感染性疾患は、不健康な食事
や運動不足、喫煙、過度の飲酒、大気汚染などが原因であることが多いです。先
進国に多い慢性疾患、いわゆる生活習慣病が原因です。4、5、8位は感染性疾患で、
医療従事者や医療施設が不足していたり、衛生環境が整っていなかったりする開
発途上国で起こりやすくなっています。

一方、所得別に分類した場合の死因は、左表とは少し異なります。例えば、低所得国（途上国）の死因トップ3は、1位が新生児固有の状態、2位が下気道感染症、3位が虚血性心疾患で、高所得国（先進国）では1位が虚血性心疾患、2位がアルツハイマー病を含む認知症、3位が脳卒中という結果です。

　③の答えであるCOPDは、慢性閉塞性肺疾患のそれぞれの頭文字をとったものです。

In 2019, there were 55.4 million deaths worldwide, and the top ten causes of death that are shown in the table accounted for 55 percent of the total. Interestingly, 7 of these top 10, ranked 1, 2, 3, 6, 7, 9, and 10, are non-communicable diseases. These are often related to unhealthy diet, lack of exercise, smoking, excessive drinking and air pollution. In developed countries, many chronic illnesses are caused by lifestyle-related diseases. The fourth, fifth, and eighth are communicable diseases, which are more likely to occur in developing countries, where there is a lack of medical personnel and medical facilities, and where sanitation is poor.

On the other hand, the causes of death when classified by income are slightly different from the above. For example, the top three causes of death in low-income (developing) countries are neonatal-specific conditions in first place, lower respiratory tract infections in second place, and ischemic heart disease in third place, while in high-income (developed) countries, ischemic heart disease is in first place, dementia including Alzheimer's disease is in second place, and stroke is in third place.

COPD, the answer to ③, is an acronym for each of the chronic obstructive pulmonary diseases.

Answer ① heart
② Stroke
③ COPD
④ Lower
⑤ conditions
⑥ lung cancers
⑦ Alzheimer's disease
⑧ Diarrheal
⑨ Diabetes
⑩ Kidney

妊婦の死者数

下の世界地図は、2017年の世界の妊婦の死者数を国ごとに5段階（3,000人以下、3,001-6,000人、6,001-9,000人、9,001-1万2,000人、1万2,001人以上）で色分けして示したものです。次の各文の内容が合っていればT、間違っていればFをつけてください。

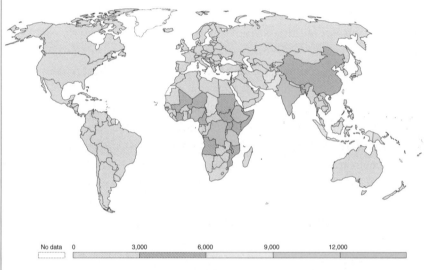

① ロシアの妊婦死者数は3,001-6,000人の間である。　　　（　　　）

② インドの妊婦死者数は1万2,001人以上である。　　　　（　　　）

③ データがない国はカナダである。　　　　　　　　　　（　　　）

④ 妊婦死者数が6,001-9,000人の間にある国は4カ国である。（　　　）

　現在、年間30万人以上の妊婦が死亡していて、2030年までにすべての国で出生10万人に対して死亡妊婦数を70人以下まで引き下げるという目標に向かって

さまざまな支援が行われています。しかし、低所得国の貧困や交通インフラの整備不足、医療従事者や施設の不足、紛争などによる治安の悪さなど多くの問題があり、先進国や大企業などからの支援がないと難しいのが現実です。

Currently, more than 300,000 pregnant women die annually, and various types of assistance are being provided for the goal of lowering this number to less than 70 per 100,000 live births in all countries by 2030. However, there are many problems, such as poverty in low-income countries, lack of transportation infrastructure, lack of medical personnel and facilities, and insecurity due to conflicts, etc., which will make it difficult to achieve the goal without support from developed countries and large corporations.

Point

地図が読めないと難しい問題です。

①は、ユーラシア大陸の北部に位置する広大な国土をもつロシアの色はうすいグレーで3,000人以下なので、間違いです。

②のインドは中国の下の、インド洋に面した南部が鋭くとがった形の国です。濃いグリーンなので、妊婦死亡者数は1万2,001人以上ということで正解です。妊婦死亡者数が最も多い国は、上位からナイジェリア（6万7,000人）、インド（3万5,000人）、コンゴ共和国（1万6,000人）、エチオピア（1万4,000人）です。

③のカナダは米国の北に位置しており、うすいグレーなのでデータがあります。地図を見ると、5段階の色分けスケールの左側に白色で示された枠があり、No data と書いてあります。データが取れなかった国は白色になっているので地図上で確認すると、北極近くに大きな島があることがわかります。グリーンランドです。ちなみに、グリーンランドの東にある小さな島はアイスランドです。

④は、妊婦死亡者数が6,001–9,000人の色がついた国を数えれば答えがわかります。インドネシアは大小の島から構成されているので一つずつ数えないように注意しましょう。その他3カ国は、チャド共和国、パキスタン、アフガニスタンです。

Answer　①F　②T　③F　④T

生活習慣病

「生活習慣病」を英語で何と言いますか？　次の中から選んでください。

① lifestyle-related disease
② unhealthy disease
③ lifelong disease

　生活習慣病とは、過度な喫煙や飲酒、運動不足、肥満、ストレスなどの生活習慣が要因となる病気のことで、例えば、がんや脳卒中、心臓病、糖尿病、高血圧、低血圧などが含まれます。生活習慣病の原因は主に個人の生活習慣とされていますが、日々の生活の乱れ以外にも、遺伝的な要因や職場・地域などの社会的な生活環境も含まれるため、国や地域・社会の環境も整える必要があるでしょう。

　Lifestyle-related diseases are caused by lifestyle factors, such as excessive smoking, drinking, lack of exercise, obesity and stress, and include, for example, cancer, stroke, heart disease, diabetes, high blood pressure and low blood pressure. Although the causes of lifestyle-related diseases are mainly attributed to the lifestyle habits of individuals, genetic factors and everyday environments, such as workplaces and communities, are also included, so national, regional and social environments must also be improved.

Point
　「病気」は英語でdisease、「生活習慣」はlifestyleで表現することができます。ちなみに②のunhealthyは「不健康な」、③のlifelongは「生涯にわたる」という意味です。

Answer　① lifestyle-related disease

生活習慣病の原因

下の図には、さまざまな語句が散らばっています。この中から、生活習慣病の原因と考えられるものを選んでください。

Tobacco

Unbalanced* diet

Good sleep

Quitting* smoking

Lifestyle-related Disease
（生活習慣病）

Overeating

Stress

Alcohol

Lack of* exercise

Refreshment and relaxation

*quitting やめること　　unbalanced バランスの悪い、偏った　　lack of ～の不足

　先進国を中心に広がっている生活習慣病。主に、たばこや酒、偏った食事、運動不足、ストレス、食べ過ぎなど、生活の質（QOL: quality of life）が低下することが、さまざま病気を引き起こしてしまいます。予防には禁煙、適量のアルコール摂取、バランスの良い食事、適度な運動、質の良い睡眠、リフレッシュしてくつろぐなどが必要です。しかし、例えば、残業続きで十分な休養が取れなかったり、職場環境によるストレスが大きかったりする場合は、環境面の見直しも必要になります。健康寿命（介助や介護を受けずに生活できる期間）が長くなるように、日頃から意識して生活したいですね。

　Lifestyle-related diseases are becoming more common, mainly in developed countries. In general, tobacco, alcohol, unbalanced diets, lack of exercise, stress, overeating and other factors that reduce quality of life (QOL) lead to various diseases. Prevention requires quitting smoking, consuming alcohol in moderation, eating a well-balanced diet, getting adequate exercise, getting good sleep and being refreshed and relaxed. However, if, for example, one does not get enough rest due to continuous overtime work, or if there is a lot of stress from the work environment, it is also necessary to examine the environment. We should be conscious of our daily lives so that our healthy life expectancy (the period during which we can live without assistance or nursing care) can be extended.

Answer ▸ Tobacco ／ Unbalanced diet ／ Overeating ／
Lack of exercise ／ Alcohol ／ Stress

超高齢化社会

「超高齢社会」の定義についての説明文があります。日本語を参考にしながら、空欄に当てはまる単語を下の語群から選んで書き入れ、文を完成させてください。

According to* the WHO and the UN, an "(①) society" refers to* a society where more than 7 percent of the population is 65 years or older, an "(②) society" is a society where more than 14 percent of the population* is above 65, and a "(③) society" is when people over 65 make up more than* 21 percent of the population.

WHO（世界保健機構）と国連によると、「高齢化社会」とは人口の7パーセントが65歳以上を占める社会のことで、「高齢社会」は人口の14パーセントを超える場合、「超高齢社会」は人口の21パーセントを超える場合と定義されています。

・super-aged　　・aged　　・aging

*according to ～によると　refer to ～を言う　population 人口　more than ～を上回る

　超高齢社会が進むと、独り暮らしか高齢夫婦のみの世帯が増える、認知症の高齢者が増えて医療や施設が逼迫する、医療費や介護費が増えるといった問題がすべて現役世代にのしかかるということになります。そのため日本の場合、国が後期高齢者の医療自己負担額を引き上げ、高齢者が長く働けるよう法律を改正するなど、問題解消に努めています。日本人の平均寿命は、男性が81.47歳、女性が87.57歳ほどですが、健康寿命は平均寿命マイナス10歳前後です。いずれ高齢者となる若い世代にとっては、介助や介護をなるべく受けずに済むよう、健康寿命と平均寿命との差をいかに縮めるかが課題になるでしょう。

As a society becomes super-aged, the number of households with only one person or elderly couples will increase, medical care and facilities will be strained by the growing number of elderly people with dementia, and medical and nursing care costs will rise. All of these problems will fall on the working-age population. In the case of Japan, the government is working to solve them by raising the co-payments for medical care for the elderly in the later stages of life and by amending laws to allow the elderly to work longer. The average life expectancy in Japan is about 81.47 years for men and 87.57 years for women, but the healthy life expectancy is about 10 years below the average life expectancy. For the younger generation who will eventually become elderly, the challenge will be how to narrow the gap between healthy life expectancy and average life expectancy so that they can receive as little assistance and nursing care as possible.

Point

　「高齢化、年をとること」はagingで表すので、①の「高齢化社会」はaging society と表現します。②の「高齢社会」はすでに高齢化が進んだ状態にあるので、「高齢の」 という意味の形容詞agedを用いてaged societyとなります。③の「超高齢社会」の 「超〜」は、「とても、ものすごく」という意味の副詞superを使います。英語には、複 数の語を組み合わせて新たな単語を作る場合には、適切な箇所にハイフンを入れると いう基本ルールがあります。主に *The Chicago Manual of Style* という文法や文章の 書き方などをまとめたスタイルブックのルールにならう場合が多いので、そのまま覚 えてしまいましょう。この場合、副詞と分詞（または形容詞）からなる語には間にハ イフンを入れるというルールから、super-agedとなります。

Answer ① aging ② aged ③ super-aged

日本の自殺者数

日本では、年間何万人が自殺していると思いますか？

① 約1万人
② 約2万人
③ 約3万人

　日本の自殺者数については、たびたびニュースなどで報道されています。2020年の自殺者数は2万1,081人、2021年では2万1,007人ですので、②の約2万人が正解です。1998年から14年間ほどは年間3万人を超えていたので、その期間と比べるとだいぶ減少しています。しかし、問題なのは自殺の原因です。

　自殺の原因・背景は、経済・生活問題、健康問題、家庭問題、学校問題、勤務問題、男女問題などさまざまです。自殺のリスクが高まるのは、これらの要因の3〜4つ以上が複合的に連鎖する中で、「生きたい」という気持ちよりも「生きたくない」という気持ちのほうが上回ってしまったときに起こります。かつては経済・生活問題が自殺の動機として最も多かったのですが、昨今では健康問題が動機の自殺者数が経済・生活問題の2倍近くに増加し、特にうつ病が大きな要因となっています。うつ病は意欲や思考力、判断力の低下を引き起こすため、いろいろな逃げ道（選択肢）を客観的に見つけることができなくなって、最終的に自分の命を絶つことを選択してしまうのです。

　うつ病やうつ傾向になる人の悩みはさまざまですが、社会人では過労や職場の人間関係に関するものが圧倒的に多く、学生では中高生が友だちとの不和や入試に関する悩み、大学生が学業不振や進路に関する悩みだそうです。

　自殺問題は一人ひとりの年代や環境、悩みの種類がさまざまで、一律に同じ対策を取ることができません。社会全体として、生きるためのさまざまな選択肢や支援先などの情報を広く浸透させていく必要があるでしょう。

　The number of suicides in Japan is often reported in the news. In 2020, it was 21,081, and in 2021 it was 21,007, so ②, about 20,000, is correct. For 14 years from 1998, the number exceeded 30,000 per year, so it has decreased considerably compared with that period. The problem, however, is the causes of suicide.

There are various causes and situations leading to suicide, including economic and lifestyle problems, health problems, family problems, school problems, work problems and gender issues. The risk of suicide increases when three to four or more of these factors are compounded in a chain of events, and when the feeling of not wanting to live outweighs the feeling of wanting to live. In the past, economic and lifestyle problems were the most common motive for suicide, but recently, the number of suicides motivated by health problems has increased nearly twice as much as the number caused by economic and lifestyle problems, with depression being a particularly significant factor. Depression causes a decline in motivation, thinking and judgment, making it impossible for people to objectively find various escape routes (options), and they ultimately choose to take their own lives.

The problems of those who suffer from depression and depressive tendencies vary widely, but in the overwhelming majority of working adults, they are related to overwork and workplace relationships, while middle school and high school students are concerned about discord with friends and entrance examinations, and university students are concerned about poor academic performance and career paths.

Suicide issues vary from person to person depending on age, environment and type of distress, and it is not possible to take uniform measures. It is necessary for society as a whole to disseminate information on various options for survival and sources of support.

Answer ② 約2万人

「すべての人に健康と福祉を」

——そのために、あなたに何ができると思いますか？

What can you do to bring about "good health and well-being"?

　一口に「すべての人に健康と福祉を」と言っても、先進国と開発途上国とでは状況が異なるため、対応も異なります。また、先進国の中でも各国独自の問題があるため、個人で何ができるのかを考えるのは、なかなか難しいでしょう。

　世界には基本的な保健医療サービスを受けられない人、医療費が払えない人、払うことで貧困に陥る人がたくさんいます。その改善策として、2012年12月12日に国連総会で、世界各国がUHC（Universal Health Coverage）を国際社会の共通目標として推進することが議決され、2015年にSDGs Goal 3のターゲットの一つにもなりました。UHCとは、「すべての人が適切な健康増進、予防、治療、リハビリなどの保健医療サービスを、支払い可能な費用で受けられる」ことを意味します。実現に向けて、感染症予防対策としての蚊帳の普及や、安価で効果のある医薬品の提供、医療従事者や診療所の整備、病院での高度医療の提供などの支援が世界各国で進められています。

　個人でできることとして思い浮かぶのは、国際医療の支援活動を行っている団体などへ寄付することでしょうか。ネット検索すると、さまざまな支援団体がヒットしますが、その実態は不透明なところもあるので、よく調べてみることをお勧めします。将来、医療や人道支援の現場で活動したいと考えている人は、民間NPOの「国境なき医師団」を調べてみるのもいいでしょう。国境なき医師団は、紛争や自然災害、貧困などで緊急に医療が必要になる場所へいち早く向かい、医療援助活動を行っています。医師や看護師以外でも、運営管理スタッフとして活動に関わることができるようです。

Even if we speak of "health and welfare for all," the situation differs between developed and developing countries, and therefore the responses will also differ. In addition, even within developed nations, each country has its own unique problems, so it can be difficult to figure out what individuals can do to help.

There are many people in the world who do not have access to basic healthcare services, who cannot afford to pay for health care or who fall into poverty by trying to pay for it. As a way to improve this situation, on December 12, 2012, the United Nations General Assembly voted to promote Universal Health Coverage (UHC) as a common goal for the international community, and in 2015, it became one of the targets of SDG 3. UHC is the "universal coverage of all people for health services, including appropriate health promotion, prevention, treatment and rehabilitation, at a cost they can afford." To make this a reality, countries around the world are providing support for the spread of mosquito nets as a preventive measure against infectious diseases, the provision of inexpensive and effective medicines, the development of healthcare workers and clinics, and the provision of advanced medical care in hospitals.

One thing that comes to mind as something individuals can do is to donate to organizations that provide support for international medical care. An internet search will turn up a variety of support groups, but the actual status of some of them is unclear, so it is recommended that you do your research carefully. If you are interested in working in the field of medicine or humanitarian aid in the future, you may want to check out Doctors Without Borders, a private non-profit organization. It goes quickly to places where urgent medical care is needed due to conflict, natural disasters, poverty, etc. and conducts medical aid activities. It seems that even those who are not doctors or nurses can get involved in their activities as operational management staff.

Goal 4

質の高い教育をみんなに
Quality Education

すべての人々への、包摂的かつ公正な質の高い教育を提供し、
生涯学習の機会を促進する。

**Ensure inclusive and equitable quality education and
promote lifelong learning opportunities for all.**

　「小学校は楽しかったですか？」「中学校ではどの教科が好きで
すか？」——質の高い義務教育を受けている日本の子どもたちは、
このような質問に何の疑問も持つことなく答えるのではないでし
ょうか。しかし世界には、日本では考えられないような理由で学
校に行けなかったり、行かない選択をしたり、行っても十分な教
育を受けられなかったりする子どもたちが大勢います。その数は、
2018年時点で2億5,840万人。教育が受けられないと読み書き
や計算といった基本的な能力を身につけることができず、将来的
にできる仕事も限られてしまい、貧困の悪循環に陥って抜け出せ
なくなってしまいます。日本では当たり前の「教育」が、世界の
国々では当たり前ではないという事実を理解し、なぜ教育が受け
られないのか、どうしたら改善できるのかを考えてみましょう。

参照：UNESCO Institute of Statistics, 2019

教育に関する用語

教育に関する言葉があります。日本語の意味を参考にして、各空欄に当てはまる語を下の語群から選んで言葉を完成してみましょう。

① education (　　　　　) = 教育格差
② (　　　　) education = 質の高い教育
③ (　　　　) education = 義務教育
④ education (　　　　) = 教育施設
⑤ (　　　　) education = 遠隔教育

・compulsory
・distance
・facilities
・gap
・quality

　「教育格差」とは、生まれ育った環境によって生まれる、学力や学歴などの格差のことです。開発途上国では家庭の経済力不足が原因で教育を受けたくても受けられない子どもたちが多くいます。一方の日本でも同じような家庭環境の格差のほか、学校によって教育の質が異なることが問題の学校間格差などが起こっていて、社会の課題になっています。
　「質の高い教育」とは、さまざまな資格をもつ教員が技術教育や職業教育の場を提供し、子どもたちに平等に知識や技能を習得させるような教育のことです。開発途上国では、働きがいのある人間らしい仕事に就くという、将来を見据えた教育のことです。

"Education gap" refers to the disparity in academic ability and educational background that is created by the environment in which a child is born and raised. In developing countries, there are many children who cannot receive an education even if they want one because their family lacks the financial resources. On the other hand, in Japan, there are similar disparities in home environments, and also a disparity between schools due to the difference in the quality of education, which is becoming a social issue.

"Quality education" refers to education in which teachers with a variety of qualifications provide technical and vocational education, and in which children acquire knowledge and skills on an equal basis. In developing countries, it means education that is focused on the future; that is, on getting a job that is rewarding and humane.

Point

③は、enforced education や mandatory education と言うこともできます。ちなみに「詰め込み教育」は force-fed education や cramming、「ゆとり教育」は more-relaxed education や lighter curriculum と表現します。

④の「施設」にはふつう複数形 facilities が用いられますが、１つの施設を表す場合には単数形の facility を使います。

⑤の「遠隔教育」は online education（オンライン授業）や remote learning（リモート授業）とほぼ同じ意味で、教員が生徒に離れた場所から授業を提供することです。「対面授業」は face-to-face education と言います。

Answer

① education (gap)
② (quality) education
③ (compulsory) education
④ education (facilities)
⑤ (distance) education

UNESCO (ユネスコ)

略称である UNESCO (ユネスコ) の正式名称は次のどれでしょうか？

① United Nations Educational, Scientific and Cultural Organization
② United Nations Education, Science and Culture Organization
③ United Nations English, Spanish and Chinese Organization
④ United Nations and Education, Science and Culture Organization

　UNESCO (ユネスコ) の英語の正式名称はUnited Nations Educational, Scientific and Cultural Organizationです。日本語名称は「国際連合教育科学文化機関」と言います。1946年11月4日にユネスコ憲章に基づいてフランスのパリで設立され、現在、日本を含む193の国と地域が加盟しています。ユネスコの目的は、世界中の人々が、人種・性・言語・宗教の差別なく、教育・科学・文化を通じて、互いに理解・協力し合いながら平和で安全に暮らすための社会づくりに貢献することで、そのためのさまざまな活動を世界規模または国単位で行っています。

　The official name of UNESCO is the United Nations Educational, Scientific and Cultural Organization. It was established in Paris, France, on November 4, 1946 under The Constitution of UNESCO and currently has 193 member countries and regions, including Japan. The purpose of UNESCO is to contribute to the creation of a peaceful and safe society in which all people of the world can live together in mutual understanding and cooperation through education, science and culture, without discrimination based on race, gender, language or religion.

Answer ① United Nations Educational, Scientific and Cultural Organization

UNESCO 提唱の教育プログラム

UNESCO が提唱する教育プログラム「持続可能な開発のための教育」の略語は次のどれでしょうか？

① SDE　　② SE　　③ ESD

Goal 4

　ESD は Education for Sustainable Development（持続可能な開発のための教育）の略語で、for 以外の語の頭文字をとって ESD です。ESD は、環境問題や人権問題、エネルギー問題など、地球上のあらゆる問題を一人ひとりの問題として捉え、身近なところから個人の意志と判断、責任でそれぞれの問題に取り組み、将来安心して暮らしていくための社会をつくる人材を育成する学習・教育活動で、SDGs を達成させるための手段のひとつです。

　ESD は、問題と向き合うために重要な6つの考え方と、問題を解決するために必要な7つの能力と態度を身につけることを目標としています。日本の学校教育にも ESD が推進され、新学習指導要領には持続可能な社会の担い手の育成について、次ページの表のような ESD の考えに沿った教育を実践できるような観点が盛り込まれています。

　ESD stands for Education for Sustainable Development, which comes from the first letters of all the words except "for." ESD treats every problem on earth, such as environmental problems, human rights problems and energy problems, as problems for each person, and tackles each problem with individual will, judgment and responsibility using things people are familiar with, so that we can live with peace of mind in the future.

　ESD aims to develop six important ways of thinking to confront problems, along with seven abilities and attitudes necessary to solve them. ESD is also being promoted in schools in Japan, and the new courses of study include perspectives on fostering leaders of a sustainable society so that students can practice education in line with ESD ideas, as shown in the table below.

問題と向き合うための６つの考え方
6 Ways of Thinking about Confronting Problems

多様性	いろいろな視点で考える	Diversity	Thinking from different perspectives
相互性	人同士はもちろん、自然や生き物と共に人は生きている	Mutuality	People live not only with each other but also with nature and other living things.
有限性	食べ物や電気などは無限ではないことを理解し、未来のために考える	Finiteness	Understanding that food, electricity and other resources are not infinite and considering the future.
公平性	国や年齢を問わず誰もが平等である	Fairness	Everyone is equal regardless of country or age.
連携性	みんなで協力すれば、大きなことを成し遂げられる	Cooperation	If we all work together, we can accomplish great things.
責任性	自分がやるべきことを考え自分で行動する	Responsibility	Think about what you should do and act on your own.

問題解決のための７つの能力と態度
7 Competencies and Attitudes for Problem Solving

疑問をもって考える力	Ability to question things when thinking
未来を想像して計画を立てる力	Ability to imagine and plan for the future
いろいろな方向から物事を見る力	Ability to see things from various perspectives
自分の気持ちや考えを伝えたり、相手の意見を聞いたりする力	Ability to communicate one's feelings and thoughts and to listen to others' opinions
みんなと協力する力	Ability to cooperate with others
つながりを意識した生活をする態度	Attitude of living with an awareness of connections
誰かのために進んで行動する態度	Willingness to act for the benefit of others

Answer ③ ESD

識字能力

literacy の意味の説明として正しいものは次のうちどれですか？

① the ability* to read, write and speak
② the ability to read, write, and numerate*
③ the ability to read and write

* ability 能力　numerate 計算する

Point

　literacy は「識字能力」という意味ですが、別の言い方をすると「読み書きができる」ということです。①は「読む、書く、話す能力」、②は「読む、書く、計算する能力」、③は「読む、書く能力」なので、正解は③です。literacy の反意語は illiteracy（非識字）で、l（エル）が２つ重なるつづりに注意しましょう。また、「読み書きのできる人、学識のある人」を literate (person)、「読み書きのできない人、教養のない人」を illiterate (person) と言います。

　基本的な計算ができることも、教育においては重要です。「基本的な計算能力」のことを numeracy と言います。また「読み書き・計算の基礎学力」を basic literacy and numeracy skills と表現します。

Answer　③ the ability to read and write

世界の識字率

世界の、読み書きができない15歳以上の人口はどのくらいだと思いますか？

① 約3.3億人
② 約5.5億人
③ 約7.7億人

　ユネスコによる「識字」の定義は、「日常生活で必要な簡単な文章を読み書きできるかどうか」で、2022年現在、読み書きができない人は世界で7億7,300万人いるといわれています。読み書きができない人の多くは、貧困や戦争・紛争、女性蔑視、学校が近くにないなどのさまざまな理由から、教育を受けずに大人になっています。とりわけ、開発途上国(サハラ以南のアフリカ諸国など)の学校に行けない6歳～14歳の子どもたちの数は約1億2,100万人にも上るとされています。

　その主な要因は貧困で、生活のために子どもが働いたり、女の子の場合、早く結婚して家事や育児に専念するために教育は必要ないという考えが根強く残っていたりします。日本ではもちろん児童労働は禁じられていますが、世界には教育を受けずに毎日畑仕事や水くみをしたり、ごみを拾って生計を立てたりしなければ生きていけない子どもたちが多くいるという現状を知っておくべきでしょう。

　UNESCO defines "literacy" as "the ability to read and write simple sentences necessary for daily life." As of 2022, there are an estimated 773 million people worldwide who cannot read or write. Many of those who cannot read and write have grown up without education for a variety of reasons, including poverty, war and conflict, disrespect for women and lack of nearby schools. In particular, the number of children between the ages of 6 and 14 who are unable to go to school in developing countries (e.g., countries in sub-Saharan Africa) is estimated to be as high as 121 million.

　The main reason for this is poverty, with children working to make ends meet and, in the case of girls, the belief that education is not necessary in order to get married early and focus on housework and childcare, which is still deeply rooted. Of course, child labor is prohibited in Japan, but it is important to know that there are many children in the world who have to work in the fields, fetch water or pick up garbage to earn a living every day without receiving an education.

Answer   ③ 約 7.7 億人

貧困と教育不足の悪循環

下の図は「貧困と教育不足の悪循環」(Vicious Cycle between Poverty and Illiteracy) を表したものです。日本語を参考にしながら、それぞれのカッコ内に当てはまる英単語を下の語群から選んでください。

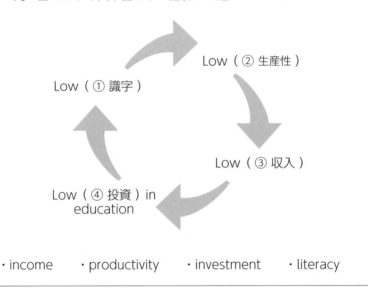

Low（① 識字）

Low（② 生産性）

Low（③ 収入）

Low（④ 投資）in education

・income　・productivity　・investment　・literacy

　貧困と教育不足の負の連鎖からわかるように、読み書きができないので⇨生産性の高い安定した仕事に就けず⇨収入が少なく⇨子どもの教育にお金をかけることができない⇨だから読み書きができない……という無限ループに陥っています。

　読み書きや簡単な計算ができないと、さまざまな職業で技術を習得するのが難しくなり、労働条件が厳しくなります。また、契約書などを読むこともできないため、知らずに過酷な労働条件下で働くことになったり、だまされて低賃金で働かされてしまったりするかもしれません。生活面でも、危険な場所の標識が読めなかったり、病気のために処方された薬の服用方法が読めなかったりすれば、命

の危険にかかわります。この悪循環を断ち切るためには、学校を建てたり、質の高い教員を増やしたりするなど、教育環境を整えることや、人々の教育への意識を高めていくことが必要になるでしょう。

As can be seen from the negative cycle of poverty and lack of education, low literacy (because someone cannot read and write) ⇨ low productivity (because someone cannot find a stable, productive job) ⇨ low income (someone does not earn much money) ⇨ low investment in education (because someone cannot spend money on their children's education) ⇨ so a person is not able to read and write...which is an endless loop.

Inability to read, write and perform simple calculations makes it difficult to acquire skills in various occupations and makes working conditions more difficult. Also, because people cannot read contracts and other documents, they may unknowingly end up working under harsh conditions or be tricked into working for low wages. In terms of daily life, not being able to read signs in dangerous places or not being able to read how to take prescribed medication for an illness can endanger one's life. To break this vicious cycle, it will be necessary to improve the educational environment and raise people's awareness of education by building schools and increasing the number of quality teachers.

Answer ① literacy ② productivity ③ income ④ investment

世界の識字率

下の世界地図は、2022年の識字率（literacy rate）を国ごとに、20パーセント未満から100パーセントまで5段階に区切って色分けして示したものです。次の各文の内容が正しければTを、間違っていればFをつけてください。

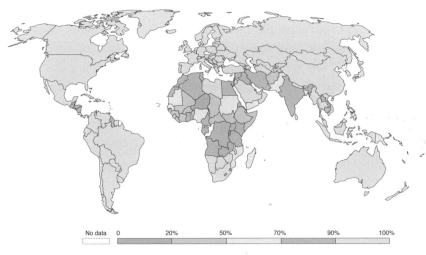

World Population Review—Literacy Rate by Country 2022を改編

① 南アフリカの識字率は50パーセント台である。　　　　（　　　）
② 識字率の最も低い国はニジェールである。　　　　　　（　　　）
③ 北朝鮮の識字率は10～20パーセントの間である。　　　（　　　）
④ チリの識字率は90～100パーセントの間である。　　　（　　　）

Point

世界の国々の位置が分かれば簡単に解ける問題です。

①の南アフリカは、アフリカ大陸の最南端に位置する国です。うすいグレーは識字率が90〜100パーセントを表すので、間違いです。

②ではニジェールの位置が問題です。識字率0〜20パーセントの濃いグリーンの国は1つだけで、アフリカのやや西寄りのサハラ砂漠の南あたりにあります。ここがニジェール共和国で、正解です。南にアルジェリアとリビア、西にマリ、東にチャド、南にナイジェリアといった国々に囲まれています。2015年に大規模調査をした際のニジェールの識字率は19.1パーセントでした。

③の北朝鮮は朝鮮半島の北部を占めています。地図で見ると色がついておらず識字率が不明です。

④チリは南米大陸の南西部にあり、南北に細長い国土の形状が特徴的です。うすいグレーで、識字率が90〜100パーセントであることがわかります。実際の調査による識字率は96.63パーセント（2015年）です。ちなみに、日本の識字率は99パーセントという調査結果が出ています。

Answer ①F ②T ③F ④T

Goal 4

日本の教育現場に関する用語

それぞれの英語の語句とその意味を線で結んでみましょう。

① tutoring school ・ ・ 教育環境

② group education ・ ・ 集団教育

③ educational environment ・ ・ 暗記学習

④ truancy ・ ・ 不登校

⑤ rote learning ・ ・ 学習塾

Point

①の「学習塾」は、「詰め込み学習」を意味するcramを使ってcram schoolと言うこともできますが、日本の教育事情に詳しくないとピンとこない外国人がいるので、補足説明が必要かもしれません。「個別指導の学習塾」はprivate-tutoring schoolと言います。

②の「集団教育」は、これまでの日本の学校での一般的なスタイルで、1クラス30〜35人の生徒が教員の話をひたすら聞く受け身の授業（passive learning）が主でしたが、最近では「主体的で対話的な深い学び」を目指すアクティブラーニング（active learning）が重視されています。主体的とは自分の意志・判断で責任をもって行動することです。

③の「教育環境」はeducation environmentと言うこともできます。

④のtruancyは「（生徒の）ずる休み、無断欠勤」などの意味を表します。school truancyと言ってもいいでしょう。「彼は不登校です」は、関連語のtruantを使ってHe is a truant.と言うか、もう少し説明調にHe refuses to go to school.と言ってもいいでしょう。

⑤の「暗記学習」あるいは「詰め込み学習」（cramming）も、日本の学習スタイルです。暗記に適した教科もあるので必ずしも悪い学習方法というわけではありません。最近の日本の学校では、疑問に思ったことを自分で調べたり、考えたりするような学習方法も多く取り入れられているようです。

① tutoring school = 学習塾

② group education = 集団教育

③ educational environment = 教育環境

④ truancy = 不登校

⑤ rote learning = 暗記学習

Goal 4

日本の不登校問題

日本における不登校の中学生の数はどのくらいだと思いますか？

① 約4万人
② 約6万人
③ 約13万人

　2020年度に行われた文部科学省の調査によると、日本の不登校の中学生は13万2,777人ということです。不登校の小学生は6万3,350人、高校生は4万3,051人なので、中学生の不登校者の数が際立って多いことがわかります。

　文部科学省による不登校の定義は、病気や経済的な理由などの特別な事情がなく、年間の欠席日数が30日以上となった状態のことです。ただし、保健室や図書室など教室外で過ごす児童・生徒や、遅刻や早退など部分登校する児童・生徒のような不登校傾向にある子どもたちを含めると、実際の数の3倍以上になると考えられています。

　不登校になる原因は、人間関係によるもの、学校生活によるもの、家庭環境によるもの、本人の問題によるものなどさまざまで、いくつかの原因が重なっている場合が多いようです。「不登校傾向にある子どもの実態調査」（日本財団、2018年）によると、不登校者の「中学に行きたくない理由のベスト10」は右表のとおりです。

　学校に行くのはなんとなくかったるい、めんどうだという気持ちは、思春期真っただ中の中学生のほとんどが感じることかもしれませんが、その気持ち以上に、中学校生活の中で自分なりに楽しいことを見つけられれば、学校へ行く気力も少しはわくのではないかと思います。なお、現在では、教育支援センターやフリースクール、不登校の生徒向けの学習塾、ネットスクールなど、民間の教育機関を利用すれば、中学校に在籍しながら自分の好きなことを突き詰めたり、自分のペースに合った学習をしたりすることが可能です。他の選択肢があって学校がすべてではないことがわかれば、気持ちも楽になるかもしれません。

According to a survey conducted by the Ministry of Education, Culture, Sports, Science and Technology in fiscal year 2020, there were 132,777 junior high school students who were not attending school in Japan. Since there were 63,350 elementary school students and 43,051 high school students who were truant, the number is strikingly high.

The definition of truancy according to the Ministry of Education, Culture, Sports, Science and Technology is a condition in which a student is absent from school for 30 days or more per year without special circumstances, such as illness or financial reasons. However, if we include students who spend time outside the classroom, such as in the nurse's room or library, and those who tend to miss school, such as those who arrive late or leave early, the actual number is believed to be more than three times higher.

The causes of truancy vary depending on relationships, school life, family environment and personal problems, and in many cases, there is a combination of causes. According to the "Survey of Children Who Tend Not to Attend School" (Nippon Foundation, 2018), the "Top 10 Reasons for Not Wanting to Go to Junior High School" for those who do not attend school are as follows:

中学に行きたくない理由のベスト10
Top 10 Reasons for Not Wanting to Go to Junior High School

1位	起きられない	No.1	Can't get up
2位	疲れる	No.2	Get tired
3位	学校に行こうとすると体調が悪くなる	No.3	Feel sick when trying to go to school
4位	授業がよくわからない・ついていけない	No.4	Don't understand or can't follow the lessons
5位	学校は居心地が悪い	No.5	Don't feel comfortable at school
6位	友達とうまくいかない	No.6	Don't get along with friends
7位	自分でもよくわからない	No.7	Don't know why myself
8位	学校に行く意味がわからない	No.8	Don't understand the meaning of going to school
9位	先生とうまくいかない・頼れない	No.9	Don't get along with teachers or can't rely on them
10位	小学校のときと比べて良い成績が取れない	No.10	Don't get good grades compared with elementary school

Most junior high school students in the midst of puberty may feel that going to school is somewhat tedious and bothersome, but if they can find something fun to do in their own way during their junior high school life, they may feel a little more motivated to go to school. Currently, private educational institutions, such as educational support centers, free schools, tutoring schools for non-attending students and online schools allow students to pursue what they like to do and learn at their own pace while still attending junior high school. A person may feel better once they realize that there are other options and that school is not everything.

Answer ③ 約13万人

日本のICT教育

日本の教育現場ではICT教育が推進されています。下の図の項目の中から真ん中のICT教育に関連があるものを選んでください。

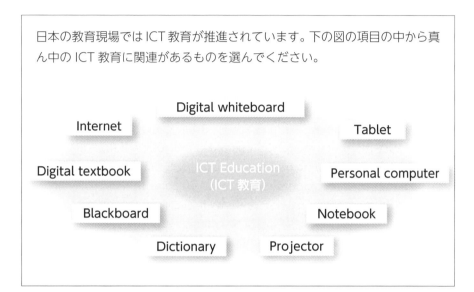

　ICT教育のICTとはInformation and Communication Technologyの単語の頭文字をとった略語で、日本語では「情報通信技術」を意味します。電子黒板やタブレット端末、アプリ、インターネットなどを活用してコミュニケーションをとる教育方法がICT教育です。

　ICT教育が進められている理由に、日本の学校でのデジタル機器の利用が世界的に見てかなり遅れていることがあげられます。その環境整備を短期間で解決しようとした文部科学省の取り組みが、児童・生徒1人に1台の学習用端末の供給と高速通信ネットワーク環境の整備の実現に向けた5年に及ぶ計画「GIGAスクール構想」です。情報化が急速に進み、児童・生徒が大きく変化する社会に対応するために、一人ひとりの能力に合わせた創造性を育む教育を目指しています。

　ICT教育の下では、紙では伝えきれない視覚的・聴覚的な情報を受け取ったり、小さいうちにITスキルを身につけることができたり、各自の能力・ペースで学習したりすることができるといったメリットがあります。一方で、キーボードを使って文字入力をするため、手書きの機会が減ってしまったり、インターネット

で簡単に調べれば知りたいことが見つかるため、自分で考える力や粘り強く物事に取り組む力が鍛えられないといったデメリットもあります。ICTを効果的に活用しながら、児童・生徒が自発的に問題を見つけ、情報を収集し、情報を見極める力を育む学習をどう取り入れていくかの対策も考えなければならないでしょう。

The "ICT" in ICT education is an acronym for the words Information and Communication Technology. ICT education is an educational method that uses digital whiteboards, tablets, apps and the internet for communication.

One of the reasons that ICT education is being promoted is that the use of digital devices in Japanese schools lags far behind the rest of the world. The Ministry of Education, Culture, Sports, Science and Technology has been trying to solve this problem in a short period of time through the "GIGA School Concept," a five-year plan to provide one learning terminal per student and to develop a high-speed communication network environment. The goal is to provide an education that fosters creativity in accordance with each student's individual abilities in order to prepare children and students for a society that is undergoing rapid changes due to the rapid progress of information technology.

In ICT education, students can receive visual and auditory information that cannot be conveyed on paper, acquire IT skills at a young age and learn at their own ability and pace. On the other hand, there are also disadvantages, such as the lack of opportunities for handwriting because students use keyboards to input text, and the fact that they can easily find what they need to know on the internet, which prevents them from developing the ability to think for themselves and persistently tackle problems. It will be necessary to consider how to incorporate learning methods that foster the ability of students to spontaneously identify problems and gather and discern information while effectively utilizing ICT.

Answer Digital whiteboard / Tablet / Personal computer / Digital textbook / Internet

「質の高い教育をみんなに」
──そのためにあなたは何ができると思いますか？
What can you do to support "quality education"?

Goal 4には、無料で公平な教育を受けられることや、初等教育の充実、男女が平等に質の高い高等教育を受けられること、教育環境や奨学金などの充実、質の高い教員を増やすことなどの目標が掲げられています。

日本では「アフリカの若者のための産業人材育成イニシアティブ」と呼ばれるプログラムがあり、アフリカの若者が日本の大学や大学院で教育を受け、日本企業でインターンシップに参加する機会を提供しています。また、JICA（国際協力機構）による「みんなの学校」プロジェクトでは、アフリカの小中学校で、保護者・教員・地域住民が行政と連携して学校を運営する取り組みが行われたりしていて、保護者や住民の教育への意識改革と子どもたちの学びの質の向上に努め、2004年の開始から現在までにアフリカ8カ国5万3,000校の学習環境が改善されるといった成果を出しています。

私たち一人ひとりができることは、教育格差問題のために活動しているNGOなどにお金を寄付することではないでしょうか。お金はそのまま、活動するNGOを支えます。ただし、ただお金を寄付するのではなく、何に使ってほしいかを明確にすることです。例えば、学校の建設や設備の拡充に使ってほしいのであれば、そこに力を入れている団体に寄付したほうがいいでしょう。また、使用済みのランドセルを、物資が不足している国々に、ノートや鉛筆などの文房具と一緒に送る団体もあります。実際に私も息子と相談してランドセルを寄付しました。インターネットで調べると、寄付を受け付けている団体がいくつか出てきます。

Goal 4 includes targets such as access to free and fair education, enhancement of primary education, equal access to quality higher education for men and women, improvement of the educational environment and scholarships as well as increasing the number of quality teachers.

In Japan, a program called the "African Business Education Initiative for Youth" provides opportunities for African youth to receive education at universities and graduate schools in Japan and participate in internships at Japanese companies. The "School for All" project by the Japan International Cooperation Agency (JICA) involves parents, teachers and local residents in elementary and junior high schools in Africa working together with the local government to manage the schools. Since its launch in 2004, the program has improved the learning environment in 53,000 schools in eight African countries.

What each of us can do is to donate money to NGOs and other organizations that are working to address educational disparities. The money will directly support the NGOs. However, we should not just donate money; we should clearly specify what we want the money to be used for. For example, if you want the money to be used for school construction or expansion of facilities, it would be better to donate to an organization that focuses on that area. There are also organizations that send used school bags along with stationery, such as notebooks and pencils, to countries where supplies are in short supply. I actually donated a school bag after discussing it with my son. If you look on the internet, you will find several organizations that accept donations.

Goal 5
ジェンダー平等を実現しよう
Gender Equality

ジェンダー平等を達成し、すべての女性および女児の
能力強化を行う。

Achieve gender equality and empower all women and girls.

　「ジェンダー平等」と言われても、「そもそもジェンダーって
何？」と思う人が多いのではないでしょうか。ジェンダーとは、
男か女かという体のつくりの違いに対して、社会的・文化的に
つくられる「男っぽさ」や「女っぽさ」といった、無意識に決め
つけられる男女の違いのことです。しかし、社会でつくられた
思い込みによるルールや習慣が男女間の不平等の問題を生んで
います。特に女の子や女性だというだけで差別されたり、社会
進出の機会を奪われて賃金格差が生じたりしています。
　本来、女性も男性も同じ人間として平等の権利をもっている
はずです。「男だから」「女だから」という決めつけによって男女
ともが苦しめられることもあります。性別にかかわらず性の多
様性をも受け入れて、誰もが平等に能力を発揮できるようにし
なければならないでしょう。

男女格差

「男女格差」を英語で何と言いますか？

① man and woman gap　② unisex gap　③ gender gap

　「男女格差」は英語でgender gapと言い、男女の経済的・社会的・文化的な不平等を意味します。男女の雇用や賃金の格差、宗教や伝統的な風習による差別など、多岐にわたる問題が含まれています。国際機関の世界経済フォーラムでは、国ごとの男女格差を政治・経済・健康・教育の４つの観点から測る「ジェンダーギャップ指数」を毎年発表しています。2022年の日本のジェンダーギャップ指数は世界146カ国中116位と、アジア諸国の中でも韓国や中国よりも低い結果で、ジェンダーの側面から見ると明らかに日本は後進国と言えます。ちなみに、②は「男女共有の、男女の区別がない」という意味です。

　The term "*danjo kakusa*" or "gender gap" refers to the economic, social and cultural inequality between men and women. The term includes a wide range of issues, such as employment and wage disparities between men and women, and discrimination based on religion and traditional customs. Every year, an international organization called the World Economic Forum (WEF) publishes the Gender Gap Index, which measures the gender gap in each country from four perspectives: politics, economy, health and education. In the Gender Gap Index, Japan ranked 116th out of 146 countries in the world in 2022, behind South Korea and China among Asian countries, clearly indicating that Japan was backward in terms of gender equality. Incidentally, the word "unisex" in ② means "shared by men and women, without distinction between them."

Answer　③ gender gap

Sex と Gender の違い

男女の体のつくりの違いから判断する性別のことを英語で sex と言い、社会的・文化的な先入観から判断する性別のことを gender と言います。次の各文はそれぞれの特徴を表しています。sex の特徴には S を、gender の特徴には G を記してください。

① Men generally* have bigger bones* than women do.　　　(　　)
② In most countries, women do more housework* than 　　(　　)
　men do.
③ In most countries, men earn* more money than 　　　　(　　)
　women do.
④ Women can menstruate,* while men cannot. 　　　　　　(　　)
⑤ In Japan, girls generally wear skirts, while boys wear 　(　　)
　slacks* for their school uniforms.

*generally たいてい、一般的に　　bones 骨格、骨、体つき　　housework 家事　　earn 稼ぐ
menstruate 生理がある　　slacks ズボン

Goal 5

Point

　①は「男性は一般的に女性より体格ががっちりしている」という意味で、男女の体つきの特徴を示しているため、正解はSです。
　②は「ほとんどの国で、女性は男性よりも多く家事をこなす」という意味です。社会的・文化的役割についての記述なので、Gです。
　③は「ほとんどの国で、男性は女性よりも多くお金を稼ぐ」です。これも社会的な先入観によるものなので、Gです。
　④は「女性には生理があるが、男性にはない」は生物学的な記述なので、Sです。
　⑤は「日本では、学校の制服として女子はたいていスカートをはくが、男子はズボンをはく」という意味です。文化的につくられた習慣なので、Gです。

Answer　①S　②G　③G　④S　⑤G

性差に関する用語

次の各語句とその意味を線で結んでください。

① gender inequality ・   ・   女性差別

② gender bias ・   ・   力（権限）を与えること

③ misogyny ・   ・   男女不平等

④ sexual harassment ・   ・   性差による偏見

⑤ empowerment ・   ・   性的嫌がらせ

Point

①の inequality は「不平等」の意味。「平等」を表す equality の頭に in- という「否定」を意味する接頭辞をつけて inequality にします。

②の gender bias は、男女の性別による差や役割について、人や社会が無意識にもつ固定観念や偏見のことです。男の子を青色や車で、女の子をピンク色やリボンで象徴したり、あえて「女性寿司職人」や「女性パイロット」と呼んだりと、日常生活の中で気づかないうちにジェンダーバイアスがかかっていることが多いのです。

③の misogyny は「女性差別」の意味で、「ミソジニー」という日本語が使われる場合もあります。説明的に discrimination against women と言うこともできます。アメリカでは、Jane Crow という架空の女性の名前が「女性差別」を意味する言葉として使われる場合があります。Jane Crow は、「アフリカ系アメリカ人を指す蔑称」の意味の Jim Crow と、「身元不明の女性、匿名の女性」に使われる Jane Doe という言葉を掛け合わせたものです。ちなみに「男性差別」は misandry と言います。

④の sexual harassment から、カタカナ語の「セクハラ」が生まれました。

⑤の empowerment は、empower（力を与える）の名詞形です。社会の中で一人ひとりが本来持っている能力を発揮して、自らの意思決定によって自発的に行動を起こすことを意味します。社会的弱者や差別されている人に対して、自らその状況を変える力を持てるように支援するという意味合いもあります。また、企業や組織で、上司が持っている権限を部下に移譲し、部下の判断で仕事を自発的にさせることで、部下

に本来持っている能力を発揮させて組織のパフォーマンスを向上させる意味合いで、empowerment という言葉が使われることもあります。

Answer
① gender inequality ＝ 男女不平等
② gender bias ＝ 性差による偏見
③ misogyny ＝ 女性差別
④ sexual harassment ＝ 性的嫌がらせ
⑤ empowerment ＝ 力（権限）を与えること

Goal 5

性差による偏見をなくす

gender bias（性差による偏見）をなくすために、差別につながる可能性のある言葉を違和感のないように性的に中立な言葉に変えたものを gender-inclusive language / gender-neutral language と言います。下の表のそれぞれの言葉を gender-inclusive language に書き換えてください。

Gendered language	Gender-inclusive language
policeman（警察官）	①
businessman（ビジネスマン）	②
steward/stewardess （スチュワード／スチュワーデス）	③
fireman（消防士）	④
ladies and gentlemen（紳士淑女）	⑤

Point

①の officer は性的に中立な言葉です。警察官にはもちろん女性もいることから、police officer が使われるようになっています。

②の business person の複数形は、business people です。

③の steward/stewardess は、最近では日本でも聞かれなくなった「客室乗務員」のことです。以前は、「男性客室乗務員」のことを steward（スチュワード）、「女性客室乗務員」のことは stewardess（スチュワーデス）と呼んでいましたが、これも性差別用語として諸外国では使われなくなり、flight attendant が使われるようになりました。日本の航空会社では一般に CA という呼称が使われているので、日本人には CA のほうが耳馴染みがあるかもしれません。CA は cabin attendant の略で、英単語としては「客船係」という意味で存在しますが、外国では飛行機の「客室乗務員」という意味ではほとんど使われることはありません。英語で飛行機の客室乗務員のことを言う場合には CA は使わず、flight attendant を使うように意識しましょう。

④のfirefighterも、消防士に女性もいることから使われるようになった言葉です。

⑤のladies and gentlemenは、以前は電車内や飛行機内などでのアナウンスで、呼びかけの言葉としてよく使われていましたが、ladiesでもgentlemenでもないと自認する人たちに配慮するために、近年ではeveryoneやall passengersといった表現が使われようになりました。

Answer
① police officer
② business person
③ flight attendant
④ firefighter
⑤ everyone

児童婚の現状

18歳未満で結婚させられている女の子は、世界中に年間どのくらいいると思いますか？

① 約12万人　　② 約120万人　　③ 約1,200万人

　18歳未満での結婚を「児童婚」と言います。18歳未満の女の子が全世界で年間1,200万人も強制的に結婚させられているとのことです。児童婚は主にアフリカやインドなど貧困地帯で、親や親戚が女の子を結婚させ、その引き換えに金品を受け取るという人身売買によって成立しています。結婚を強いられた女の子は自由や教育の機会を奪われるだけでなく、体が未発達のまま妊娠・出産するため、命を落とすリスクも高くなります。また、夫からの暴力や虐待の被害に遭いやすく、さまざまな意味で悪影響を受けています。貧困や、国・地域に根強く残る好ましくない慣習、不十分な法整備、大人の認識不足などの問題が改善されなければ、児童婚はなくならないでしょう。

Child marriage is the marriage of children under the age of 18. Twelve million girls under the age of 18 are forcibly married each year worldwide. Child marriage is mainly practiced in poverty-stricken areas, such as Africa and India, where girls are trafficked by parents or relatives who force them to marry in exchange for money. Girls forced into marriage are not only deprived of their freedom and educational opportunities, but also face a high risk of death due to pregnancy and childbirth while their bodies are still undeveloped. They are also vulnerable to violence and abuse by their husbands, which negatively affects them in many ways. Child marriage will not disappear unless problems such as poverty, undesirable practices that persist in various countries and regions, inadequate legislation and lack of awareness among adults are corrected.

Answer　▷　③ 約1,200万人

性差別問題

世界には考えられないような性差別が存在します。次のうち、本当にあるものはどれだと思いますか？

① 女性が自動車を運転することが禁止されている。
② 女性が夫の許可なく海外へ行くことができない。
③ 女児が生まれると 24 時間以内に殺してしまう慣習がある。
④ 男性のみが土地を所有・管理することができる。

①はサウジアラビアの一部の保守的な地域で実際にある慣習で、女性は自動車の運転免許を持つことができず、父親や夫の同伴がなければ遠くへ外出できません。

②はイスラム法に従ったイランの慣習で、既婚女性は夫の許可なく海外へ行くことができません。未婚女性も40歳までは父親の許可が必要です。

③はインドの一部の農村に存在する非常に深刻な問題です。インドでは結婚の際に花嫁の父親が花婿の家族に巨額な持参金を贈るならわしがあり、女の子は貧困家庭にとって経済的な負担とみなされています。自治体や警察もこの慣習は把握しているものの、個々の家族の問題として介入に難色を示しています。また、都市部の中流層では、出生前の性別検査をして、妊婦が女児を妊娠していることがわかると中絶する家庭もあるようです。

④はタンザニアやレソト、スーダン北部などに残る慣例で、法的には平等に権利が与えられているにもかかわらず、実際には女性は土地を所有することを禁じられています。

① is the **actual practice** in some conservative areas of Saudi Arabia, where women are not allowed to have a driver's license for a car and cannot go far away from home without being accompanied by their father or husband.

② is an Iranian practice according to **Islamic law**, where married women are not allowed to go abroad without the permission of their husbands.

Unmarried women also need their father's permission before the age of 40.

③ is a very serious problem that exists in some rural villages in India. In India, it is customary for the father of the bride to give a huge dowry to the groom's family at the time of marriage, and girls are considered an economic burden for poor families. Local authorities and police are aware of this practice, but are reluctant to intervene as it is considered to be a matter for individual families. In addition, some families in urban middle-class areas have abortions when a prenatal sex test reveals that the pregnant woman is carrying a girl.

④ is a practice that remains in Tanzania, Lesotho and northern Sudan, where women are actually prohibited from owning land, even though they are legally entitled to equal rights.

Answer　すべて本当である。

少子化問題

「少子化」を英語で何というのが適当でしょう。

① declining birthrate
② inclining birthrate
③ baby boom

「少子化」とは、出生数の減少や、高齢者に対する子どもの割合の低下を意味します。

現在の日本は高齢化にともなって、生まれてくる子どもの数が減少する状態が続いています。2021年に生まれた子どもの数は過去最少の81万1,604人で、6年連続で減少しています。この傾向は国の推計より6年早く、超高齢化の日本が超少子化へと進んでいることは明らかでしょう。

少子化の原因は、結婚に価値を見出せなかったり、独身生活のほうに利点があったりするなどの考え方の変化や、晩婚化による晩産化、出産・育児・教育への経済的不安、結婚や出産後の就労継続の難しさ、子育て世代の男性の長時間労働と家事・育児への不参加などがありますが、これらを改善し育児を支える社会制度が整っていないことが問題なのです。家族手当などの経済的支援はもとより、結婚・出産後も女性が働くことができるよう、保育施設を充実させたり、男性の育児参加への意識改革や育児休業制度を整備したりといった支援も進めなければなりません。また今後は、結婚という法制度にとらわれずに子どもを生みたいカップルなどへの支援を行う制度を確立するなど、今までには考えられなかった政策が必要になってくるかもしれません。

The term "declining birthrate" refers to a decrease in the number of births and the ratio of children to the elderly.

In Japan today, the number of children being born continues to decline as the population ages: the number of children born in 2021 was the lowest on record at 811,604, a decline for the sixth consecutive year. This trend is six years ahead of what the country estimated, and it is clear that Japan's super-aging population is moving toward a super-low birthrate.

The causes of the declining birthrate include changes in attitudes, such as not placing value on marriage, the advantages of single life, late childbearing due to later marriages, economic concerns about childbirth, childcare and education, difficulties in continuing to work after marriage and childbirth, and long working hours and nonparticipation in housework and childcare by men of child-rearing age. The problem is that there is no social system in place to deal with these issues and support child-rearing. In addition to economic support, such as family allowances, we need to improve childcare facilities so that women can work after marriage and childbirth, raise awareness of men's participation in childcare and establish a childcare leave system. In the future, it may also be necessary to establish previously unthinkable policies, such as establishing a system to support couples who want to have children without being bound by the legal system of marriage.

Point

①のdecliningは「減少している」、birthrateは「出生率」という意味です。もう少し簡単にlow birthrateと言うこともできます。②のincliningはdecliningの反意語で「増加している」です。③のbaby boomは赤ん坊の出生が一時的に急増する現象のことで、日本では第1次ベビーブーム（1947〜1949年）に約270万人、第2次ベビーブーム（1971〜1974年）に約210万人の新生児が誕生しました。

Answer ① declining birthrate

多様性に関する用語

次の各語句とその意味を線で結んでみましょう。

① diversity　　　　・　　　・　多様性を受け入れて生かすこと

② inclusion　　　　・　　　・　（人種・宗教などの）少数派（民族）

③ LGBTQ+　　　　・　　　・　身体障がい者

④ minority　　　　・　　　・　性的少数派

⑤ the disabled　　・　　　・　多様性

Point

　①の diversity は「ダイバーシティー」とカタカナ語で使われることもあります。性別や人種、年齢、国籍、障がいの有無などで差別することなく、一人ひとりが持つ違いを認め・尊重することを意味します。

　②の inclusion にはダイバーシティーと似たような意味もありますが、性別や人種、年齢、国籍、障がいの有無などで差別することなく、それぞれが個性や能力を発揮できる場を与えることを意味します。

　③の LGBTQ+ は「エル・ジー・ビー・ティー・キュー・プラス」と読み、多様なセクシュアリティーの人たちを表現する言葉です。L = lesbian（レズビアン：女性として女性を好きになる人）、G = gay（ゲイ：男性として男性を好きになる人）、B = bisexual（バイセクシャル：男女どちらにも性的な感情が向く人）、T = transgender（トランスジェンダー：心と体の性が一致しない人）、Q = queer/questioning（クイア：もともとは「風変わりな、奇妙な」といった同性愛者への侮蔑語で、現在は型にはまらない性の捉え方を一括りにした表現／クエスチョニング：自分の性がどちらなのか、またどちらの性に魅かれるのか定まっていない人）のそれぞれの頭文字をとっています。最後の + = plus は、その他のセクシュアリティーを表していて、常に新しいセクシャルマイノリティーに開放的でいようとするポジティブな意味が込められています。LGBT や LGBTQ、複数形の LGBTQs なども広く使われています。また、国連機関などでは、LGBTQ+ を包括した言葉、SOGI（Sexual Orientation and Gender

Identity：どの性を向いていて自分がどの性と認識しているかということ）が使われるようになっています。

　④のminorityの反意語はmajority（多数派）です。

　⑤のdisabledは「身体に障がいのある」という意味の形容詞です。形容詞にtheをつけると「〜の人々」という意味になります。

　　① diversity = 多様性

　　② inclusion = 多様性を受け入れて生かすこと

　　③ LGBTQ+ = 性的少数派

　　④ minority = （人種・宗教などの）少数派（民族）

　　⑤ the disabled = 身体障がい者

無償労働の問題点

家事や育児、家族の介護などの仕事のことを（　　　　）work と言います。
この空欄に当てはまる単語は次のどれだと思いますか？

① house
② unpaid
③ overtime

　無償労働の問題点は、必要不可欠な労働であるにもかかわらず対価が支払われ
ないことと、その多くを担っているのが女性だということです。国連女性機関に
よると、無償労働の評価額は各国の国内総生産（GDP）の10 〜 39パーセント相
当の規模があり、製造業や運輸業などよりも経済に貢献するはずの値だというこ
とです。また、平成30年に公表された内閣府経済社会総合研究所の調査では、日
本人女性の１年間の家事活動の貨幣評価額は193万5,000円でした。
　一方、労働に費やす時間を見ると、女性は男性の約2.5倍の時間を家事などの
無償労働に使っています。賃金労働に費やす時間が無賃労働のために奪われてし
まうため、必然的に女性は男性よりも収入が少なくなり、男女格差が生まれる結
果となります。いまだに多くの国に「家事は女性がするもので、男性は外で働き
家計を支える」という慣習があります。これは男性の意識のみならず、女性にも
「結婚したら家庭に入るものだ」と思っていたり、「夫の給料で楽をしたい」と考
えたりする人がいるからではないでしょうか。無償労働のような男女の不平等を
改善するには、男女共に意識を変えて協力し合い、女性が自立し社会参加できる
環境が必要でしょう。

　The problem with unpaid work is that it is essential labor that is not
compensated, and that most of it is done by women. According to an organization
called UN Women, the value of unpaid work is equivalent to between 10 and
39 percent of the gross domestic product (GDP) of each country, so it must be
contributing more to the economy than the manufacturing or transportation

industries do. In addition, according to a survey by the Economic and Social Research Institute of the Cabinet Office published in 2018, the monetary value of Japanese women's housework activities for one year was 1,935,000 yen.

On the other hand, looking at the time spent on labor, women spend about 2.5 times more time than men on unpaid work, such as housework. Since the time spent on paid work is limited by unpaid work, women inevitably earn less than men, resulting in a gender gap. In many countries, there is still a custom that "housework is done by women, and men work outside to support the household." This is not just because of men's mindsets. Women, too, often think things like "I joined my husband's family when I got married" or "I want to live an easy life with my husband's salary." In order to reduce gender inequality and things like unpaid work, it will be necessary for both men and women to change their mindsets and cooperate with each other, and to create an environment in which women can become independent and participate in society.

Point

　家事や育児、家族の介護のように、時間と労力を使っているにもかかわらずお金を受け取ることができない仕事のことを、unpaid work（無償労働）と言います。unpaid は「無給の、無報酬の」という意味です。①を用いて housework と言えば「家事」を指します。③の overtime work は「残業」という意味です。また、賃金が支払われる仕事は paid work と表現されます。

Answer ② unpaid

ノンバイナリージェンダー

性別を表す代名詞（he や she）のことを gender pronouns と言いますが、最近では男女 2 択のジェンダーにとらわれないノンバイナリージェンダー（nonbinary gender）が浸透しつつあります。nonbinary の人を表す代名詞は次のどれだと思いますか？

① they
② y'all
③ X

Point

they はもともと三人称複数に使われる代名詞ですが、英語辞典にも "used to refer to a single person whose gender identity is nonbinary"（性自認がノンバイナリーな人に言及するときに使われる）という意味が新たに加わり、they がノンバイナリーの人を表す三人称単数の代名詞として使われていることが示されています。ただし、このノンバイナリーの they を日本語で訳すとなると、「彼、彼女」ではないためになかなか表現しがいものがあります。

② の y'all は you all の短縮形で、「あなた方、君たち」という意味です。もともとアメリカ南部の人たちが使っていた言葉で、「ヨー（ル）」と伸ばして発音します。

③の X は「自分の性が男女どちらにもはっきりと当てはまらない人」のことを表すアルファベットです。見た目や性的指向は問われません。オーストラリアのパスポートの性別欄には、2011 年から M（男性）と F（女性）に X（不確定）が加えられたり、アメリカでも 2022 年からパスポートの申請時の性別欄で X が選択可能になったりと、インクルーシブな政策が進められています。

Answer　① they

「ジェンダー平等を実現しよう」
──そのためにあなたは何ができると思いますか？
What can you do to bring about "gender equality"?

　ジェンダーの不平等は、古くからの社会的・文化的な慣習に起因する問題であり、長い歴史の中で人々に植え付けられてきた無意識下の問題でもあるため、かなり複雑で、問題解決に時間がかかることは確かです。しかし、ジェンダー問題を改善させることは、貧困の減少や教育問題の改善にもつながるため、ジェンダー平等の実現は必要不可欠です。

　私たちにできることは限られているかもしれませんが、必要なことはまず、どんな問題があるのかを「知ること」、そして知り得た知識を周りの人に「伝えること」です。国や社会、企業が行う支援や活動、取り組みの中に、個人が参加できるものがあれば、参加してみるのもいいでしょう。また、身の回りで言えば、家事を分担するといった小さなことが、ジェンダー平等の取り組みにつながります。さらに、「男だから」「女だから」という考えに縛られることなく、多様な性のあり方を認識し、常に公平な意識をもって人と接してみることも、日常的にできる取り組みでしょう。

　Gender inequality is a problem that stems from long-standing social and cultural practices, and reflects an unconscious attitude that has been instilled in people over a long period of time, so the problem is quite complex and will certainly take time to solve. However, it is essential to achieve gender equality because improving gender issues will also lead to reductions in poverty and improvements in educational issues.

　What we can do may be limited, but what is necessary is first to "know" what problems exist, and then to "communicate" the knowledge we have gained to those around us. If there are supports, activities or initiatives provided by the government, society or companies that individuals can participate in, it is a good idea to get involved. Also, in terms of our immediate surroundings, small things, such as sharing household chores, can lead to gender equality efforts. Furthermore, recognizing the diversity of gender without being bound by the idea of "because I am a man" or "because I am a woman," and always trying to interact with people with an unbiased attitude would be an effort that can be made on a daily basis.

Goal 6

安全な水とトイレを世界中に
Clean Water and Sanitation

すべての人々にとっての水と下水道設備の利用可能性と
持続可能な管理を確保する。

**Ensure availability and sustainable management of water
and sanitation for all.**

　「水の惑星」とも呼ばれる地球。実際、地球の表面の3分の2が水ですが、その約97パーセントを海水が占めているため、実際に人々が飲み水や生活用水として使える川や湖の水（淡水）は、わずか0.01パーセントでしかありません。まさに水は限られた貴重な資源なのです。

　また、私たち日本人は何の問題もなくきれいな水を毎日使うことができますが、世界では4人に1人が不衛生な水を飲んで命を落としたり、3人に1人が衛生的な水洗トイレを使えません。世界で深刻な水とトイレの問題を知り、改善策を考えてみましょう。

参照：国土交通省「世界の水資源」
日本ユニセフ協会「6.安全な水とトイレを世界中に」

地球の水資源

下の図は、地球の水資源の割合を表したものです。日本語を参考にして、それぞれのカッコ内に当てはまる語句を下の語群から選んでください。

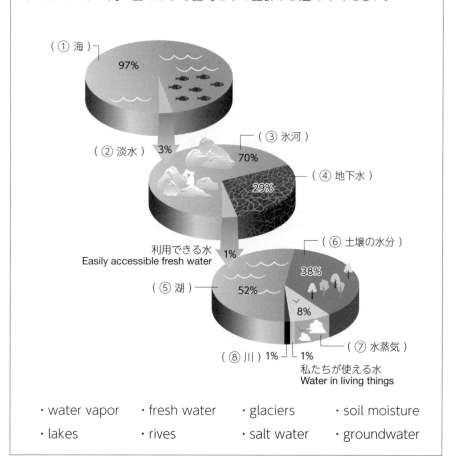

(① 海)

97%

(③ 氷河)

(② 淡水) 3%

70%

(④ 地下水)

29%

利用できる水
Easily accessible fresh water 1%

(⑥ 土壌の水分)

38%

(⑤ 湖) 52%

8%

(⑦ 水蒸気)

(⑧ 川) 1% 1%

私たちが使える水
Water in living things

・water vapor　　・fresh water　　・glaciers　　・soil moisture

・lakes　　・rives　　・salt water　　・groundwater

この章の冒頭でも述べたとおり、地球の97パーセントは海水（＝塩水）で、淡水はわずか3パーセントです。その3パーセントのうちの70パーセントが氷河で

29パーセントが地下水、残りの1パーセントが使える水ということになります。ところが、実際にはこの1パーセントのうち、水蒸気や土壌の水分が46パーセント、水質が悪い湖や川が53パーセントもあるため、私たちが使えるのはその中のわずか1パーセントに過ぎないのです。地球の水の量をバスタブ1杯分（200リットル）に換算してみると、なんとスプーン1杯分（20ミリリットル）なのです。気候変動や人口増加、それに伴う水資源の消費増加など、水不足はますます深刻になっています。各国では、生態系を崩さないようにしながら、海水や不衛生な水を、技術を駆使して使えるようにするシステムの開発が進められています。

As mentioned at the beginning of this chapter, 97 percent of the earth's surface is salt water, and only 3 percent is fresh water. Of that 3 percent, 70 percent is in the form of glaciers, 29 percent is groundwater, and the remaining 1 percent is usable water. In reality, however, of this 1 percent, 46 percent is water vapor and soil moisture, and 53 percent is lakes and rivers of poor quality, so only 1 percent of that is usable. The earth's usable water supply is equivalent to one spoonful (20 milliliters) of water in a bathtub (200 liters). Water scarcity is becoming increasingly serious due to climate change, population growth and the resulting increase in consumption of water resources. Countries are developing systems to make seawater and unsanitary water usable through the use of technology, while ensuring that ecosystems are not disrupted.

Point

「地球の水資源」を英語でEarth's water resourcesと言います。図のようにさまざまな資源からなるのでresourcesと複数形になります。

Answer　① salt water　② fresh water　③ glaciers　④ groundwater
⑤ lakes　⑥ soil moisture　⑦ water vapor　⑧ rivers

水の大切さ

下の語句を正しい順に並び替えて「人は水がなければ約3日間しか生きることができません」という文を完成させてください。

about / a person / three days / live / water / can /without /
for / only / .

　人は、食べ物がなくても体内の脂肪や、さらに筋肉までをもエネルギーに変えることができるため、水と睡眠をとっていれば2～3週間は生きられます。逆に、水がなければおよそ3日間で死んでしまいます。人の体内にある水の量は体重のおよそ55~60パーセントで、体重50キロの人だと約30リットルの水を体内に蓄えていることになります。そのうちの2パーセント程度が失われると口や喉の渇きを感じ、6パーセントが失われると頭痛や眠気を引き起こして情緒が不安定になります。約10パーセントが失われると筋肉のけいれんや体温の上昇などの脱水症状を起こし、汗や尿が出なくなったり、血液の循環が悪くなったりします。そして体内の水分の約20パーセントがなくなると死んでしまいます。まさに、水は人々にとって生きていくために必要不可欠な要素なのです。

　Even without food, a person can convert fat and even muscle into energy, and can live for two to three weeks with water and sleep. Without water, on the other hand, they will die in about three days. The amount of water in the human body is about 55-60 percent of body weight, meaning that a person weighing 50 kilograms has about 30 liters of water stored in their body. If the body loses about 2 percent of this amount, the mouth and throat feel thirsty, and if 6 percent is lost, headaches and drowsiness occur, causing emotional instability. When about 10 percent is lost, dehydration occurs, including muscle cramps and increased body temperature, which can lead to loss of sweat and urine and poor blood circulation. And when about 20 percent of the body's water is lost, people die. Water is truly an essential element for people to survive.

Point

　英語の語順の基本は「主語→動詞」です。そして動詞のあとに「目的語」や「補語」「修飾語」などを加えていきます。この文では、「人は（主語）／〜しか生きることができません（動詞）／水がなければ（修飾語）／約3日間（修飾語）」という語順で考えます。

Answer　A person can only live without water for about three days.

水に関する用語

次の単語とその意味を線で結んでください。

① sewerage ・ ・ 公衆衛生

② a lack of safe water ・ ・ 安全でない水

③ water supply ・ ・ 安全な水の不足

④ unsafe water ・ ・ 上水道、飲料水の供給設備

⑤ sanitation ・ ・ 下水道（設備）、下水処理

　使用済みの汚れた水は、下水道を通って下水処理施設まで運ばれ、有害物質などを処理して、海や川へ排水されます。

　世界に水道水をそのまま飲める国はわずか15カ国しかなく、ほとんどの国では水質に問題があったり、味に癖のある硬水だったりで、水道がない国すらあります。また、水そのものが不足している国もあります。日本の水のように水質が良く、そのまま飲めるのはまれです。

　安全な水を飲むことのできない人々が世界に約22億人いると言われています。開発途上国の中には、虫やごみが浮いた川で水をくみ、飲料水として使っているところがありますが、ごみなどを取り除き煮沸したとしても安全とは言えず、体が未発達な子どもたちは頻繁に下痢を起こしたり、命を落としたりすることさえあります。

　Used and dirty water is carried through the sewage system to sewage treatment facilities, where it is treated for harmful substances and discharged into the sea or rivers.

　There are only 15 countries in the world where you can drink tap water directly from the tap, and most of them have water quality problems or hard water with a peculiar taste, and there are many countries that do not even have tap water. There are also countries where water itself is in short supply.

Rarely is the water as high quality and drinkable as Japanese water.

It is estimated that there are approximately 2.2 billion people in the world without access to safe drinking water. In some developing countries, water is drawn from rivers with floating insects and debris and used as drinking water, but even if the debris is removed and the water is boiled, it is not safe, and children, whose bodies are not yet fully developed, frequently suffer from diarrhea or even die.

①の sewerage とよく似た sewage という語は、家庭から流れる「下水、汚水、汚物」のことを指します。

②の a lack of 〜は「〜の不足」を意味します。

③は waterworks とも言います。

⑤の sanitation は、下水処理をすることで公衆衛生を守り、安全な環境を維持するということです。同じような意味で hygiene もありますが、こちらは病気を予防するために清潔な状態を保つ「衛生状態」のことです。

Answer

① sewerage = 下水道（設備）、下水処理

② a lack of safe water = 安全な水の不足

③ water supply = 上水道、飲料水の供給設備

④ unsafe water = 安全でない水

⑤ sanitation = 公衆衛生

Goal 6

水不足の原因

下の図の中央の「水不足の原因」の周りには、さまざまな語句が散らばっています。この中から、水不足の原因だと考えられるものを選んでください。

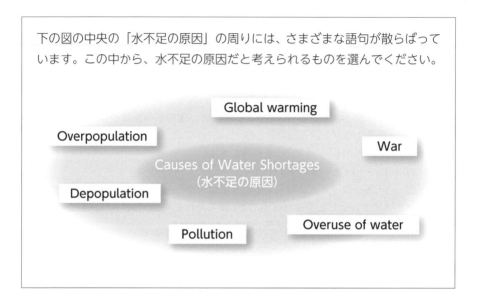

世界の水不足の原因はさまざまですが、主要な原因の一つに世界的な人口増加が挙げられます。人が増えれば、生活用水や製造業などの工業用水の使用量も増えるため、水が足りなくなるのは当然のことでしょう。

さらに、地球温暖化や水質や土壌の汚染も世界の水不足に影響を及ぼしています。二酸化炭素などによって地球温暖化が進むと、洪水や干ばつなどの異常気象が起こりやすくなります。洪水は一時的に水不足を解消するように思われますが、大量の水が土地に流れ込むことでさまざまな施設を破壊し、生活機能が失われてしまいます。また、流れ込んだ水そのものも汚染されているので使うことはできません。

水質や土壌汚染も深刻な問題です。上下水道のインフラが整っていないと、川や池に排泄物や生活ごみが直接流れ込んだり、工場からの化学物質が含まれた汚染水が垂れ流しの状態だったりします。安全な水にアクセスできない地域では、自宅から遠く離れた水場まで、子どもが何時間も歩いて水くみをしなければならず、子どもの教育の機会を奪うといった別の問題も生じています。

There are many causes of water shortages in the world, but one of the major ones is global population growth. As the number of people increases, so does the amount of water used for daily life and industrial purposes, such as manufacturing, so it is only natural that water will become scarce.

In addition, global warming and water and soil pollution are also contributing to the world's water shortages. As global warming increases due to carbon dioxide and other factors, extreme weather events, such as floods and droughts, are more likely to occur. Floods may sound like they would temporarily relieve water shortages, but the large amounts of water flowing over the land destroy various facilities that are needed to support people's everyday lives. In addition, the water itself that flows over the land is contaminated and cannot be used.

Water and soil contamination are also serious problems. If the water supply and sewerage infrastructure are not in place, excrement and household waste will flow directly into rivers and ponds, and polluted water containing chemicals from factories will be discharged. In areas without access to safe water, another problem arises when children must walk for hours to fetch water from water sources far from their homes, depriving them of educational opportunities.

Answer Global warming／Overuse of water／Pollution／Overpopulation

Goal 6

開発途上国の水事情

近くに水源がない開発途上国の女性や子どもたちは毎日約何キロメートル
を歩いて水くみをしていると思いますか？

① 約2キロメートル
② 約4キロメートル
③ 約6キロメートル
④ 約8キロメートル

　開発途上国には、毎日必要な水をくみに行かなければ生活ができない人々がいます。その役割を担うのが女性や子どもたちで、平均して往復約6キロメートルの距離を毎日歩いて水を運んでいます。底がしっかりとした靴を履かずに、素足やゴムサンダル履きで歩きます。1回に20リットルの水を運んだとしても、1人が1日に使用する最低限の量にしかならないため、家族の分も確保するためには何往復もしなくてはなりません。重い水の容器を頭に乗せたり、背中に担いだりしながら、石が転がる未舗装の道を何時間もかけて歩くことは、とりわけ女性や子どもにとっては過酷であり危険を伴います。

　また、やっと手に入れた水は汚れで濁っています。煮沸をしたとしても安全な飲み水にはほど遠く、下痢や感染症を引き起こしたり、最悪の場合は命を落とすことにつながったりします。

　このように、水くみは女性や子どもたちの貴重な時間と労力、さらには命までをも奪っています。水くみをしないですめば、子どもたちはその時間に学校に行き、女性たちは収入を得る仕事をして経済活動に参加することができます。各国のNGOでは、支援先の人々と一緒に、住んでいる場所の近くに井戸や貯水タンクを設置して、短時間で安全な水を確保できるよう支援しています。

　In developing countries, there are people who have to go to get the water they need every day for their daily life. Women and children are responsible for this task, and they walk an average of about 6 kilometers round trip every day to get water. They often do this barefoot or in rubber sandals instead of wearing shoes with solid soles. Even if they carry 20 liters of water at a time, it is only enough for one person to use for a day, so they must make several round trips to get enough for their families. Walking for hours over rocky dirt roads carrying heavy water containers on your head or on your back can be harsh and dangerous, especially for women and children.

In addition, the water that is finally obtained is often muddy with dirt. Even if the water is boiled, it is far from safe to drink and can cause diarrhea, infection or in the worst case, death.

Therefore, lack of access to clean water is both a drain on the precious time and energy of women and children, and a threat to their lives. If water fetching were eliminated, children could go to school during this time, and women could participate in economic activities by doing income-generating work. NGOs in various countries are working with the people they support to install wells and water tanks near where they live to help them secure safe water in a short period of time.

Answer ③ 約6キロメートル

Goal 6

世界のトイレ事情

世界では何人に 1 人が衛生的なトイレを使えずにいるでしょうか？

① 3 人
② 5 人
③ 10 人
④ 20 人

　世界には、トイレのない生活を送っている人が約20億人います。さらに、安全かつ衛生的なトイレを使うことのできない人が、開発途上国を中心に約42億人います。実に、約3人に1人がいわゆる「トイレ」以外で用を足しているのです。例えば、野外で地面に穴を掘って用を足し、終わったら土をかぶせて埋めたり、池や川で排泄したり、バケツに排泄して汚物を屋外に捨てたりするなどです。このような排泄方法は飲み水の汚染にもつながり、赤痢やコレラ、腸チフスといった感染症を招くことにもなります。実際に、不衛生な水が原因の下痢性疾患で毎日800〜1,000人の乳幼児が亡くなっています。

　水とトイレの問題を抱えている地域では、上下水道のインフラ整備や、水を使わず微生物の力で排泄物を処理するバイオトイレの開発・普及の努力が行われていますが、急激な人口増加もあってなかなか追いつかないのが現実です。

There are about 2 billion people in the world who live without toilets. Furthermore, approximately 4.2 billion people, mainly in developing countries, do not have access to safe and hygienic toilets. In fact, about one in three people relieve themselves in a place other than the so-called "toilet." For example, they may dig a hole in the ground outdoors and cover it with soil when they are done, defecate in a pond or river, or use a bucket and dispose of the waste outdoors. This method of excretion also leads to contamination of drinking water, leading to infectious diseases, such as dysentery, cholera and typhoid fever. In fact, 800 to 1,000 infants die every day from diarrheal diseases caused by unsanitary water.

In areas where water and toilet problems exist, efforts are being made to improve water and sewage infrastructure and to develop and spread bio-toilets that use microorganisms to dispose of waste without the use of water, but the reality is that it is difficult to keep up, partly due to rapid population growth.

Answer　①3人

UNICEF

UNICEF（ユニセフ）の正式名称は次のどれでしょうか？

① United Nation's Children's Fund
② United Nations Childrens Fund
③ United Nations Children's Fund
④ United Nation's Children's Funds

UNICEFの英語の正式名称はUnited Nations Children's Fund（国際連合児童基金）です。「あれ？ 頭文字をとってもUNICEFにはならないぞ!?」と思った人は鋭いですね。1946年12月11日に設立された国連の補助機関UNICEFは、当初はUnited Nations International Children's Emergency Fund（国際連合国際児童緊急基金）と名付けられていました。その頭文字をとったのがUNICEFという呼称です。

戦後の緊急援助を、子どもを対象に行っていましたが、子どもの権利の保護など緊急援助以外の幅広い活動をするために、1953年に正式名称が現在のものに変わりました。略称には、当初のUNICEFがそのまま使われています。現在では主に、「子どもの権利条約」の普及活動と、開発途上国や戦争・紛争地域で被害を受けている子どもの支援活動を中心とし、物資の援助と子どもの親に対するさまざまな啓発活動に力を入れています。

UNICEF's official name in English is United Nations Children's Fund. Some people may think, "What? The letters in that don't match with UNICEF!?" UNICEF, a subsidiary agency of the United Nations established on December 11, 1946, was originally named the United Nations International Children's Emergency Fund. That is what the acronym stands for.

In 1953, the official name was changed to the current one in order to cover a wider range of activities other than emergency relief, such as the protection of children's rights. The original name UNICEF is still used as an acronym.

Today, UNICEF's main activities are the dissemination of the Convention on the Rights of the Child and support for children affected by war and conflict in developing countries, with an emphasis on material assistance and various educational activities for parents.

Answer ③ United Nations Children's Fund

Goal 6

日本の水使用量

下の円グラフは、日本の家庭における水の使用量の割合を目的別に示したものです。空欄にあてはまるそれぞれの目的・用途を下の語群から選んでください。

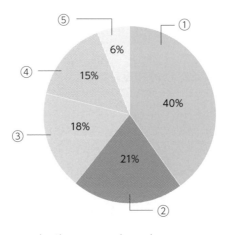

・toilet   ・bath   ・laundry
・kitchen   ・face-washing and other

　水の用途は主に、生活用水、工業用水、農業用水の3つに分けることができます。生活用水は、洗濯や調理、風呂などの家庭用水とオフィスや飲食店、ホテルなどで使われる都市活動用水に二分されます。

　円グラフは東京都水道局が2015年に実施した家庭用水の使われ方の調査をもとにしています。最も使用量の多いのが風呂（約40パーセント）、以下トイレ（約21パーセント）、炊事（約18パーセント）、洗濯（約15パーセント）、洗面・その他（約6パーセント）と続きます。生活用水の使用量の推移は、1998年頃が増加のピークでしたが、節水の技術進歩などによって緩やかな減少傾向になっています。

　日本人の1日の水の平均使用量は1人約300リットルと言われています。開発途上国では1人が1日15リットルほどの水を使用していることを考えると、私た

ちがいかにぜいたくに使っているかがわかるでしょう。水が豊富な日本でも、温暖化や梅雨時期の小雨、急勾配の地形によって淡水が海へ流れてしまうなどの理由から水不足になってしまう可能性があります。身近なところから少しずつ水の使い方を工夫して、無理のない節水を心がけるといいでしょう。

Water uses can be divided into three main categories: domestic water, industrial water and agricultural water. Domestic water is divided into two categories: domestic water used for washing, cooking, bathing, etc., and urban water used in offices, restaurants, hotels, etc.

The pie chart is based on a survey of household water usage conducted by the Tokyo Metropolitan Government Bureau of Waterworks in 2015. The largest use of water is for bathing (about 40 percent), followed by toilets (about 21 percent), cooking (about 18 percent), laundry (about 15 percent), and washing and other (about 6 percent). The trend of daily water consumption peaked around 1998, but has been on a gradual downward trend due to technological advances in water conservation and other factors.

The average daily water consumption of Japanese people is said to be about 300 liters per person. Considering that one person in developing countries uses about 15 liters of water per day, this shows how extravagant we are in our use of water. Even in Japan, where water is abundant, there is a possibility of water shortages due to global warming, light rains during the rainy season and steep terrain that causes fresh water to flow into the sea. It is a good idea to start with the familiar and gradually devise ways to use water and try to conserve water in a reasonable manner.

Goal 6

Answer　① bath　② toilet　③ kitchen
④ laundry　⑤ face-washing and other

水ストレス

下の世界地図は、2018年の水ストレス（water stress）の割合を国ごとに5段階（No stress / Low / Medium / High / Critical）で色分けして示したものです。次の各文に、内容が正しければ T、間違っていれば F をつけてください。

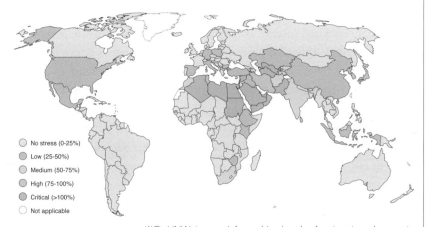

○ No stress (0-25%)
○ Low (25-50%)
○ Medium (50-75%)
● High (75-100%)
● Critical (>100%)
○ Not applicable

出典：UNWater.org: Infographic—Levels of water stress by country

① アラビア半島の国々の水ストレスは重大である。　　　　（　　　）

② モンゴルの水ストレスは 25 〜 50 パーセントである。　　（　　　）

③ カナダの水ストレスは 25 パーセント以下である。　　　（　　　）

④ スリランカの水ストレスは高い。　　　　　　　　　　　（　　　）

　水ストレスとは、日常生活の中で水の需要に対して供給がひっ迫している状態のことを表します。

　① アラビア半島はアフリカ大陸とアジアの中間に位置する巨大な半島で、アラブ首長国連邦、イエメン、オマーン、カタール、サウジアラビアの国々からなり

ます。 地図の色から判断すると、Critical（重大）に分類されているのでTです。

　②　モンゴルは中国とロシアに挟まれた国です。No stress（ストレスなし）なのでFです。

　③　北米のカナダは水ストレスが0 〜 25パーセントを示す色に分類されているので、Tです。

　④　スリランカはインドの南東にある小さな島国です。分かりづらいですが、High（高い）に分類されるため、Tです。

　地図を見ると、北アフリカのあたりで水ストレスが重大であることがわかります。水が豊富な日本は水ストレスとは無関係だと思われがちですが、低いながらもストレスがあります。原因は日本の食料自給率の低さに関係しています。食料は、小麦にしても牛肉にしても、大量の水を使って生産されます。そうした食料の多くを輸入に頼っている日本は、同時に大量の水も輸入していると考えられるため、水ストレスが生じるのです。

Water stress is a condition in which the demand for water for daily life is in excess of the supply.

　①　The Arabian Peninsula is a huge peninsula located between the African continent and Asia, made up of the countries of the United Arab Emirates, Yemen, Oman, Qatar and Saudi Arabia. Judging from the color of the map, it is classified as Critical, so it is true.

　②　Mongolia is a country sandwiched between China and Russia. It has no stress, so the answer is False.

　③　Canada, a North American country, is colored to indicate 0-25 percent water stress, so it is True.

　④　Sri Lanka is a small island country southeast of India. It is hard to tell, but it is classified as high, so the answer is True.

The map shows that water stress is critical around North Africa. People tend to think that since Japan has an abundance of water, water stress has nothing to do with it, but there is some, albeit low. The cause is related to Japan's low food self-sufficiency. Food, whether wheat or beef, is produced using large amounts of water. Japan, which relies on imports for much of such food, is thought to be importing large amounts of water at the same time, which causes water stress.

Answer　　① T　② F　③ T　④ T

バーチャルウォーター

輸入品の生産に必要な水のことをバーチャルウォーター（virtual water）と言います。ハンバーガー1個に必要なバーチャルウォーターは何リットルだと思いますか？

① 約140リットル
② 約400リットル
③ 約1,500リットル
④ 約2,400リットル

　バーチャルウォーターは間接ウォーターと呼ばれることもあります。小麦やレタス、牛肉、チーズなど、ハンバーガーのそれぞれの食材を生産するのに、産地では大量の水を必要とします。産地の状況にもよりますが、ハンバーガー1個にはおよそ2,400リットルの水が使われていると考えられます。仮にハンバーガーの材料のすべてを輸入していると考えた場合、バーチャルウォーターは2,400リットルということになります。他の食材では、例えばステーキ1枚に4,650リットル、牛乳1杯に200リットル、リンゴ1個に70リットルの水が使われています。このように、たとえ食材の生産に自国の水を使っていないとしても、食材を輸入すれば、その輸入産品を通じて国外の水を使っていることになり、その土地の水不足の問題にもかかわっていることになります。

Virtual water is also sometimes referred to as "indirect water." A large amount of water is required in the production area to produce each ingredient of hamburgers, such as wheat, lettuce, beef and cheese. Depending on the conditions in the producing region, it is estimated that approximately 2,400 liters of water are used to produce one hamburger. If we assume that all of the ingredients for a hamburger are imported, the virtual water consumption would be 2,400 liters. For other ingredients, for example, 4,650 liters of water are used for a steak, 200 liters for a glass of milk and 70 liters for an apple. Thus, even if you do not use your own water in the production of foodstuffs, if you import foodstuffs, you are using water from outside your country through the imported products, and you are also involved in the local water scarcity problem.

Answer ④ 2,400 リットル

Goal 6

「安全な水とトイレを世界中に」
——そのためにあなたは何ができると思いますか？
What can you do for the goal of "clean water and sanitation"?

　各国の政府や企業、支援団体によって、上下水道の整備や井戸・トイレの設置、海水から真水を作る技術の開発・供与などの国際協力が続けられています。単に施設を作って提供するだけでなく、現地の人々に技術を教えたり、その土地に合った解決策を一緒に考えて導入したり、子どもたちに教育の一環として衛生習慣を伝えたりと、将来的に現地の人々が自分たちの知識と技術で水と衛生環境を整えていけるような支援活動を行っています。

　個人でできる取り組みは、よく言われている「節水」を意識することではないでしょうか。顔を洗うときに蛇口の水を出しっぱなしすると、1分間で約12リットルの水がむだになっています。シャワーの水を3分間出しっぱなしにすれば、約36リットルの水が流れます。節水を意識して水を有効利用することで水道代も節約できます。例えば、歯を磨くときに水をコップにくんでから使えば、それだけでも約5リットルの水が節約でき、3人家族の場合、朝晩の歯磨きで1カ月に約220円の節約になります。

　また、食器やフライパンなどの油汚れを洗うときには、最初にキッチンペーパーなどで油分を拭き取っておくと、使う水や洗剤の量が少なくて済むうえ、下水に油を流し込まないようにすることで地球全体を水質汚染から守ることもできるでしょう。

　バーチャルウォーターのことを考えると、なるべく輸入品に頼らず国内あるいは地元で生産されたものを購入すれば、国・地域の振興にもつながっていくでしょう。

International cooperation is being continued by governments, companies and aid organizations in various countries to improve water supply and sewage systems, install wells and latrines, and develop and provide technology to produce fresh water from seawater. We not only build and provide facilities, but also teach local people about the technology, work with them to develop and implement solutions that suit their local needs and teach children hygiene practices as part of their education so that in the future local people can use their own knowledge and skills to improve water and sanitation.

One of the most important things that individuals can do is to be aware of the often-mentioned "water conservation." If you leave the faucet running when you wash your face, you are wasting about 12 liters of water per minute. If you leave the water running in the shower for 3 minutes, about 36 liters of water will be used. By being conscious of water conservation and using water effectively, you can save money on your water bill. For example, if you use a cup of water when brushing your teeth, you can save about 5 liters of water, and for a family of three, you can save about 220 yen a month by brushing your teeth this way morning and night.

Also, when washing dishes, pans and other greasy items, if you first wipe off the grease with paper towels, you will use less water and detergent, and you will also protect the entire planet from water pollution by not pouring oil into the sewage system.

In terms of virtual water, if we purchase domestic or locally produced products instead of relying on imported ones as much as possible, we will also be helping our country and region.

Goal 6

Goal 7

エネルギーをみんなに、そしてクリーンに
Affordable and Clean Energy

すべての人々に、安価かつ信頼できる持続可能な
近代的エネルギーへのアクセスを確保する。

**Ensure access to affordable, reliable, sustainable
and modern energy for all.**

　もしもこの瞬間に停電になったら、私たちの生活はどうなる
でしょうか？　電気を必要とする室内の明かり、パソコン、エ
アコン、冷蔵庫、電子レンジ、IH調理器具、スマホの充電器、
テレビやラジオも使えなくなります。ほぼ日常生活を送ること
は不可能です。しかし、世界ではおよそ7億7,000万人が電気
のない生活を送っています。いまだに薪や炭を燃やして料理を
している人が25億人以上もいるのです。Goal 7は、枯渇の可
能性があり地球環境に良くないエネルギーから、誰もが自由に
使える地球にやさしい再生可能なエネルギーへの利用に切り替
えることを目指しています。エネルギーに関するさまざまな課
題を知って、私たちに何ができるか考えてみましょう。

参照：IEA Access to electricity/Access to clean cooking
—SDG7: Data and Projection

エネルギーに関する用語

次の各語句とその意味を線で結んでください。

① run out　　　　　　•　　　　　•　停電

② consumption　　　•　　　　　•　充電

③ blackout　　　　　•　　　　　•　底をつく、尽きる

④ save　　　　　　　•　　　　　•　消費（量）

⑤ battery charge　•　　　　　•　節約する、守る

Point

　①の run out は of を伴って run out of ～の形で「～がなくなる、不足する」という意味を表します。例えば、「時間がない」ことを表すのに、「時間」を主語にすると Time is running out. で、「人」を主語にすると We are running out of time. と言うことができます。use up や be exhausted も「使い果たす、使い尽くす」という意味で使われます。

　②の consumption は consume（消費する、使い切る）の名詞形です。consumption の反意語は production（生産、製造）です。

　③の blackout は「一時的に意識を失うこと、失神」という意味でも使われます。「機能[供給]が停止する、故障する」という意味の outage や failure を用いれば、power [electricity/gas/water] outage というように、電気、ガス、水などについて具体的に表現することができます。

　④の save は「データをセーブする」「食べる量をセーブする」など、日本語としてもよく使われ、「助ける、取っておく、保存する、貯金する」などさまざまな意味をもつ単語です。

　⑤で「バッテリーを充電する」と言いたいときには、charge a battery と言います。

Answer　　① run out = 底をつく、尽きる　② consumption = 消費（量）
　　　　　　　③ blackout = 停電　④ save = 節約する、守る
　　　　　　　⑤ battery charge = 充電

世界の燃料事情

世界の人口のうち、およそどのくらいの人が薪や炭を使って料理していると
思いますか？

① 3分の1
② 5分の1
③ 5分の3

　世界の人口は約80億人。本章の冒頭にも記したとおり、薪や炭を燃やして料理
をしている人は25億人以上います。つまり、世界の人口の約3分の1の人々がい
まだに電気やガスを使えず、薪や炭、灯油などの危険で非効率な燃料を使って調
理しています。屋内で薪や炭などを使う場合、十分に換気しなければ一酸化炭素
中毒を引き起こします。また、煙やすすは有害物質を含んでいることがあり、人
体に悪影響を及ぼします。このような状況は開発途上国の農村部、特にサハラ以
南のアフリカの地域に多く見られ、家屋内の空気汚染が原因で女性や子どもを中
心に年間約49万人が死んでいます。さらに、IEA（国際エネルギー機関）による
と、新型コロナウイルスの影響で物流の混乱やエネルギー価格の高騰が起こって
貧困層が増えてしまい、アジアやアフリカの途上国では約5,000万人が再び薪や
炭、灯油などを使い始めているそうです。

　The world's population is approximately 8 billion. As noted at the beginning
of this chapter, more than 2.5 billion people burn wood or charcoal to cook.
In other words, about one-third of the world's population still does not have
access to electricity or gas and cooks with dangerous and inefficient fuels,
such as wood, charcoal and kerosene. Indoor use of wood or charcoal can
cause carbon monoxide poisoning if there is not adequate ventilation. In
addition, smoke and soot can contain toxic substances that are harmful
to the human body. This situation is common in rural areas of developing
countries, especially in sub-Saharan Africa, where about 490,000 people,

mostly women and children, die annually due to air pollution inside their homes. Furthermore, according to the International Energy Agency (IEA), COVID-19 has caused logistical disruptions and energy price hikes that have increased the number of poor people, and about 50 million people in developing countries in Asia and Africa have begun using firewood, charcoal, kerosene and other energy sources again.

Answer　① 3分の1

地球温暖化

地球温暖化（global warming）の意味を説明した文があります。日本語を参考にしながら、各空欄に当てはまる語句を下の語群から選んで文を完成させてください。

Global warming: a gradual increase in world temperatures caused by greenhouse gases, such as (①), that are collecting in the air around (②) and stopping heat from escaping into (③).

地球温暖化：二酸化炭素などの温室効果ガスが空気に包まれて地球の周囲を覆うことで、熱が大気圏の外に出ていかなくなり、地球全体の温度が徐々に上昇すること。

・the earth
・carbon dioxide
・space

　地球温暖化は、18世紀半ばの産業革命以降に人間が化石燃料を使い始めたことや、森林が伐採によって減少したことが原因です。動植物などの死骸や残留物が長い年月をかけて変化してできた化石燃料は、世界のエネルギー源の約90パーセントを占めていて、私たちにとっては大切な資源なのですが、これを燃やすことで発生するガスが環境に悪影響を及ぼします。例えば、自動車や工場から排出される化学物質は大気を汚染し、大気中の水分と反応して酸性雨を作り出します。また、大気中の温室効果ガスの濃度が上がると温室効果が強まり、地球の温度を上昇させてしまいます。これにより、21世紀末までに世界の平均気温は20世紀末に比べ2.8℃上昇し、海面水位は30センチメートルから1メートル上昇すると予測されています。わずかな気温の上昇でも、沿岸部が洪水の被害に遭ったり、森林火災のリスクが上がったり、農作物の生産量が低下したりと、さまざまなと

ころに悪影響が現れるのです。

　また最近では、温暖化よりも気候変動という言葉をよく耳にします。気候変動は長い期間持続する気候の変化を意味し、太陽の活動周期が変調をきたしたり、火山が噴火したりするなどの自然が原因による変化と、地球の大気のメカニズムを変化させる人間の活動が原因のものとがあります。近年の地球温暖化は人為的な要因によるものが大きく、気候変動も後者の意味合いが強くなっています。

Global warming is caused by the fossil fuel use by humans that has been happening since the Industrial Revolution began in the mid-18th century, and by deforestation. Fossil fuels, which are formed by the transformation of dead animals, plants and other residues over a long period of time, account for about 90 percent of the world's energy sources and are an important resource for us, but the gases produced by burning them have a negative impact on the environment. For example, chemicals emitted by automobiles and factories pollute the atmosphere and react with moisture in the air to create acid rain. In addition, as the concentration of greenhouse gases in the atmosphere increases, the greenhouse effect is intensified, causing the earth's temperature to rise. As a result, the global average temperature is projected to rise 2.8°C by the end of the 21st century, and sea levels will rise by between 30 cm and 1 meter. Even a small increase in temperature will have a negative impact in many areas, such as causing coastal flooding, increased risk of forest fires and reduced crop yields.

　Also, these days we hear the term "climate change" more often than "global warming." Climate change refers to long-lasting climatic changes, which can be caused by natural factors such as modulation of the sun's activity cycle or volcanic eruptions, or by human activities that alter the mechanisms of the earth's atmosphere. Global warming in recent years has been largely due to anthropogenic factors, and the term "climate change" is increasingly associated with the latter.

Answer　　① carbon dioxide　② the earth　③ space

温室効果ガス

温室効果ガス（greenhouse gas）の主なものとして二酸化炭素、メタン、亜酸化窒素、フロンなどがあります。それぞれの温室効果ガスとその発生源を線で結んでください。

① Carbon dioxide
　 二酸化炭素

② Methane
　 メタン

③ Dinitrogen monoxide
　 一酸化二窒素

④ CFCs
　 フロン類

Refrigerators, Air conditioners
(A/C) and Aerosols

Oil, Coal and Natural gas

Cattle and Agriculture

Gasoline and Fertilizer

　主な温室効果ガスには、二酸化炭素、メタン、亜酸化窒素、フロンなどがあります。それぞれの発生源にどのようなものがあるか確認してみましょう。

　①の二酸化炭素（CO_2）は温暖化への影響度が一番大きいガスで、IPCC（気候変動に関する政府間パネル）第5次評価報告書の2010年の数値によると、ガス別排出量の割合が76パーセントです。二酸化炭素は石油、石炭、天然ガスなどの化石燃料やプラスチックなどの固形廃棄物を燃やすことで大量に発生します。二酸化炭素は炭酸飲料の中にも入っており、私たちが息を吐くときにも出ていきます。まさに私たちの生活と切っても切れない関係がある物質です。

　②のメタン（CH_4）は英語では「ミーセイン[méθeɪn]」と発音します。農業分野で見てみると、日本では稲作のプロセスで発生するメタンの割合が44.4パーセントと最も高いのですが、世界では牛やヤギなどの家畜のゲップが発生源の77.7パーセントを占めています。

　③の一酸化二窒素（N_2O）はガソリンを燃やしたときや家畜のふんからも発生

しますが、その多くは堆肥や化学肥料が土壌中の微生物によって分解されるときに多く発生します。

　クロロフルオロカーボン類はCFCsと略され、エアコン、冷蔵庫、スプレー缶などの冷媒として使われています。無毒性・不燃性で便利な物質ですが、オゾン層を破壊し地球温暖化に悪影響があるとして国際協定・法律で大幅放出が禁止されています。

Major greenhouse gases include carbon dioxide, methane, nitrous oxide and CFCs. Let's review the sources of each of these.

Carbon dioxide (CO_2), ①, is the gas with the largest impact on global warming, accounting for 76 percent of emissions by gases, according to 2010 figures from the Fifth Assessment Report of the Intergovernmental Panel on Climate Change (IPCC). Carbon dioxide is produced in large quantities by burning fossil fuels, such as oil, coal and natural gas, as well as solid waste, such as plastics. Carbon dioxide is also found in carbonated beverages and is released when we exhale. It is truly a substance that is inextricably linked to our daily lives.

Methane (CH_4) in ② is pronounced [méθeɪn] in English. In the field of agriculture, the rice cultivation process accounts for 44.4 percent of the methane gas produced in Japan, but in the world, 77.7 percent of the methane is burps produced by cattle, goats and other livestock.

Dinitrogen monoxide (N_2O), mentioned in ③, is also generated when gasoline is burned and from livestock feces, but most of it is produced when compost and chemical fertilizers are decomposed by microorganisms in the soil.

Chlorofluorocarbons, abbreviated as CFCs, are used as refrigerants in air conditioners, refrigerators and spray cans. Although they are non-toxic, non-flammable and convenient, the release of CFCs is prohibited by international agreements and laws because of their harmful effects on the ozone layer and global warming.

> **Answer**　① Oil, Coal and Natural gas
> ② Cattle and Agriculture
> ③ Gasoline and Fertilizer
> ④ Refrigerators, Air conditioners (A/C) and Aerosols

温室効果ガスの役割

温室効果ガスには太陽からの熱を封じ込めて地表を温める役割があります。
もしこの温室効果ガスがなければ、地球の表面温度は何度になると思います
か？

① − 90℃
② − 19℃
③ 19℃
④ 90℃

　温室効果ガスとは、大気圏にある二酸化炭素やメタンなどのガスの総称です。
太陽からの熱（赤外線）を封じ込めて地表を温める役割をもっています。地表の平
均温度は約14℃なのですが、もしこの温室効果ガスがなければ、− 19℃になっ
てしまいます。地球温暖化の原因としてネガティブなイメージがありますが、実
は地球に欠かすことのできないガスなのです。しかし、その量が増えすぎると地
球の大気の温度が上昇し、その結果、異常気象が発生しやすくなるなどの気候変
動につながったり、生態系に影響を及ぼしたりすることになります。

　Greenhouse gases are a general term for gases such as carbon dioxide and
methane in the atmosphere. They are responsible for warming the earth's
surface by trapping heat (infrared radiation) from the sun. The average
temperature of the earth's surface is about 14℃, but if it were not for these
greenhouse gases, it would be -19℃. Although it has a negative image as a
cause of global warming, carbon dioxide is in fact an indispensable gas for
the earth. However, if the amount increases too much, the temperature of the
earth's atmosphere rises, and the resulting climate change leads to abnormal
weather and affects the ecosystem.

Answer　②　− 19℃

145

再生可能エネルギー

「再生可能エネルギー」を英語で何と言いますか？

① renewable energy
② green energy
③ clean energy

「再生可能エネルギー」とは、太陽（光・熱）エネルギーや風力エネルギーといった、繰り返し使えるエネルギー源のことで、ほかには水力エネルギー、地熱、バイオエネルギー、海洋エネルギー、そして水素と酸素を利用した化学エネルギーがあります。

2019年度における主要9カ国の再生可能エネルギーの使用の割合で、日本は8位（18パーセント）でした。1位のカナダ（66パーセント）と比べると、まだまだ化石燃料に頼っていることがわかります。再生可能エネルギーは季節や天候によって発電量が左右されることと、エネルギーを蓄積する手段の確保が難しいことがあるため、なかなか安定した供給ができないのが現状です。

②のgreen energyと③のclean energyも、「再生可能エネルギー」と同じ意味に捉えられがちですが、少し違いがあります。green energyは太陽や風、地熱、バイオマスといった自然由来で環境にやさしいエネルギーのことです。水力発電は森林を伐採しダムを作ることで環境を破壊するのでgreen energyに相当しない、と言う人もいます。

一方、clean energyは空気を汚さずに作られる、排ガスゼロのエネルギーのことです。太陽、風、水の力を利用して作られるエネルギーに加え、潮の満ち引きや地熱を利用したエネルギーがあり、どれもきれいな空気を保ったままエネルギーを作ることができます。この2つのエネルギーには微妙な違いはありますが、ほとんど同じと考えてよいでしょう。

Renewable energy refers to energy sources that can be used repeatedly, such as solar (light and heat) and wind energy; others include hydroelectric, geothermal, bioenergy, ocean energy, and chemical energy, which uses hydrogen and oxygen.

Japan ranked eighth (18 percent) in the percentage of renewable energy use in the nine leading countries in fiscal year 2019, compared with Canada (66 percent), which ranked first, indicating that Japan still relies heavily on fossil fuels. Renewable energies are difficult to supply in a stable manner, partly because the amount of power generated depends on the season and weather conditions, and partly because it is difficult to secure the means to store energy.

Green energy in ② and clean energy in ③ tend to be regarded as having the same meaning as "renewable energy," but there is a slight difference. Green energy is energy that is naturally derived and environmentally friendly, such as solar, wind, geothermal and biomass. Some say that hydropower is not green energy because it requires destruction of the environment by clearing forests and building dams.

On the other hand, clean energy is energy that is produced without polluting the air and with zero emissions. In addition to energy produced by the sun, wind and water, there is also energy produced by tides and geothermal energy, all of which can produce energy without polluting the air. There are subtle differences between these two types of energy, but they can be considered almost identical.

Answer   ① renewable energy

Goal 7

再生可能エネルギーの発電効率

「太陽光」「風力」「水力」の3つは発電効率の高い再生可能エネルギーです。次の図の①〜③に、発電効率（%）の高い順にsolar、wind、waterを入れてください。

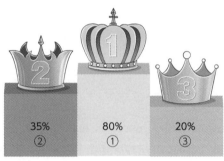

| 35%
② | 80%
① | 20%
③ |

　発電効率とは、再生可能エネルギーをどのくらいの割合で電気エネルギーに変換できたかを指します。再生可能エネルギーを利用して発電するには電気エネルギーに変換しなければなりませんが、変換の途中で摩擦損失が起きるため、発電効率は下がります。発電効率が最も高いのは水力発電で、摩擦損失を加えても80パーセント変換することができます。2位は風車を回して発電機で電気エネルギーに変換する風力エネルギーです。発電効率は最大で45パーセントほどですが、平均すると35パーセントくらいです。3位は太陽光エネルギーで20パーセントと、意外と低い発電効率です。一般家庭や企業などへの太陽光パネルの普及はかなり進んでいますが、気温が25℃以上だと発電効率が低くなったり、パネル表面に汚れや影があると効率が下がったりします。仮に、地球全体に降り注ぐ太陽光を100パーセント電力に変換できるとしたら、世界の年間消費エネルギーをわずか1時間ほどでまかなえると考えられています。地球温暖化を逆手にとって、水力をしのぐエネルギーになってほしいですね。

Generation efficiency refers to the percentage of renewable energy that can be converted into electrical energy. In order to generate electricity from renewable energy, it must be converted into electrical energy, but frictional losses occur during the conversion process, reducing the generation efficiency. At 80 percent, hydropower has the highest generational efficiency, even with frictional losses. This is followed by wind energy, which is converted into electrical energy by spinning windmills and using generators. The generation efficiency is up to 45 percent, but the average is about 35 percent. Third is solar energy, with a surprisingly low efficiency rate of 20 percent. Although solar panels are becoming more widely used in homes and businesses, they are less efficient when the temperature is above 25°C (77°F) or when the surface of the panel is dirty or shaded. If 100 percent of the sunlight falling on the entire planet could be converted into electricity, it is thought that the world's annual energy consumption could be met in just one hour. I would like to see this energy source surpass hydroelectric power as a way to reverse global warming.

Answer ① water ② wind ③ solar

Goal 7

化石燃料の将来

下のグラフは化石燃料について、今後採掘が可能と予想される期間（可採年数）を表したものです。各空欄に当てはまる化石燃料の種類を下の語群から選んでください。

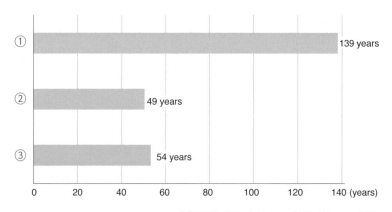

出典：BP Statistical Review of World Energy 2021

・natural gas　　・oil　　・coal

　化石燃料は将来的には枯渇してしまうと言われています。可採年数の割り出し方は、確認可採埋蔵量÷年間生産量です。これでおおよその採掘可能な年数がわかります。①は石炭で、139年の寿命です。②は天然ガスで49年、③は石油で、54年で枯渇すると予想されています。今後ますますエネルギーを消費していくと、この可採年数はもっと短くなり、厳しい状況になっていくでしょう。過剰消費を抑えて、再生可能エネルギーの割合を増やしていくことが急務です。

　Fossil fuels are expected to run out in the near future. The method of calculating the minable years is Proved Minable Reserves divided by Annual Production Volume. This gives you an approximate number of minable years. ① is coal, which has a lifespan of 139 years. ② is natural gas, and ③ is oil, which is expected to run out in 54 years. As we consume more and more energy in the future, this minable life will become even shorter and the situation will become more difficult. There is an urgent need to curb excessive consumption and increase the share of renewable energy.

Point

　「枯渇する」は英語でrun outと言います。「化石燃料はいつなくなってしまうのでしょうか？」は、When will fossil fuels run out? と表現できます。depleteも「（資源などを）枯渇させる」という意味で、Our fossil fuels will be depleted by 2060.（化石燃料は2060年までに枯渇するでしょう）のように使います。

Answer　① coal　② natural gas　③ oil

Goal 7

151

化石燃料の輸入元

右の円グラフ (pie chart) は日本の化石燃料の輸入元をまとめたものです。①〜⑤に入る国名を下から選んでください。

- Australia
- Indonesia
- Malaysia
- Saudi Arabia
- UAE

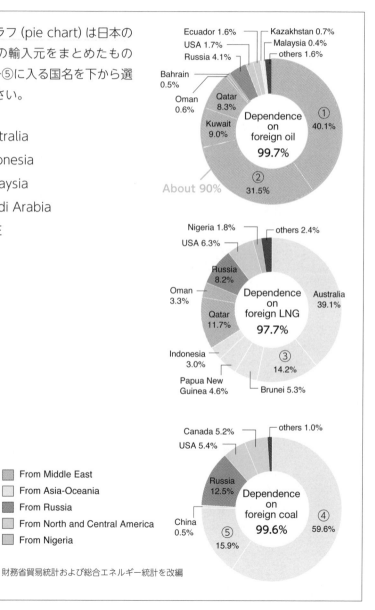

Ecuador 1.6%
USA 1.7%
Russia 4.1%
Kazakhstan 0.7%
Malaysia 0.4%
others 1.6%
Bahrain 0.5%
Oman 0.6%
Qatar 8.3%
Kuwait 9.0%

Dependence on foreign oil
99.7%

① 40.1%
② 31.5%
About 90%

Nigeria 1.8%
USA 6.3%
others 2.4%
Russia 8.2%
Oman 3.3%
Qatar 11.7%
Indonesia 3.0%
Papua New Guinea 4.6%

Dependence on foreign LNG
97.7%

Australia 39.1%
③ 14.2%
Brunei 5.3%

Canada 5.2%
USA 5.4%
others 1.0%
Russia 12.5%
China 0.5%

Dependence on foreign coal
99.6%

④ 59.6%
⑤ 15.9%

- From Middle East
- From Asia-Oceania
- From Russia
- From North and Central America
- From Nigeria

財務省貿易統計および総合エネルギー統計を改編

152

日本では、国内で産出・確保できるエネルギー資源が主に原子力、太陽光、風力に限られています。日本はエネルギー自給率がわずか11.2パーセント（2020年度）で、主要なエネルギー資源をほぼ海外からの輸入に頼っています。

In Japan, energy resources that can be produced and secured domestically are mainly limited to nuclear, solar and wind power. With an energy self-sufficiency rate of only 11.2 percent (in fiscal year 2020), Japan relies almost exclusively on imports of major energy resources from overseas.

Point

　原油の約90パーセントを中東地域から輸入していて、海外依存度が99.7パーセントです。①と②には色分けから判断して中東の国名が入ることから、Saudi ArabiaとUAEに絞ることができます。UAEはUnited Arab Emiratesの略で、アラブ首長国連邦のことです。③にはLNG（＝liquefied natural gas：液体天然ガス）の輸入元としてアジア・オセアニアの国名が入りますが、AustraliaとIndonesiaはそれぞれ円グラフの中にあるので、Malaysiaを選びます。日本の天然ガスの海外依存度は97.7パーセントと、原油の依存度と同様に高い割合です。石炭（coal）もアジア・オセアニアからの輸入がほとんどで、④と⑤にはAustraliaとIndonesiaがそれぞれ入ります。

Answer　　①Saudi Arabia　②UAE　③Malaysia　④Australia　⑤Indonesia

温暖化対策の世界目標

2015年に採択された「パリ協定」（The Paris Agreement）では、地球温暖化対策の世界目標として、産業革命前からの平均気温の上昇を「何℃」に抑えることに合意しましたか？

① 1.5℃
② 2.0℃
③ 2.7℃

　「パリ協定」は2020年以降の気候変動問題に関する多国間の国際的な合意で、2015年12月にパリで開かれた「国連気候変動枠組条約第21回締約国会議（COP21）」で採択されました。その5年前、2010年のCOP16では、産業革命後の気温上昇を2℃以内に抑える「2℃目標」が設定されていたのですが、COP21ではさらなる努力目標として「1.5℃目標」が掲げられました。

　2℃だった目標をたったの0.5℃下げただけですが、このわずかな差でも生態系や人間の生活、経済への影響に大きな違いが現れます。平均気温が2℃上がることで、2100年までに海面水位が世界平均で約10センチメートル上昇したり、昆虫や動植物の生息域の失われる割合が2倍以上に増えたり、水不足によって生活に支障をきたす人の割合が50パーセント増えたりするのです。

　この「1.5℃目標」を達成するためには、2030年の二酸化炭素排出量を2010年比で45パーセント減らし、さらに2050年までに二酸化炭素排出量をプラスマイナスゼロの状態にしなければなりません。しかし、たとえ各国が2030年に向けて立てた温室効果ガス排出削減目標をすべて実行したとしても、14パーセントの増加が試算されています。IPCC（気候変動に関する政府間パネル）第6次評価報告書によると、1850年〜2020年の世界の平均気温がすでに1.09℃上昇したということです。このままいくと、今世紀末までに2.8℃上昇する見通しで、「1.5℃目標」には程遠い状況です。削減を進めつつも、温暖化に適応するための新たな

アプローチが必要なのかもしれません。

The Paris Agreement is a multilateral international agreement on post-2020 climate change issues, adopted at the 21st Conference of the Parties (COP21) to the United Nations Framework Convention on Climate Change held in Paris in December 2015. Five years earlier, at COP16 in 2010, a "2°C target" was set to limit the post-industrial temperature increase to within 2°C. At COP21, a "1.5°C target" was set as a further goal.

This is only a 0.5°C reduction from the 2°C target, but even this small change will make a big difference in the impact on ecosystems, human life and the economy. A 2°C increase in average temperature will raise sea levels by an average of about 10 cm by 2100, more than double the rate of loss of habitat for insects, plants and animals and increase the proportion of people whose lives will be affected by water shortages by 50 percent.

In order to achieve the 1.5°C target, we must reduce carbon dioxide emissions in 2030 to 45 percent lower than the levels in 2010, and further reduce carbon dioxide emissions to zero (carbon neutral/carbon neutrality) by 2050. However, even if all of the greenhouse gas emission reduction targets set by each country for 2030 are implemented, the increase is estimated to be 14 percent. According to the IPCC (Intergovernmental Panel on Climate Change) Sixth Assessment Report, the global average temperature for the period from 1850 to 2020 has already increased by 1.09°C. If this trend continues, the temperature is expected to rise by 2.8°C by the end of this century, which is far from the 1.5°C target. While promoting emission reductions, a new approach may be needed to adapt to global warming.

Answer ① 1.5°C

Goal 7

「エネルギーをみんなに そしてクリーンに」

──そのためにあなたは何ができると思いますか？

What can you do to support the goal of "affordable and clean energy"?

2022年7月、国連は世界の人口が2022年11月までに80億を突破する見込みだと発表し、実際に11月15日には80億人突破を発表しました。貧困問題が深刻なインドの人口が、人口大国の中国を抜いて1位になると予測されており、ますます薪や炭、灯油などを使う人が増え、空気汚染や環境破壊問題が深刻になるでしょう。地球温暖化は化石燃料の使用だけでなく、人口増加や貧困、先進国と途上国の技術格差など、さまざまな問題がからみ合いながら長いスパンで表面化しました。生活環境を産業が発達する前の状態に戻すことは現実的ではないため、先進国が化石燃料の使用を減らして再生可能エネルギーを導入したり、途上国へ電気やガスなどのインフラ支援を行ったりするなど、地球温暖化の進行を率先して抑制する努力をしなければなりません。

エネルギー資源を海外に頼っている日本に住む私たちに、何ができるのでしょうか？　小さなことですが、節電する、自動車のアイドリングストップを実行する、化石燃料の使用を減らすためにリサイクル品を活用する、緑を育てるなど、少しずつ行動することは可能です。また、気候変動の影響によって起こり得るさまざまな災害に適応できるよう、対策や備えを強化にしておくことも大事です。集中豪雨や洪水、土砂災害などの災害時の避難場所や家族との連絡方法などを確認しておくと安心です。

In July 2022, the United Nations announced that the world's population was expected to surpass 8 billion by November 2022, and on November 15, they actually announced that it had reached the 8 billion mark. The population of India, which has serious poverty problems, is projected to overtake China, the world's most populous country, to become number one in terms of population. More and more people will use firewood, charcoal and kerosene, and air pollution and environmental destruction problems will become more serious. Global warming has surfaced over a long span of time due to a combination of various problems, including not only the use of fossil fuels but also population growth, poverty and the technology gap between developed and developing countries. Since it is not realistic to return our living environment to the state it was in before the development of industry, developed countries must take the initiative in curbing the progress of global warming by reducing the use of fossil fuels, introducing renewable energy and providing infrastructure support, such as electricity and gas, to developing countries.

What can we, as people living in Japan, which depends on foreign countries for energy resources, do? It may seem insignificant, but we can take small actions such as saving electricity, not idling our cars, using recycled products to reduce the use of fossil fuels and growing greenery. It is also important to strengthen measures and preparedness so that we can adapt to the various disasters that could occur as a result of climate change. It is a good idea to check where to evacuate and how to contact your family in case of disasters, such as torrential rain, floods and landslides.

Goal 7

Goal 8
働きがいも経済成長も
Decent Work and Economic Growth

包括的かつ持続可能な経済成長、およびすべての人々の完全かつ生産的な雇用と働きがいのある人間らしい雇用（ディーセント・ワーク）を促進する。

Promote sustained, inclusive and sustainable economic growth, full and productive employment and decent work for all.

　世界では1億6,000万人の子どもたち（5〜17歳）が学校に行かずに働いています。そのうち約半数が危険を伴う場所で働いています。学校に行きたいのに、生活のために働かなくてはならないのです。一方、新型コロナウイルスの影響も重なって世界の雇用環境が悪化し、2020年には失業率が6.5パーセントに達しました。働きたいのに仕事がなかったり、子どもを預ける場所がないために働けなかったり、障がいがあるために職に就けなかったりする人もいます。仕事があって働いていても、長時間労働や人間関係によってストレスや健康問題を抱える人たちがいます。経済を発展させながら働きやすい環境でやりがいのある仕事をするために、私たちに何が必要なのかを考えてみましょう。

参照：UNICEF Child labour 2021
UN SDGs Report 2021 Goal 8

ILO（国際労働機関）

ILO（国際労働機関）の正式名称は次のどれでしょうか？

① International Labor Organization
② Intercontinental Labour Organization
③ International Labour Organization

　ILO（国際労働機関）は1919年に国際連盟によって創設され、1946年に国際連合の最初の専門機関となりました。スイスのジュネーブに本部を構え、日本を含む187カ国が加盟しています。国際労働基準を制定し、すべての人が働きがいのある人間らしい仕事に就くことを目指して、働き方や生活条件の向上、雇用機会の増進、雇用環境や社会保障の充実、政府・労働者・使用者間の対等な対話の推進、労働者の権利の保障と尊重などに取り組む活動を行っています。

　The International Labour Organization (ILO) was founded by the League of Nations in 1919 and became the first specialized agency of the United Nations, in 1946. Headquartered in Geneva, Switzerland, the ILO has 187 member countries, including Japan. It establishes international labor standards and aims to improve working and living conditions, enhance employment opportunities, improve the employment environment and social security, promote equal dialogue between governments, workers and employers, and guarantee and respect workers' rights, with the aim of ensuring that all people have access to fulfilling and humane work.

Point

　ILO（国際労働機関）の正式名称は③の International Labour Organization です。Labour（労働）にはuが入っています。国連では主にイギリス英語を使用しているため、ここでは labour が使われています。アメリカ英語のつづりはuの入らない labor で、例えば「アメリカ合衆国労働省」は US Department of Labor と表記されます。

Answer　③ International Labour Organization

経済成長に関する用語

次の各語句とその意味を線で結んでください。

① economic growth ・　　　・　労働

② employment ・　　　　　・　最低賃金

③ work ・　　　　　　　　・　働きがいのある人間らしい仕事

④ decent work ・　　　　・　経済成長

⑤ minimum wage ・　　　・　雇用

　適正な収入や安全な労働環境、社会的保障などが奪われると経済が停滞する、と言われています。Goal 8は、労働者がそのような不利な立場に置かれることなく、長期的かつ平等な就労機会を獲得することを目指し、持続可能な経済成長を推進するものです。

　働きがいのある人間らしい仕事は、ILOの活動目標にもうたわれています。この言葉は、「男女平等および非差別に基づき、労働者の人権を尊重した公正で好ましい条件での仕事」という意味で、1999年のILO総会で初めて用いられました。

It is said that deprivation of decent income, safe working conditions and social security can lead to economic stagnation, so Goal 8 promotes sustainable economic growth by ensuring that workers are not placed at a disadvantage and have long-term, equal access to work opportunities.

Fulfilling and humane work is also a goal of the ILO's activities. The phrase "work under fair and favorable conditions, based on gender equality and non-discrimination, and respecting the human rights of workers" was first used at the ILO General Conference in 1999.

Goal 8

②のemploymentは「（長期的に）人を雇うこと」を意味します。hiringやengagementも同じく「雇用」ですが、これらは「（一時的に、短期間）雇うこと」という意味合いが強い単語です。

③のworkは、仕事全体を表したり、専門性を伴わない業務や雑務などを指したりします。似たような意味の単語にjobがありますが、こちらは一つ一つの作業や特定の業務、専門的な職業を表します。

④のdecentには、社会的に認められている基準やルールに当てはまる「まっとうな、ちゃんとした、妥当な」という意味があります。

⑤のminimum（最低の）の反意語はmaximum（最高の）です。wageは「働いた分に応じて支払われるお金（時給や日給など）」のことで、似たような意味のsalaryは「月ごとに支払われるまとまったお金（固定給）」を指します。また、wageとsalaryの両方の意味をあわせ持つ単語にpayがあります。

Answer

① economic growth ＝ 経済成長

② employment ＝ 雇用

③ work ＝ 労働

④ decent work ＝ 働きがいのある人間らしい仕事

⑤ minimum wage ＝ 最低賃金

英語になった日本の労働状況

次の日本語のうち、英語の辞書に載っている言葉はどれだと思いますか。

① sankei（3K）
② burakku kigyo（ブラック企業）
③ ikigai（生きがい）
④ karoshi（過労死）

　選択肢に挙げた言葉を『コリンズ英語辞典』(https://www.collinsdictionary.com) で調べてみると③のikigaiと④のkaroshiが載っています。

　③のikigaiは "reason for living"（生きる意味）と定義されています。ikigaiという言葉については、海外メディアでたびたび取り上げられたり、2017年に日本在住のスペイン人が書いた*Ikigai: The Japanese Secret to a Long and Happy Life*がベストセラーとなったりしたのをきっかけに広まるようになりました。「生きがい」の概念は非常にあいまいですが、「生きる喜びや張り合い（を感じるもの）」などが一般的な解釈でしょう。英語ではよくQOL（quality of life）という言葉が使われます。これは「生活・人生の質」という意味で、生活や人生における満足度を示す概念です。心身の健康ややりがいのある仕事、充実した余暇など、さまざまな観点からQOLの高さが評価されます。ikigaiと似たような考え方と言えるかもしれません。

　④のkaroshiは、2002年に『オックスフォード英語辞典』に初めて掲載されました。『コリンズ英語辞典』には "(in Japan) death caused by overwork" という定義で載っていて、日本について悪い印象を与えるような日本語として世界中に知られています。実際、過労死は日本で社会問題になっています。日本では労働基準法で、標準的な労働時間（35 ～ 40時間／週）に加えて時間外労働（残業）が月に45時間、年に360時間を限度とするなどと決められています。しかし、必要な場合には複数月平均で80時間以内、あるいは月に100時間未満の残業が認められています。2021年、WHO（世界保健機構）とILO（国際労働機関）は、こう

した日本の状況について、国際的に見ればまだ労働時間が長すぎるので、さらなる規制の見直しが必要だ、と発表しています。

If you look up the words listed as options in the *Collins English Dictionary* (https://www.collinsdictionary.com), you will find ③ *ikigai* and ④ *karoshi*.

The word "*ikigai*" in ③ is defined as "reason for living." *Ikigai* is often mentioned in the foreign media, and in 2017, *Ikigai: The Japanese Secret to a Long and Happy Life*, written by a Spanish man living in Japan, became a bestseller. The concept of "*Ikigai*" is very ambiguous, but a common interpretation is "the joy and satisfaction of living." In English, the term QOL (quality of life) is often used. QOL means "quality of life," and is a concept that indicates the level of satisfaction in life. Quality of life is evaluated from a variety of perspectives, including mental and physical health, rewarding work, and fulfilling leisure time. It may be said to be similar to the concept of *ikigai*.

Karoshi ④ first appeared in the *Oxford English Dictionary* in 2002. The *Collins English Dictionary* defines *karoshi* as "(in Japan) death caused by overwork," and it is known throughout the world as a Japanese word that gives a negative impression of the country. In fact, death from overwork is a social problem in Japan. In Japan, the Labor Standards Act stipulates that overtime work in addition to standard working hours (35-40 hours/week) should be limited to 45 hours per month and 360 hours per year. However, when necessary, overtime is allowed for an average of no more than 80 hours per multi-month period or fewer than 100 hours per month. In 2021, the World Health Organization (WHO) and the International Labor Organization (ILO) announced that the working hours in Japan are still too long by international standards and that further regulatory review is needed.

Point

　①の「3K」は仕事が「キツい（kitsui）」「汚い（kitanai）」「危険（kiken）」と、劣悪な労働環境を指す言葉です。また②の「ブラック企業」は、パワハラや違法労働などが横行していても適切に対処しない会社を表す言葉です。

Answer　③ ikigai（生きがい）　④ karoshi（過労死）

児童労働事情

世界で子どもたちの何人に 1 人が児童労働（child labor）に従事している
と思いますか？

① 5 人
② 10 人
③ 15 人
④ 20 人

　この章の冒頭でも述べたように、世界では5歳〜17歳の子ども 1 億6,000万人
が日常的に働いています。全世界の子どものじつに10人に1人に相当します。そ
して、その約半数の7,900万人の子どもたちは、過酷な肉体労働など心身の発達
に悪影響を及ぼすような危険な労働に従事しています。

　労働に従事する子どもが最も多い地域はサハラ以南のアフリカの農村部で、全
体の23.9パーセントを占めており、その大部分が家族の営む農業を手伝っていま
す。貧困家庭が収入を増やすために子どもを外で働かせることもありますが、子
どもの賃金は安いので、早朝から夜まで働いたとしてもわずかな額にしかなりま
せん。子どもは1日の大半を労働に費やすことになり、学校へ行けないのです。
子どもが望んで仕事をするはずはないので、児童労働は強制労働にあたります。

　ILO（国際労働機関）とUNICEF（ユニセフ）の予測によると、新型コロナウイ
ルスの影響によって貧困が急増し、2022年末までにさらに900万人もの子どもた
ちが児童労働に陥る危険があるといいます。それが現実とならないためにも、貧
困家庭に向けた社会的保護の拡大や、子どもの労働に依存しないようにするため
の大人への適正な仕事の促進などが、急務となっています。

　As noted at the beginning of this chapter, 160 million children between the
ages of 5 and 17 work on a daily basis worldwide. This is equivalent to 1 in
10 children around the world. About half of them (79 million) are engaged in
hazardous work, such as hard physical labor, which is detrimental to their

physical and mental development.

The areas with the largest number of children engaged in labor are rural parts of sub-Saharan Africa, accounting for 23.9 percent of the total, and most of them help their families with agriculture. Poor families sometimes send their children to work outside the home to increase their income, but children's wages are so low that even if they work from early morning to late at night, they earn only a small amount of money. The child spends most of the day working and is unable to go to school. Child labor is considered forced labor because the child would never willingly work.

The International Labour Organization (ILO) and UNICEF estimate that the impact of COVID-19 has led to a sharp increase in poverty, putting an additional 9 million children at risk of having to perform child labor by the end of 2022. To prevent this from becoming a reality, there is an urgent need to expand social protection for poor families and promote decent work for adults to prevent dependence on child labor.

Answer ② 10人

失業問題

次の英語の意味を表す単語を下の語群から選んでください。

A situation in which someone does not have a job

・employer
・employee
・unemployment
・homeless

　世界的に人口の増加が加速し、2020年には失業者数が2億2,000万人に達しました。特にアフリカの人口が増加し雇用が足りなくなっているため、貧困から飢餓への負の連鎖も加速しています。ILO（国際労働機関）によると、新型コロナウイルスの影響による労働時間や直接雇用の減少によって、2023年までにコロナ危機前の失業率に戻ることはなく、依然として高い状態が続くということです。

　2020年の先進国の失業率を見てみると、カナダで9.46パーセント、イタリアで9.16パーセント、アメリカで8.05パーセント、フランスで8.01パーセントと軒並み高い割合ですが、日本の失業率は2.80パーセントにとどまっています。新型コロナウイルスの影響で解雇が増えたとしても、日本の失業率は以前とさほど変わらないのです。そのカラクリは、仕事を一時的に休んでいる休業者が600万人もいることにあります。休業者は、収入が大幅に減ったとしても失業者とは見なされず、失業率に反映されないのです。また、従業員の雇用が法律で手厚く守られているため、企業は仕事が減っても簡単には従業員を解雇できず、ときには従業員が低賃金で責任の重い仕事に長時間従事するといった問題も起きています。

　このように、日本は実際には雇用に関する問題が多い国です。簡単には解決できませんが、労働を多くの従業員に分配することで、長時間労働や失業の不安がある程度解消するのではないでしょうか。

Goal 8

Population growth is accelerating worldwide, with the number of the unemployed reaching 220 million by 2020. Especially in Africa, where the population is increasing and there is a shortage of employment, the vicious cycle of poverty and hunger is accelerating. According to the International Labour Organization (ILO), unemployment will not return to pre-coronavirus-crisis levels by 2023 and will continue to remain high due to the reduction in working hours and direct employment caused by the coronavirus.

Looking at unemployment rates in developed countries in 2020, the rates are high across the board: 9.46 percent in Canada, 9.16 percent in Italy, 8.05 percent in the United States and 8.01 percent in France, while the unemployment rate in Japan is only 2.8 percent. Even if the number of dismissals increases due to the effects of the coronavirus, the unemployment rate in Japan will not change much from before. The reason lies in the fact that there are about 6 million people who have been put on temporary leave from their jobs and may never return. Even if their income is significantly reduced, they are not considered unemployed and their absence is not reflected in the unemployment rate. In addition, because workers' employment is strongly protected by law, companies cannot easily lay off employees even if they lose their jobs, sometimes leading to problems such as employees working long hours at low wages and with great responsibility.

Thus, Japan is actually a country with many employment-related problems. Although there is no easy solution, distributing labor to a larger number of employees would probably eliminate some of the concerns about long working hours and unemployment.

> ### Point
>
> A situation in which someone does not have a job は「仕事がない状態」という意味です。語群にある employer（雇用主）、employee（従業員）、unemployment（失業［状態］）、homeless（住む家のない）のうち、この意味と同じなのは unemployment です。

Answer   unemployment

人身取引に関する用語

人身取引に関する言葉があります。日本語の意味を参考にして、空欄に当てはまる語を下の語群から選んで言葉を完成してください。

① (　　　　　) trafficking ＝ 人身売買
② forced (　　　　　) ＝ 強制結婚
③ (　　　　　) harvesting ＝ 臓器摘出
④ (　　　　　) exploitation ＝ 性的搾取
⑤ forced (　　　　　) ＝ 強制労働

　・labor
　・marriage
　・sexual
　・human
　・organ

①の「人身売買」と「人身取引」は同じような意味ですが、「人身売買」は主に女性や女児の性的搾取を目的とするもので、「人身取引」は性的搾取や臓器売買、強制労働など幅広い目的を含みます。世界で4,030万人が人身取引の被害に遭っていると言われ、2,490万人が強制労働を、1,540万人が強制結婚をさせられています。そして人身取引の被害者の4人に1人が子どもだということです。

②の「強制結婚」とは、結婚する当事者の一方または両方が、同意せずに、あるいは意志に反して結婚させられることです。UNICEFによると、18歳未満で結婚した女性は現在、世界に推定6億5,000万人いるといわれています。特にアフリカでは、経済的な理由から女の子と金品を交換して生活費を得る家庭が多く、女児の3人に1人が強制結婚の被害に遭っています。

③の「臓器摘出」も人身取引の一つで、子どもの臓器が強制的に摘出されて市

Goal 8

169

場で売られるといった実態があります。臓器移植を必要とする人が違法に臓器買うことがあり、臓器を提供する側も貧困が原因で子どもの人身取引を行って金品を受け取り、子どもは臓器を摘出されて命を落としてしまうこともあります。

④の「性的搾取」や性的虐待は秘密裏に行われることが多いため、なかなか実態をつかみづらいところがありますが、世界で推定480万人の女性や子どもたちが被害に遭っています。被害者は主に売春やポルノなど商業的性的搾取によって、心身に傷を負ったり、望まない妊娠や性感染症の危険にさらされたりしています。「搾取」を意味するexploitationは、営利的・利己的な目的で人や集団を利用するといった侮蔑的な意味合いを含んでいます。

⑤の「強制労働」は、意志に反して課せられる労働のことで、古代の奴隷労働と同じような状況であるため"現代の奴隷"とも呼ばれることもあります。

① "Sex trafficking" and "human trafficking" are similar in meaning, but "sex trafficking" is mainly used for the sexual exploitation of women and girls, while "human trafficking" includes a wide range of purposes, such as sexual exploitation, organ trafficking and forced labor. It is estimated that 40.3 million people worldwide are victims of trafficking in persons, 24.9 million have been forced into labor and 15.4 million have been forced into marriage. One in four victims of trafficking is a child.

② "Forced marriage" is when one or both parties to a marriage are forced to marry without their consent. According to UNICEF, there are currently an estimated 650 million women worldwide who were married before the age of 18. In Africa, in particular, many families exchange money and goods for girls for economic reasons, and one in three girls is a victim of forced marriage.

③ "Organ harvesting" is another form of trafficking in persons, and children's organs are sometimes forcibly removed and sold on the market. People who need transplants sometimes buy organs illegally, and on the donor's side, there is trafficking in children so that people living in poverty can receive money and goods. Children often lose their lives when their organs are removed.

④ "Sexual exploitation" and sexual abuse are often carried out in secret, so it is difficult to get a clear picture of the actual situation, but an estimated 4.8 million women and children are victims worldwide. Victims suffer physical and mental trauma, unwanted pregnancies and the risk of sexually transmitted diseases, mainly due to commercial sexual exploitation, such as prostitution and pornography. "Exploitation," has pejorative connotations, such as taking advantage of a person or group of people for commercial or selfish purposes.

⑤ "Forced labor" is work imposed against one's will, sometimes also called "modern slavery" because the situation is similar to ancient slave labor.

> **Point**
>
> traffickingは「不正取引、密売」という意味です。
> harvestingは「(作物などの)収穫」という意味でよく使われますが、「(動物の)捕獲」や「(臓器や細胞の)摘出、採取」という意味もあります。

Answer
① (human) trafficking ＝ 人身売買
② forced (marriage) ＝ 強制結婚
③ (organ) harvesting ＝ 臓器摘出
④ (sexual) exploitation ＝ 性的搾取
⑤ forced (labor) ＝ 強制労働

Goal 8

G7各国の労働時間

下の「G7各国の労働時間」のグラフを見て、次の各文の内容が正しければ
Tを、間違っていればFをつけてください。

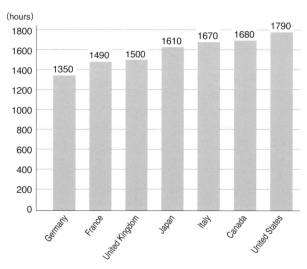

出典：OECD (2022), Hours worked (indicator). doi: 10.1787/47be1c78-en (Accessed on 18 July 2022)

① 日本の労働時間はイタリアよりも短い。　　　　　　　　　　（　　　　）
② 労働時間が最も長いのはカナダである。　　　　　　　　　　（　　　　）
③ ドイツの労働時間は1,490時間である。　　　　　　　　　　（　　　　）
④ フランスとイギリスの労働時間はほぼ同じである。　　　　　（　　　　）

　グラフによると、日本の労働時間はG7の中でちょうど中間です。日本は長時間労働が深刻だと言われる国なので、この結果を意外に感じる人が多いでしょう。これは、このデータが正社員だけでなくパートタイム労働者の労働時間も含んでいるからです。日本では少子高齢化で人手不足となり、企業はパートタイム労働者の枠を広げてきました。その結果、労働時間の短いパートタイム労働者の数が

増え、全体の平均労働時間が減っているのです。

According to the graph, Japan's working hours are right in the middle of the G7. Many people may find this result surprising since Japan is a country where long working hours are said to be a serious problem. This is because the data includes the working hours of not only full-time employees but also part-time workers. In Japan, the declining birthrate and aging population have resulted in a labor shortage, and companies have been expanding the number of part-time workers. As a result, the number of part-time workers with shorter working hours has increased, and the overall average hours worked has decreased.

Point

①では、日本の1,610時間に対してイタリアが1,670時間なので、Tが正解です。

②では、最も労働時間の長い国が1,790時間のアメリカなので、Fが正解です。

③では、ドイツの労働時間が1,350時間なので、Fが正解です。

④では、フランスの労働時間が1,490時間、イギリスが1,500時間でほぼ同じですから、Tが正解です。

Answer　①T　②F　③F　④T

民間企業における障がい者就業率

日本には民間企業で働く障がい者がどのくらいいると思いますか？

①約 9 万人
②約 35 万人
③約 58 万人

　2021年度における日本の障がい者の数は964万7,000人で、そのうち民間企業で働く人は57万8,292人です。障がい者が差別なく安定して就職することを目的とする「障害者雇用促進法」では、企業に障がい者雇用率に相当する人数を雇用する義務が課せられています。従業員が43.5人以上いる民間企業の場合の法定雇用率は2.3パーセントです。2020年に発表された障がい者雇用率は2.15パーセントと過去最高値を更新しましたが、法定雇用率には届きませんでした。

　障がいには身体障がい、知的障がい、精神障がいなどの種類があり、それぞれの障がいの程度もさまざまですが、自立して仕事をし、その対価を受け取りたいと考えている障がい者はたくさんいます。一方、企業側は、障がい者にどのような仕事を任せたらいいのか、現場でしっかり障がい者を教育できるのか、障がい者は他の社員とうまく関われるのかなど、さまざまな疑問や悩みがあり、積極的な障がい者の雇用が難しいこともあります。しかし、企業側の人手不足対策として障がい者を雇用することが生産性の向上につながったり、ワークシェアリングで業務の効率を改善したりといったメリットもあるため、周囲の理解や協力のもとで障がい者雇用を浸透させる必要があるでしょう。

The number of **persons with disabilities** in Japan in fiscal 2021 was 9,647,000, of which 578,292 worked in the **private sector**. The Act to Facilitate the Employment of Persons with Disabilities, which aims to ensure stable employment for persons with disabilities without discrimination, imposes on companies the obligation to employ a number of persons with disabilities based on a legally mandated rate. For private companies with 43.5

or more employees, this is 2.3 percent. The employment rate for persons with disabilities announced in 2020 was 2.15 percent, the highest ever, but still short of the legally mandated rate.

Although there are different types of disabilities, such as physical, intellectual and mental disabilities, and the degree of each disability varies, there are many people with disabilities who want to work independently and receive compensation for their efforts. On the other hand, companies also have various questions and concerns, such as what kind of work to entrust to people with disabilities, whether they can train them well onsite and whether they can relate well to other employees, sometimes making it difficult to proactively hire people with disabilities. However, since hiring people with disabilities as a measure to address labor shortages can also have benefits, such as improving productivity and work efficiency through work sharing, it is necessary to promote the employment of people with disabilities with the understanding and cooperation of those around them.

Answer ③約58万人

ワークライフバランス

働きすぎの問題を抱える日本では、働き方だけでなく、ワークライフバランス（work-life balance ＝ 仕事と生活の調和）も見直されています。下の図はワークライフバランスを構成する要素を表したものです。日本語を参考に、各要素を表す英単語を書いてください。

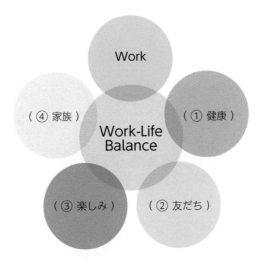

ワークライフバランスは1990年代初頭、東西冷戦後の不況にあえいでいたアメリカで考え出された概念で、「仕事とプライベートをバランスよく両立させること」を言います。日本でも近年、政府が働き方改革（働く人が個々の事情に合った多様で柔軟な働き方を自分で選択できるようにするための改革）の実施を促し、企業や団体が取り組みを進めています。その中で、働き方だけでなく、私生活の充実によって仕事がうまくいく、また逆に仕事がうまくいくことで私生活も潤うという、仕事と生活の相乗効果の関係が重視されています。
　　上の図のように、生活に欠かせないものとして健康、いろいろなことを話せる友だち、自分を元気にするような楽しみ、ライフステージごとの家庭・家族があり、

それらが仕事とうまく調和できるとワークライフバランスが整っていることになります。ここで重要なのは、仕事と私生活をきっちり分けたり、両者の時間や比率を決めたりするものではないということです。仕事で成果を上げるためのスキル習得を生活の中で行ったり、充実した生活から仕事に生かせるヒントが生まれたりするからです。

ワークライフバランスの考え方は、社会人だけでなく、学校に通う子どもたちにも応用できます。実際、スクールライフバランスという言葉もあるくらいです。一方に傾いていて支障が出ている人は、できることからバランスを整えてみるのがいいかもしれません。

Work-life balance is a concept conceived in the United States in the early 1990s, during the post-Cold War recession, and refers to "striking a balance between work and private life." In recent years, in Japan as well, the government has encouraged the implementation of work-style reforms (which allow workers to choose diverse and flexible work styles that suit their individual circumstances), and companies and organizations have been promoting initiatives. In these reforms, there is an emphasis on not just how people work, but on how a fulfilling private life enhances one's work life and, conversely, how one's personal life can be enriched by work.

As shown in the diagram above, the essential elements of life are health, friends with whom one can talk about various things, enjoyment that energizes one, and home and family at each stage of life. When these are harmonized well with work, one has a good work-life balance. The important point here is that it is not about separating work and personal life exactly, or determining the time or ratio between the two. Rather, it is about learning the skills necessary to achieve results at work and figuring out how to apply these skills to your work life through a fulfilling lifestyle.

The concept of work-life balance can be applied not only to working adults but also to children in school. In fact, there is even a term called school-life balance. If you are leaning toward one side and it is interfering with your life, you may want to try to find things in your life that you can do to achieve a balance.

Answer ① Health ② Friend ③ Fun ④ Family

Goal 8

AI に変わってしまう職業

AI やロボットが導入されることで、日本で 2030 年ごろまでになくなる可能性のある職業を、次から選んでください。

Counselors

Taxi drivers

General office workers

Bank employees

Teachers

Security guards

Doctors

2015年、英国のオックスフォード大学と野村総研の共同研究の結果として、日本の労働者の約49パーセントが就いている職業が、10 ～ 20年後にAIやロボットに取って代わられる可能性があると発表されました。

ITの進化には業務の効率化や人為的エラーを防ぐメリットがあるため、当然AIやロボットに置き換えられる仕事もあります。例えば、車両の自動運転技術が進化すれば、タクシーの運転手や電車の車掌などは必要なくなるかもしれません。また、キャッシュレス化が進むことで、銀行員の窓口業務や数字のチェック業務が不要となる可能性があります。監視カメラやセンサー技術の向上によって24時間監視できるシステムや巡回警備ロボットを導入できれば、警備員が代替されることになるでしょう。その他、スーパーやコンビニの店員、ホテルの受付係などもいらなくなる可能性があるようです。

一方で、人でなければできない仕事もあります。医師や看護師、保育士などは、機械が苦手とする臨機応変な対応を必要とします。また、常に他の人とコミュニケーションを取りながら仕事をする教員や営業担当者、コンサルタント、また、

相手の感情を理解することが求められるカウンセラー、クリエイティブな発想が必要なクリエイターなどは、機械による代替が難しい職業と言えるでしょう。

In 2015, a joint study by the University of Oxford in the UK and Nomura Research Institute Ltd. found that jobs occupied by about 49 percent of the Japanese workforce could be done by AI and robots in 10 to 20 years.

Some jobs will naturally be replaced by AI and robots since the evolution of IT has the advantage of improving work efficiency and preventing human error. For example, as vehicle self-driving technology evolves, cab drivers and train conductors may no longer be needed. In addition, the trend toward cashless transactions may eliminate the need for bank tellers and number-checking services. Security guards will be replaced by 24-hour monitoring systems and patrolling security robots if surveillance cameras and sensor technology improve. In addition, supermarket and convenience store clerks and hotel receptionists may also become unnecessary.

On the other hand, there are some jobs that can only be done by people. Doctors, nurses and childcare workers, for example, need to be resourceful, which machines are not good at. Teachers, salespeople and consultants, who work while constantly communicating with others, counselors, who need to understand the emotions of others and creators, who need to think creatively, are occupations that are difficult to replace with machines.

> **Answer** Taxi drivers ／ General office workers ／
> Bank employees ／ Security guards

「働きがいも経済成長も」
──そのためにあなたは何ができると思いますか？
What can you do to support the goal of "decent work and economic growth"?

　働きがいがあって、十分な収入が得られる仕事をディーセントワークと言います。働く人の権利が守られ、安心して安定した生活と仕事を得ることを誰もが望んでいますが、児童労働を強いられる人や低賃金で長時間労働をする人、職を失う人、ブラック企業で働く人などが多くいるのが現実です。

　私たちにできるのは、ワークライフバランス（学生はスクールライフバランス）を意識して効率的に働く癖をつけることです。政府や企業の取り組みに期待するよりも、まずは自分で取り組めるところから意識改革をするといいのではないでしょうか。また、児童労働に加担しないために、海外の安い商品を選ばずフェアトレード商品を選んでみるのもいいでしょう。フェアトレードでは生産者の労働環境や生活水準が保障されるとともに、環境・社会・経済の観点から10の基準が設けられていて、児童労働や強制労働の撤廃が目標となっています。

　さらに、地域の経済活性化のためにも、地産地消を心がけましょう。地域によっては、野菜販売ロッカーを設けたり、週末に朝市を開いたりするところがあります。地元産の新鮮な食材を味わえるだけでなく、地元生産者の支援にもつながります。

　Decent work is that which is worthwhile and provides sufficient income. Everyone wants the rights of workers to be protected and for them to have secure and stable lives and jobs, but the reality is that there are many people who are forced to work as child laborers, who work long hours for low wages, who lose their jobs or who work for companies that exploit their workers.

　What we can do is develop the habit of working efficiently with an awareness of work-life balance (school-life balance for students). Rather than relying on the government or companies to take action, it would be better to first change our mindset by starting with what we can do ourselves. It is also a good idea to choose fair trade products instead of cheap ones from overseas in order not to be complicit in child labor. Fair trade guarantees the working environment and standard of living of the producers, and has 10 standards from environmental, social and economic perspectives, with the goal of eliminating child labor and forced labor.

In addition, local production for local consumption should be encouraged to stimulate the local economy. Some communities set up vegetable sales lockers or hold morning markets on weekends. This not only allows people to taste fresh local produce, but also supports local producers.

Goal 8

Goal 9

産業と技術革新の基盤をつくろう
Industry, Innovation and Infrastructure

強靭（レジリエント）なインフラ構築、包括的かつ持続可能な
産業化の促進およびイノベーションの推進を図る。

**Build resilient infrastructure, promote inclusive and
sustainable industrialization and foster innovation.**

　日本では、電気もガスも水道もトイレも当たり前に使っています。スマートフォンやタブレットを使ってインターネットを楽しむ子どもたちもたくさんいます。整備された道路や鉄道があるからこそ流通網も発達して欲しいものがすぐに手元に届くのです。しかし、世界にはまだまだインフラが整備されず不便な生活を送っている人々がいます。たとえば、アラブ首長国連邦が100パーセントのインターネット普及率であるのに対しエリトリアはわずか1.31パーセントと大幅なデジタル格差が存在します。
　災害などに強く安定したインフラを整備し、より便利で豊かな暮らしを実現するために必要なことを考えてみましょう。

参照：Global Note 世界のインターネット普及率
国別ランキング・推移（2022）

インフラとは？

「インフラ」を英語で何と言いますか？

① infrastructure
② inflation
③ influence

　「インフラ」は英語のinfrastructureが元になってできた言葉です。インフラストラクチャーは「（社会の）基盤、生活の基盤となる設備」の意味で、電気・ガス・水道・道路・鉄道・インターネットなど、日々の生活を支える基盤となるもののことです。それがないと日常生活に支障が出てくるものを指します。

　The word "*infura*" is derived from the English word "infrastructure." Infrastructure means "the framework and facilities that form the basis of society," such as electricity, gas, water, roads, railroads and the internet, which are the foundations of our daily lives. It refers to things that our lifestyles would be difficult without.

Point

　②のinflationは「インフレ」のことで、物の値段が上がり続け、相対的に貨幣価値が下がった状況のことです。反意語はdeflation（デフレ）です。
　③のinfluenceは「影響、影響力」という意味です。最近よく見聞きする「インフルエンサー」はinfluencerと書き、「社会的に大きな影響力をもつ人」のことを指します。

Answer　① infrastructure

産業基盤に関する用語

次の単語とその意味を線で結んでください。

① growth　　　　　　　　　　　・　　　　　・　技術革新

② technological innovation　　・　　　　　・　産業化

③ industrialization　　　　　　・　　　　　・　回復力、復元力

④ development　　　　　　　　・　　　　　・　成長

⑤ resilience　　　　　　　　　・　　　　　・　開発、発展

Point

　①のgrowthには、生物の「成長」、細胞などの「増殖」といった意味がありますが、経済や文明、文化などの「発展」を表すときにも使われます。ほかに、advancement（進歩、向上）、buildup（体制などが増強すること）、build-out（技術などの発展・成長）なども同じような意味です。

　②は、新たな技術を生み出し、そこから新たな価値のあるものをつくって社会に大きな変化を起こすことです。

　③は、一般的に、農業中心の社会から工業中心の社会に変わることを意味します。「工業化」と言われることもあります。

　④のdevelopmentには、growthと同じように「成長」という意味もありますが、質的に変化するイメージを持っており、「より良くなる、さらに発展する」という意味合いがあります。

　⑤のresilienceは、最近「レジリエンス」と日本語化されてよく見聞きします。元々は物体に外側から力を加えて変形させ、力を取り除くと元に戻るような「回復力、復元力」といった性質を意味する言葉ですが、「立ち直りの早い、ストレスに強い、逆境をうまく乗り越えられる」ような人を「レジリエンスのある人」などと表現することもあります。災害時にダメージを受けやすいインフラを、技術開発を進めてレジリエンスのあるものに整備することが求められています。

Answer

① growth ＝ 成長

② technological innovation ＝ 技術革新

③ industrialization ＝ 産業化

④ development ＝ 開発、発展

⑤ resilience ＝ 回復力、復元力

アフリカの交通インフラ

アフリカ諸国では交通インフラの状態が悪化しています。サハラ以南のアフリカの道路舗装率は何パーセントだと思いますか？

① 9 パーセント
② 14 パーセント
③ 23 パーセント
④ 35 パーセント

　アフリカ諸国の鉄道や幹線道路は旧植民地時代に建設・整備されたものがほとんどで、独立後は各国の維持・管理不足で鉄道・道路・港湾の交通インフラの状態が悪化しています。その中でも、サハラ以南のアフリカ諸国の道路舗装率はわずか9パーセントだと言われています。各国で交通規制が異なり、その共通化にも困難をきたしています。また、鉄道は老朽化して機能が低下しているため、輸送量が低下しています。さらに、大型貨物船が入れる港湾が少なく、少数の特定の国際港湾に船が集中してしまうため、待ち時間の長さが問題になっています。

　このように、アフリカ諸国では各国・地域の交通インフラの状態が悪化していたり、未整備だったりすることで輸送コストや時間がかかり、結果としてアフリカの経済成長の妨げとなっています。鉄道・道路・港湾それぞれのインフラ整備を改善しつつ、アフリカ大陸全土の交通規制を統一し、越境交通整備を円滑に進めることが必要不可欠です。

　Most of the railroads and highways in African countries were constructed and maintained during the former colonial period, and after independence, the condition of the transportation infrastructure of railroads, roads and ports deteriorated due to lack of maintenance and management in each country. It is said that just 9 percent of roads in sub-Saharan African countries are paved. Traffic regulations differ from country to country, making it difficult to standardize them. In addition, railroads are aging and losing functionality, resulting in a decline in traffic volumes. Furthermore, there are few ports that can accommodate large cargo ships, and ships are concentrated in a few specific international ports, making long waiting times a problem.

Thus, the deteriorating or underdeveloped state of national and regional transportation infrastructures in African countries is making transportation costly and time-consuming, and as a result, is hindering Africa's economic growth. It is essential to improve the respective infrastructures of railroads, roads and ports while unifying traffic regulations across the African continent and facilitating the development of cross-border traffic.

Answer ① 9 パーセント

自然災害の経済損失トップ3

下の表は1998年以降20年の間に、自然災害による甚大な経済的損失が
あった上位3カ国とその経済損失額をまとめたものです。空欄の上位3カ国
を下の国名から選んで書き込んでください。

Top 3 Countries in terms of Absolute Loss (billion US$), 1998–2017

①		$944.8 billion
②		$492.2 billion
③		$376.3 billion

出典：国連国際防災戦略事務局 (UNISDR)・災害疫学研究センター (CRED) "Economic Losses, Poverty &
Disasters 1998-2017"

・Japan　　・USA　　・India　　・China　　・Puerto Rico

　地震や津波、洪水、干ばつ、暴風雨などの自然災害によって環境が脅かされる
と、経済にも大きな損害が出てしまいます。1998年から2017年までの20年間で
自然災害による甚大な経済的損失があった上位3カ国とその経済損失額は、1位
がアメリカ（9,448億ドル）、2位が中国（4,922億ドル）、3位が日本（3,763億ドル）
です。ちなみに、4位以降は順にインド、プエルトリコ、ドイツ、イタリア、タイ、
メキシコ、フランスとなっています。

　1位のアメリカはハリケーンによる被害が甚大で、経済損失額も2位の中国の
約2倍です。アメリカでは排水設備や電力網などの改修が不十分なため、すぐに
大規模停電や広域かつ長期的な断水などが起こってしまいます。そこで2021年
11月、超党派によるインフラ投資・雇用法が成立し、総額約1兆ドルを投じて道
路や橋、都市の公共交通機関、鉄道・港湾・空港などの整備や、上下水道設備の
改修、高速インターネット回線の強化、未来に向けたクリーンエネルギーの開発・
整備が行われる予定です。

　2位の中国は毎年の豪雨によって洪水や土砂崩れ、堤防の決壊、建物の倒壊な

どの甚大な被害を受けています。また、近年では電子決済が急速に普及しているため、水害で停電が起こると、買い物ができなくなったりタクシーや地下鉄に乗れなくなったりといった二次被害もかなり深刻になっていて、劣化したインフラの改修に加え通信システムの強化が急務となっています。

　地震や津波、台風などの被害が多い日本が3位です。2004年の中越地震では経済損失が約3兆円、2011年の東日本大震災では約16.9兆円、関西国際空港が水没した2018年の台風21号の経済損失は約2兆5,000億円に達しました。台風による水害や土砂災害、地震や津波の被害を防ぐインフラの整備・強化が進められていますが、ハザードマップの作成や防災情報の高度化推進、災害時緊急事業の対応体制の強化など、地域の防災力を高める取り組みも行われています。

When the environment is threatened by natural disasters, such as earthquakes, tsunamis, floods, droughts and storms, economies can suffer significant damage. The top three countries and their economic losses due to natural disasters over the 20-year period from 1998 to 2017 were the United States ($944.8 billion), China ($492.2 billion) and Japan ($376.3 billion). Incidentally, from fourth place onward, in descending order, were India, Puerto Rico, Germany, Italy, Thailand, Mexico and France.

The US, in first place, suffered tremendous damage from hurricanes, and the amount of economic loss was about twice that of second-place China. In the US, the drainage system and power grid are inadequately repaired, resulting in immediate large-scale power outages and widespread, long-term water outages. In November 2021, the Bipartisan Infrastructure Law (Infrastructure Investment and Jobs Act) was enacted, which will invest a total of approximately $1 trillion to improve roads, bridges, urban public transportation, railways, ports, airports, etc., upgrade water and sewage systems, ensure stable high-speed internet access and develop and improve clean energy for the future.

China, in second place, suffers tremendous damage from annual torrential rains that cause floods, landslides, levee failures and building collapses. In addition, since electronic payments have rapidly become more common in recent years, other problems, such as the inability to shop or take cabs and subways when power is cut off due to flooding, are quite serious, making it imperative to both repair deteriorated infrastructure and maintain telecommunications systems.

Japan ranks third in terms of damage from earthquakes, tsunamis and typhoons: the 2004 Chuetsu Earthquake caused economic losses of about 3 trillion yen, the 2011 Great East Japan Earthquake caused about 16.9 trillion yen in losses, and Typhoon No. 21 in 2018, which submerged parts of Kansai International Airport, caused economic losses of about 2.5 trillion yen. While infrastructure is being developed and strengthened to prevent flooding and landslides caused by typhoons and damage from earthquakes and tsunamis, efforts are also being made to enhance local disaster preparedness by creating hazard maps, promoting the advancement of disaster prevention information and strengthening the response system for emergency disaster management projects.

Answer ① USA ② China ③ Japan

後発開発途上国の研究者の数

産業の生産性を上げるためにはイノベーションを促進させることが重要ですが、後発開発途上国には研究者が不足しています。こうした国では人口100万人当たり何人の研究者がいると思いますか？

① 63人
② 1,098人
③ 3,739人

　後発開発途上国は、開発途上国の中でも特に開発が遅れている国々のことで、アフリカや東南アジアの内陸部に集中しています。SDGsのGoal 9には、途上国内の技術開発・研究・イノベーションを支援することや、すべての国でイノベーションと科学研究を促進させることがターゲットとして盛り込まれていますが、途上国では国を豊かにするハイテク産業が育ちにくいのが現状です。その原因の一つに研究開発費と研究者の不足があります。研究者の数については、世界平均で人口100万人当たり②の1,098人と言われていますが、後発開発途上国ではわずか63人です。ちなみに先進国の100万人当たりの研究者の数は③の 3,739人です。

　産業の生産性を向上させるには、国内の貧富の差を解消するとともに先進国との格差も縮めなければならないのですが、研究開発費や研究者が不足しているとイノベーションが促進されません。その他、イノベーションに必要な知識や情報をリアルタイムで収集できるインターネット環境が整備不足だったり、イノベーションを発展させるための対策や取り組みに消極的だったりすることも、途上国でハイテク産業が育ちにくい原因となっています。

Least developed countries are those nations that are particularly underdeveloped, even among developing countries, and they are concentrated in the interior regions of Africa and Southeast Asia. Goal 9 of the SDGs includes targets to support technology development, research and innovation within developing countries and the promotion of innovation and scientific research in all countries. However, it is difficult for high-tech industries that enrich countries to grow in developing countries. One of the reasons for this is lack of R&D funds and researchers. The global average number of researchers is said to be 1,098 per million people ②, while the number is only 63 in the least developed countries. Incidentally, the number of researchers per million people in developed countries is ③ 3,739.

In order to improve industrial productivity, the gap between rich and poor within a country must be eliminated, and the gap with developed countries must be narrowed, but innovation cannot be promoted if funds for R&D and researchers are lacking. Other factors that make it difficult for high-tech industries to grow in developing countries include lack of internet infrastructure that enables real-time collection of knowledge and information necessary for innovation, and a reluctance to introduce measures and initiatives to develop innovation.

Answer ① 63 人

Goal 9

下の棒グラフは、2022 年 1 月現在の世界のインターネット利用者数の国別ランキングです。棒グラフを見ながら、次の英語の質問に答えてください。

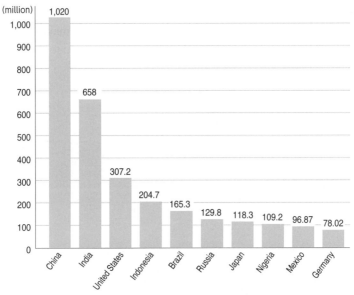

出典：© Statista 2022

① Does Mexico have more internet users than Germany?

② Which country has the second-most internet users in the world?

③ Is the number of China's internet users approximately* five times* that of Japan?

④ How many internet users are there in Nigeria?

*approximately およそ、約　　〜times 〜倍

中国がインターネット利用者数で世界一、インドが2位ということに驚くかもしれませんが、中国もインドも総人口が多いため、必然的にインターネットの利用者数も多くなります。しかし、インターネットの普及率で見ると中国は70.4パーセントで、90パーセント台に達しているアメリカや日本よりも低いのです。これは主に、高齢者層にインターネットの利用が普及していないためで、政府は高齢者にも使いやすいデバイスやアプリを開発し、利用を促進しています。

You may be surprised to learn that China has the largest number of internet users in the world and that India is in second place, but both China and India have large total populations, which inevitably leads to large numbers of users. However, China's internet penetration rate of 70.4 percent is lower than that of the US and Japan, which have rates in the 90 percent range. The situation in China is mainly due to the fact that internet use is not widespread among the elderly population, and the government is promoting its use by developing devices and applications that are easy for the elderly to use.

Point

①は「メキシコにはドイツよりもインターネット利用者が多くいますか？」という質問です。メキシコは9位、ドイツは10位なので、Yesで答えます。

②は「世界で2位のインターネット利用者数はどの国ですか？」という質問です。棒グラフの上から2番目はインドなので、Indiaと答えます。

③は「中国のインターネット利用者数は日本の約5倍ですか？」という質問です。中国のインターネット利用者数が10億2,000万人なのに対し、日本は1億1,830万人です。約5倍ではなく約9倍の数の人がインターネットを利用しているので、Noを使って答えます。

Answer ① Yes, it does. ② India ③ No, it isn't. ④ 109.2 million

情報格差を英語で説明

情報格差 (digital divide) の意味を説明した英文があります。日本語を参考にしながら、空欄に当てはまる単語を下の語群から選んで文を完成させてください。

Digital divide: the (①) between people who have (②) access to the (③) and those who do not.

情報格差：インターネットに簡単にアクセスできる人とそうでない人との間に生じる差

・internet

・gap

・easy

　情報格差は、そのまま「デジタルデバイド／デジタルディバイド」と言うこともあります。2021年度の世界のインターネット普及率は、先進国で90パーセント、発展途上国で57パーセント、後発開発途上国で27パーセントと、国の間で大きな開きがあります。デジタル情報へのアクセスの可否に差があるということは、デジタル化が進んだ現代社会において、教育・社会・経済などさまざまな場面で格差を生むことにつながります。

　また、国家間の情報格差問題に加えて、ひとつの国の中でも情報格差が発生するという問題があります。たとえば、動画コンテンツやオンラインゲームの利用度が高くニュースサイトを見ない人と、動画コンテンツやオンラインゲームの利用度は低いがニュースサイトの利用度は高い人では、ネットの利用目的が違うので、入手する情報の種類・内容に格差が生じます。また、スマホやタブレットを自由に操れる人でも、パソコンの知識や技能がなければ職場で文書などを作成することができません。生まれ育った環境によっては、Wi-Fi設備に投資する余裕

がなかったり、スマホやパソコンを持てない人もいるでしょう。このようにICT（情報通信技術）を利用できない人を情報弱者と言います。国や自治体は情報格差を解消するために、ICT活用のサポートや、無料端末の設置、IT業界全体の人材育成といった取り組みを行い、情報弱者を減らす必要があります。

The digital divide is sometimes referred to directly as the "digital divide." In fiscal year 2021, the global internet penetration rate was 90 percent in developed countries, 57 percent in developing countries, and 27 percent in the least developed countries, showing a wide gap between nations. This gap in access to digital information leads to disparities in various aspects of modern society, including education, society and the economy.

In addition to the problem of information disparity between countries, there is also the problem of information disparity within countries. For example, a person who uses video content and online games frequently and does not visit news sites, and a person who uses video content and online games less but uses news sites more, have different purposes for using the internet, resulting in a disparity in the type and content of information they obtain. In addition, even those who can freely use smartphones and tablets cannot create documents at work if they do not have computer knowledge and skills. Depending on the environment in which they live, some may not be able to afford to invest in Wi-Fi equipment or have access to smartphones or computers. People who do not have access to ICT (information and communication technology) are referred to as the "information poor." In order to eliminate the information gap, national and local governments need to support the use of ICT, provide free devices and develop human resources in the IT industry to reduce the number of information-poor people.

Answer ① gap ② easy ③ internet

身の回りのAI

近年、AI（artificial intelligence）が身近なところに使われるようになってきました。下の図の中からAIが使われているものを選んでください。

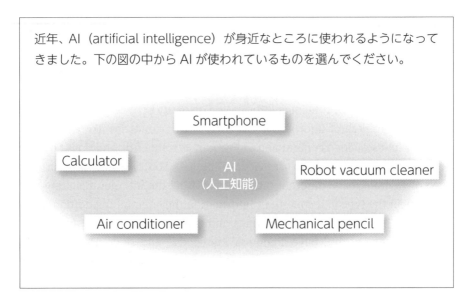

AI（人工知能）はその名の通り、人間の知的能力の一部を、ソフトウェアを用いて人工的に再現したものです。データとして蓄積したパターンをもとに、状況に応じて最適化することができるのが特徴で、日常生活での快適さを追求する目的でAIが導入された製品がいくつかあります。

よく知られているのはスマートフォンなどに搭載されている音声アシスタント機能です。話しかけると返答してくれたり、質問に対する情報をインターネット上で検索して教えてくれたりします。ロボット掃除機もAIを搭載した製品として有名です。部屋の大きさや障がい物の場所の情報を収集しながら、内蔵カメラでごみを検知して掃除をしてくれます。エアコンにもAIが搭載されています。人の体温や動きによる温度変化に瞬時に反応して、自動的に快適な温度調節を行うため、人がリモコンなどを使って調節する必要がありません。

その他、自動運転システムを搭載した自動車や会話のできる介護ロボット、災害時に救助活動を行えるレスキューロボットなど、人間では困難な場所や人手が

必要な場所などで活躍するためのAIの研究開発が行われています。

　AI (Artificial Intelligence), as the name implies, is an artificial reproduction of some of the intellectual abilities of humans using software. It is characterized by its ability to optimize itself in response to situations based on patterns accumulated as data, and there are many products in which AI has been introduced to make daily life more comfortable.

　A well-known example is the voice assistant function in smartphones and other devices. When you talk to it, it responds to your questions, or searches the internet for information to answer them. Robot vacuum cleaners are another well-known AI-equipped product. They use built-in cameras to detect debris and clean while collecting information on the size of the room and the location of obstacles. Some air conditioners are also equipped with AI. They instantly react to temperature changes caused by a person's body temperature and movement, and automatically adjust the temperature to a comfortable level, eliminating the need for a person to use a remote control to adjust them.

　Other examples of AI research and development include automobiles equipped with self-driving systems, nursing care robots that can talk and robots that can perform rescue operations in the event of a disaster.

Answer　Smartphone ／ Robot vacuum cleaner ／ Air conditioner

ネットの産業革命

第一次産業革命 (the First Industrial Revolution) は蒸気機関の発明によって産業に発展をもたらしました。すべてのものがネットにつながることでさまざまな産業構造の変化が生み出されるという現在の産業革命は、第何次に位置していると思いますか？　正しい序数を選んで空欄に入れてください。

the (　　　　) Industrial Revolution

① Second
② Third
③ Fourth
④ Fifth

　電話機や電球が発明された第二次産業革命、コンピューターやインターネットの登場でデジタル革命を起こした第三次産業革命、それに続くのが現在進行中の第四次産業革命で、Industry 4.0とも呼ばれています。
　第四次産業革命は、大量の情報をAIが解析し、AIが自ら学習して最適な行動をとることが可能となる産業社会を目指しています。たとえば、「モノのインターネット」と呼ばれるIoTという手段で、あらゆるものがインターネットを介して通信するようになります。つまり、外出先からお風呂を沸かしたり、ドアの開閉を知ることで人の行動を把握したりといったように、家電製品や各種装置を、取り付けられたセンサーからの情報をもとに遠隔制御したり、離れた装置間でデータを送受信したりすることが可能になります。その他、3Dプリンターや、カメラ・超音波センサー・GPSなどを搭載した自動運転車、物質を原子や分子スケールで自在に制御するナノテクノロジーや、医療や農業、環境分野で利用されることが多いバイオテクノロジーなども第四次産業革命の特徴的なイノベーションと言えます。さらに、このイノベーションを通じて、サイバー空間とフィジカル空間を高度に融合させた便利で質の高い生活を送ることのできる人間中心の「超

スマート社会」Society 5.0が、最終的な未来の社会像とされています。

　日本には、内閣府による「ムーンショット目標1〜9」という計画があります（https://www8.cao.go.jp/cstp/moonshot/target.html）。これは、2050年までに科学技術を用いて人々が社会・環境・経済の3領域で幸福で豊かな暮らしを送れることを実現しようというものです。目標1では、「人が体・脳・空間・時間の制約から解放された社会を実現」することを目指すために、2030年までに1人10体以上のサイバネティックアバター（人口頭脳をもつ分身ロボット）を所有できる基盤を構築し、2050年までに10体のアバターと共に体・脳・空間・時間の制約を超えた新しい生活様式を確立、アバターたちがサイバー空間とフィジカル空間で自由自在に活動する、というかなりギョッとするような計画です。

The Second Industrial Revolution, which saw the invention of the telephone and the electric light bulb, was followed by the Third Industrial Revolution, which saw a digital revolution with the advent of computers and the internet, and is now being followed by the ongoing Fourth Industrial Revolution, also known as Industry 4.0.

The Fourth Industrial Revolution aims to create an industrial society in which a large amount of information is analyzed by AI (artificial intelligence), enabling it to learn and make optimal actions on its own. For example, everything will be able to communicate via the internet by means of IoT, which refers to the "internet of things." In other words, it will be possible to remotely control home appliances and various devices based on information from attached sensors, and to send and receive data between remote devices, allowing us to heat a bath from outside the house or know when a door is open or closed. Other innovations characteristic of the Fourth Industrial Revolution include 3D printers, self-driving cars equipped with cameras, ultrasonic sensors, or GPS, nanotechnology to freely control materials on the atomic and molecular scale and biotechnology that is often used in the medical, agricultural and environmental fields. Furthermore, through these innovations, the ultimate vision of society in the future is Society 5.0, a human-centered "super-smart society," where people can lead convenient and high-quality lives through a sophisticated fusion of cyberspace and physical space.

Japan has a plan called "Moonshot Goals 1-9" (Moonshot for Human Well-being) by the Cabinet Office (https://www8.cao.go.jp/cstp/moonshot/target.html). This plan aims to use science and technology to help people

Goal 9

201

lead happy and prosperous lives in the three domains of society, environment and the economy by the year 2050. Goal 1 aims to "realize a society in which people are free from the constraints of body, brain, space and time." In order to achieve this goal, each person will own at least 10 cybernetic avatars (alter ego robots with artificial brains) that improve their perception and physical and mental abilities for specific tasks by 2030 and go far beyond that by 2050. However, it is a rather frightening plan.

Answer ③ Fourth

持続可能なインフラ

自然のもつ機能を活用しながら持続可能なインフラ整備や土地利用などを
推進する概念を英語で何と言いますか？

① blue infrastructure
② green infrastructure
③ gray infrastructure

　グリーンインフラは、自然環境のもつ多様な機能を、ヒートアイランドや気候
変動、洪水など、社会におけるさまざまな課題を解決するために活用し、持続可
能な国土・都市・地域づくりを進める取り組みのことです。テクノロジーとのハ
イブリッドで進めることで、同時に自然環境の保全と再生を行うことができます。
SDGsのGoal 9のターゲットに、「資源をよりむだなく使えるようにし、環境に
やさしい技術や生産の方法をより多く取り入れて、インフラや産業を持続可能な
ものにする」というものがあり、グリーンインフラの活用はGoal 9を達成するた
めの基盤と言えます。

　グリーンインフラはもともとアメリカで発案されたインフラ整備手法で、欧米
を中心に取り組みが進められています。日本では、防災・減災、地域振興、環境
を考えた取り組みが中心になっています。たとえば、ヒートアイランド現象緩和
のための都市部の屋上緑化施設整備や、浸水対策として雨水を有効活用した雨水
浸透型花壇の設置、津波の減災として自然の堤防である砂丘を保全する埋設護岸
整備など、地域の特徴をふまえた社会課題の取り組みです。

　Green Infrastructure is an initiative to promote sustainable land, city
and regional development by utilizing the diverse functions of the natural
environment to solve various social issues, such as heat islands, climate
change and flooding. Hybrid technology can simultaneously conserve and
regenerate the natural environment. SDG 9 is to "make infrastructure and
industry sustainable by using resources more sparingly and incorporating

more environmentally friendly technologies and production methods. The use of green infrastructure is the foundation for achieving Goal 9.

Green infrastructure is a method of infrastructure development originally conceived in the United States, and it is being promoted mainly there and in Europe. In Japan, efforts are focused on disaster prevention and mitigation, regional development and environmental considerations. For example, rooftop greening facilities in urban areas to mitigate the heat island effect, rainwater infiltration flower beds to effectively utilize rainwater to prevent flooding and buried revetments to preserve dunes as natural levees for tsunami mitigation are initiatives to address social issues based on local characteristics.

<blockquote>

Point

　greenという単語には、「緑（色）の」という意味の他に、「若々しい」「未熟な、経験の浅い」や「環境［地球］にやさしい、環境問題意識の高い」という意味もあります。
　③のgray infrastructureは、コンクリートの人工構造物を用いた従来型の社会基盤のことを指します。

</blockquote>

Answer　② green infrastructure

「産業と技術革新の基盤をつくろう」
──そのためにあなたは何ができると思いますか？
What can you to support the goal of "industry, innovation and infrastructure"?

　Goal 9は、事故や災害が起きても容易に復興できるようなインフラを整備し、持続可能な社会で安心・安全に暮らすための技術を向上させて経済の発展につなげることを目標としています。インフラが不十分な開発途上国に向けて、先進国の政府や企業、民間団体は長期的な計画のもとに整備・支援を進めながら、同時にメンテナンスなどのケアを行ったり、支援先の人々に技術援助を行ったりしています。

　先進国である日本ではインフラが整っているように見えますが、ほかの先進国と比べるとICT技術の普及で遅れをとっています。これは、新型コロナウイルス感染症発生当初の教育機関の一斉休校時のオンライン教育や、緊急事態宣言下での企業のリモートワーク導入時などに露呈しました。行政や医療のICT化が進めば、私たちの生活はより快適なものになりますが、実際にはなかなか改革が進まず、本当にデジタル基盤が整うのはまだ先になりそうです。

　では、私たち一人ひとりにはいったい何ができるのでしょうか。開発途上国にインフラ整備に充てる寄付金を送るのもいいかもしれません。しかし、寄付金が本来使われるべきところに届かなかったり、汚職が原因で一部のお金が利権者に渡ってしまったりする可能性もあるため、信頼できる団体や企業を通じて送るのがいいでしょう。また、現地の活動をサポートしている日本の団体でボランティアをしてみるのもいいかもしれません。イベントやセミナーなどがあれば参加し、現地で活動するスタッフの話を聞いて知識を深めることができます。さらに、これからのデジタル社会を生き抜くうえで必須なのは、ITやICTの知識や技術と、論理的・創造的思考力と問題解決力を養うためのプログラミング的思考です。近い将来、社会や企業を変革させるような人材になれるよう、スキルを身につけてみましょう。

Goal 9 aims to develop infrastructure that can be easily recovered after an accident or disaster, and to improve technology for people to live safely and securely in a sustainable society, leading to economic development. For developing countries with inadequate infrastructure, governments, companies and private organizations in developed countries are promoting development and support based on long-term plans, while at the same time providing maintenance and other forms of care and technical assistance to the people they support.

Although Japan, as a developed country, appears to have a well-developed infrastructure, it lags behind other developed countries in the diffusion of ICT technology. This was exposed in such cases as online education during the simultaneous closure of educational institutions at the beginning of the outbreak of the COVID-19 pandemic, and the introduction of remote work by companies under the state of emergency that was declared. The more ICT is used in government and health care, the more comfortable our lives will be, but, in reality, reforms have been slow to occur, and it will be some time before a truly digital infrastructure is in place.

So, what can each of us do to help? Sending donations to developing countries for infrastructure development may be a good idea. However, there is a possibility that the money will not be used as it should be, or that some of it will be given to special interests due to corruption, so it is better to send the money through trusted organizations or companies. It may also be a good idea to volunteer with a Japanese organization that supports local activities. If there are events or seminars, you can attend and listen to the staff working in the area to deepen your knowledge. Furthermore, what is essential to survive in the digital society of the future is IT and ICT knowledge and skills, as well as computational thinking to develop logical and creative thinking and problem-solving skills. Why not acquire these skills so that you can become the kind of person who can transform society and companies in the near future?

Goal 10
人や国の不平等をなくそう
Reduced Inequalities

各国内および各国間の不平等を是正する。

Reduce inequality within and among countries.

　これまで、Goal 1 では貧困による格差、Goal 4 では教育における格差、Goal 5 ではジェンダー格差、Goal 7 や Goal 9 では技術やデジタルの格差などについて触れてきました。先進国と途上国といった国家間における貧富の差はもちろんですが、ひとつの国の中にも所得、人種、宗教、国籍、障がいの有無などによるさまざまな不平等が存在します。これらの不平等を減らすことが、貧困や教育、ジェンダーなどの格差問題の解決にもつながります。格差、不平等、差別、偏見などを生む原因やそれによって起こる問題について考えながら、平等な世界をつくるにはどうしたらいいのか考えてみましょう。

不平等に関する用語

次の単語とその意味を線で結んでください。

① nationality   ・   ・   慣習

② race   ・   ・   国籍

③ observance   ・   ・   外見、見た目

④ appearance   ・   ・   宗教

⑤ religion   ・   ・   人種

Point

　①のnationalityはnational originと言われることもあります。「国籍による差別」はnationality discriminationと言います。「フランスと日本の二重国籍を持っています」と言う場合はcitizenshipを用いて、I have [hold] dual citizenship in France and Japan.と言うことができます。dualは「二重になっている」という意味です。

　②のraceは、肌や髪の毛の色など、身体的特徴による人の分類のことで、黒色人種（Negroid）、白色人種（Caucasoid）、黄色人種（Mongoloid）、黒褐色人種（Australoid）が四大人種と呼ばれています。肌の色から、黒人のことをblack（アメリカではAfrican Americanも一般的）、白人をwhite（Caucasianも一般的）と呼ぶことがありますが、アジア人をyellowと呼ぶのは侮蔑的なので避けるべきです。AsianやEast Asianなどがよいでしょう。また、「有色人種」を表すcoloredという言葉も、白人以外の人をひとくくりにした差別的な表現とみなされるので避けるべきです。また、「人種差別主義者」のことをracistと言います。

　③のobservanceは、宗教的・伝統的な慣習や儀式のことを表します。customにも「慣習、風習、習わし」という意味がありますが、local custom（地元の風習）やSpanish custom（スペインの習慣）などのように使われる、より地域的・社会的な意味合いが強い単語です。世界各地に伝わる伝統的な慣習も、女性差別や経済格差を広げる要因になっています。

　④のappearanceは、looksとも言い換えられます。「彼は見かけでは判断できない

よ」は You can't judge him by his appearance [looks]. と、「彼女のことを外見で判断してはだめだよ」は Don't judge her by her appearance [looks]. と表現できます。

⑤の religion は「宗教」の意味です。近年では世界の多くの国で信教の自由が保障されていますが、いまだに発展途上国やイスラム国家などの一部では宗教的迫害（religious persecution）が問題になっています。

Answer
① nationality ＝ 国籍
② race ＝ 人種
③ observance ＝ 慣習
④ appearance ＝ 外見、見た目
⑤ religion ＝ 宗教

コロナ感染症以降の大富豪

新型コロナウイルスのパンデミック下の世界で、何人が新たに「大富豪」の仲間入りをしたと思いますか？

① 10人
② 176人
③ 573人
④ 1,458人

　国際NGOの「オックスファム」の発表によると、2019年に始まった新型コロナウイルス感染症の蔓延下で、保有資産が10億ドルを超える億万長者が新たに573人増えたといいます。そして、その大半を、食品・農業分野、燃料分野、製薬分野、テクノロジー分野などの企業の経営者が占めているということです。燃料や食品などの価格が高騰して消費者が苦しむ一方で、それらの価格上昇によって利益を得て億万長者になったのです。製薬業界では新たに40人が大富豪になったということで、明らかにワクチンビジネスの特需のご利益と言えます。

　一方で、このパンデミック下で、新たに1億6,000万人が貧困状態へと追いやられていること、そして世界の最貧困層で収入が減ったことで毎日2万1,000人の死者が出ていることも事実で、貧富の差がさらに拡大していることは明らかです。富裕層の税負担が軽すぎるという経済システムに欠陥があると言う専門家もいますが、富裕層は税制上の優遇措置を受けるなどして「賢く」合法的に節税しているため、富裕層に関わる各国の法律が変わらない限り今後も貧富の差はなくならないでしょう。

　According to the international NGO Oxfam, 573 new billionaires, whose holdings exceed $1 billion, have been created during the COVID-19 pandemic that began in 2019. That means the majority of them are managers of companies in the food and agriculture, fuel, pharmaceutical and technology sectors. While consumers suffer from rising prices of fuel and food, they have become billionaires by profiting from those price hikes. In the pharmaceutical industry, 40 people have become new billionaires, clearly benefiting from the special demand in the vaccine business.

On the other hand, it is also true that 160 million people have been pushed into poverty during the pandemic, and that 21,000 people die every day due to reduced income among the world's poorest people, clearly widening the gap between the rich and the poor. Some experts say that the economic system is flawed in that the tax burden on the wealthy is too light, and since the wealthy are "clever" and legally save taxes by taking advantage of tax incentives, the gap between the rich and the poor will not disappear in the future unless the laws in various countries concerning the wealthy are changed.

Answer ③ 573人

富の再分配

Goal 10 の目標を達成させるためには、富の再分配をする必要があると言われています。日本語を参考にしながら、各空欄に当てはまる単語を選んで文を完成させてください。なお、空欄①に入る単語は語頭を大文字に変えてください。

(　①　) of (　②　) is necessary to stop inequality.
不平等をなくすためには富の再分配が必要です。

- ・wealth
- ・distribution
- ・redistribution
- ・wealthy
- ・redistribute
- ・distribute

　国際NGOの「オックスファム」によると、世界で最も裕福な26人が、世界の総人口のうち所得の低い半数に当たる38億人の総資産と同額の富を握っているそうです。所得格差が広がると経済成長が鈍化するので、富裕層の人々と水準以下で暮らす人々の格差をなくすためには富の再分配が必要になります。国家間も同様で、先進国と途上国との不平等をなくすには世界規模での富の再分配が重要になってきます。

　富の再分配は税制、福祉、社会保障、公共事業などによって、経済的に貧しい人に富を届けることです。貧富の差を縮めて社会の不平等をなくすことを目指すものです。例えば、日本の健康保険制度では、健康で収入の多い若者が保険料を多く払い、収入が少ない高齢者は低い負担率で病院を利用できます。これが可能になるのは、制度に再分配的な側面があるからだと言えます。一方で、現在、国

212

家間の富の再分配に関しては世界規模の仕組みがないため、世界上位1パーセントの超富裕層の資産が世界全体の個人資産の40パーセントを占めるといったことが起きているのです。

According to the international NGO Oxfam, the 26 richest people in the world hold wealth equal to the total assets of 3.8 billion people, the lowest-income half of the world's population. As income inequality widens, economic growth slows, so wealth redistribution is necessary to eliminate the gap between the richest people and those living below the poverty line. The same applies to nations. To eliminate inequality between developed and developing countries, it is important to redistribute wealth on a global scale.

Wealth redistribution is the delivery of wealth to the economically poor through taxation, welfare, social security and public works. It aims to reduce the gap between the rich and the poor and eliminate social inequality. For example, in Japan's health insurance system, young people who are healthy and have high incomes pay higher premiums, while elderly people with low incomes can use hospitals at lower rates. This is possible because of the redistributive aspect of the system. On the other hand, there is currently no global mechanism for the redistribution of wealth among nations, and this is why the assets of the top 1 percent of the world's super-rich account for 40 percent of the world's total personal assets.

Point

「富の再分配」は英語でredistribution of wealthです。redistributionは名詞でre（再び）＋distribution（分配）に分解できます。redistributeは「再分配する」という意味の動詞です。wealthは名詞で「富、財産、裕福であること」などの意味です。反対語はpovertyです。wealthyは形容詞で「裕福な、富んだ」という意味です。

Answer　①Redistribution　②wealth

国際移民の分布

下の円グラフは 2020 年における国際移民の移民先の分布を地域別に示したものです。①〜③に当てはまる地域名を選んでください。

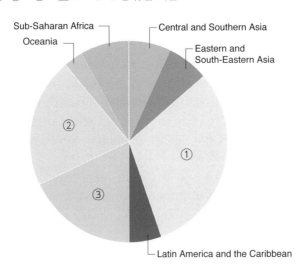

Sub-Saharan Africa
Oceania
Central and Southern Asia
Eastern and South-Eastern Asia
①
②
③
Latin America and the Caribbean

出典：UN DESA, Population Division (2020b). International Migrant Stock 2020.

・Europe

・North America

・Northern Africa and Western Asia

2020年の1年間に人々が世界のどの地域に移住しているかを表している円グラフです。移民の数が最も多いのはヨーロッパで8,700万人、2番目は北米で5,900万人、3番目は北アフリカと西アジアで5,000万人です。

国別で最も多い移住先はアメリカで、2020年には5,100万人を受け入れており、全体の18パーセントを占めています。その他の国で移民の受け入れ数が多いのはドイツ（1,600万人）、サウジアラビア（1,300万人）、ロシア（1,200万人）などです。

2020年の全世界の国際移民の数は2億8,100万人で、インドネシアの総人口とほぼ同数です。これほど多くの人々が他国へ移住する主な理由は貧困と失業で、もともと住んでいた国・地域では仕事がなくて生きていけないために職を求めて

脱出するのです。しかし、安全な秩序を保った移住ではなく、非合法かつ危険な入国方法で国を移動したり、違法労働に従事したりする不法移民が問題となっています。不法移民は就職できずに貧困を抜け出せないまま人身売買されることもあります。合法的に他国へ入国した移民も、社会保障や医療を受けられなかったり、不当な賃金で働かされたりします。

　移民を受け入れている国では、警備を強化したり、強制送還を行ったりして不法入国者を排除しながら、一方で正規の移民に対する権利保護や社会経済的福祉の適用などの政策を導入しています。しかし、これ以上移民を増やさないために、先進国は移民排出国に対して、自国で働いて十分に生活できるような環境を整えるための継続的な開発支援を行っていく必要があるでしょう。

The pie chart shows which regions of the world people were migrating to in the year 2020. The largest number of migrants went to Europe, with 87 million, followed by North America, with 59 million, and North Africa and West Asia, with 50 million.

On a country basis, the largest destination for immigration is the United States, which received 51 million immigrants in 2020, accounting for 18 percent of the total. Other countries with large numbers of immigrants included Germany (16 million), Saudi Arabia (13 million) and Russia (12 million).

In 2020, the total number of international migrants worldwide was 281 million, roughly equal to the total population of Indonesia. The main reasons that so many people migrate to other countries are poverty and unemployment; they escape in search of work because they cannot survive without work in the country or region where they originally lived. However, the problem is not safe and orderly immigration, but illegal immigrants who move between countries using illegal and dangerous immigration methods or who engage in illegal labor. Illegal immigrants may be trafficked without being able to find employment and escape poverty. Immigrants who enter other countries legally may also be denied social security and medical care or forced to work for unfair wages.

Countries that accept immigrants have introduced policies, such as increased security and deportation, to keep illegal immigrants out, while at the same time protecting the rights of and providing socioeconomic welfare to regular immigrants. However, in order to prevent further migration, developed countries will need to provide ongoing development assistance to migrant-displacing countries to create an environment in which people can work and live comfortably in their own countries.

Answer ① Europe ② Northern Africa and Western Asia ③ North America

BLM（人種差別抗議運動）

2020年5月に起きた「ジョージ・フロイド事件」をきっかけに、アメリカで広まった人種差別抗議運動BLMはどのような言葉を略したものですか？

2020年5月、アメリカのミネソタ州でアフリカ系アメリカ人のジョージ・フロイドが、白人の警察官に8分46秒もの間首を圧迫されて死亡するという事件がありました。これを受けて全米で抗議デモが行われたときに、SNS上で#blacklivesmatter（黒人の命は大切だ）というハッシュタグが拡散されて、BLMという言葉とともに抗議運動が広まりました。

しかし、BLM運動の大元のきっかけは、2012年にフロリダ州で起きた自警団によるアフリカ系アメリカ人の高校生トレイボン・マーティンの射殺事件でした。マーティンは武器を所持していなかったにもかかわらず不審者とみなされて自警団の男性に射殺され、男性は正当防衛が認められて無罪となりました。この判決について、アメリカの活動家がBlack Lives Matterという言葉を用いてSNSに投稿し、それを見た知人の活動家がハッシュタグをつけて発信したのがBLM運動の始まりです。現在、アメリカのみならずヨーロッパや東アジアなど世界各国でBLM運動が行われています。

日本には、先住民族のアイヌが不当な扱いを受けていた過去があります。また、近年ではヘイトスピーチ（特定の集団や個人を差別したりけなしたりする発言）も問題になっています。世界ではアパルトヘイトやユダヤの迫害など、昔から人種や民族の差別があり、世代を超えて受け継がれてなくならないのが現実です。国連は1965年に「人種差別撤廃条約」を採択し、現在181カ国が締約して条約に基づいた人種差別の撤廃を目指した取り組みを行っています。国ごとの地道な啓発・広報活動も重要です。

In May 2020, an African American man, George Floyd, was asphyxiated by a white police officer for 8 minutes and 46 seconds in the US state of Minnesota until he died. When protest demonstrations were held across the US in response, the hashtag #blacklivesmatter (black lives matter) was used on social networking sites, and the protest movement spread under the term BLM.

However, the original impetus for the BLM movement came from the 2012 shooting death of Black high school student Trayvon Martin by a vigilante group in Florida. Martin was shot and killed by a vigilante because he was deemed suspicious, even though he was not carrying a weapon, and the man was found not guilty by reason of self-defense. The BLM movement began when an American activist posted about this verdict on a social media site using the term Black Lives Matter, and an activist he knew saw it and sent it out with the hashtag. Today, the BLM movement is active not only in the US, but also in Europe, East Asia and other countries around the world.

Japan has a history of mistreating the indigenous Ainu people. In recent years, hate speech (statements that discriminate or denigrate certain groups or individuals) has also become an issue. The reality is that there has always been racial and ethnic discrimination in the world, such as apartheid and Jewish persecution, and it has been passed down from generation to generation. The United Nations adopted the International Convention on the Elimination of All Forms of Racial Discrimination in 1965, and currently 181 countries are parties to the Convention and are working toward the elimination of racial discrimination based on the agreement. Continued awareness-raising and public relations activities in each country are also important.

Answer   Black Lives Matter

主要国の男女賃金格差

次のグラフは主要先進国のフルタイム労働者の男女間賃金格差を示したものです。①～④に当てはまる国名を下から選んでください。

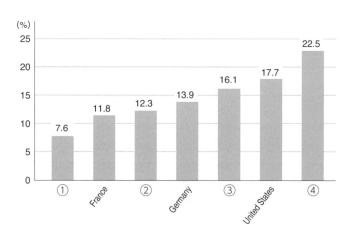

出典：OECD. Gender Gap of Leading Nations (2020)

・Japan　　・Italy　　・United Kingdom　　・Canada

　経済協力開発機構（OECD）によると、調査した42カ国・地域の中で日本は、韓国、イスラエルに次いでワースト3位でした。上の主要7カ国の男女間の賃金格差のグラフは、男性の賃金と女性の賃金との格差を示したもので、割合が大きいほど格差が開いていることになります。OECD加盟国の平均が11.6パーセントであるのに対し、日本の男女間の賃金格差は22.5パーセントです。つまり、日本の男女間の賃金格差は、他の7カ国に比べてかなり大きいと言えます。

　賃金の格差が生まれる原因は、いまだに社会における男女の役割分担に慣習やしきたりなどが根強く残っていること、育児や介護などの制度・サービスが十分に整備されていないこと、女性を適正に評価する仕組みが欠けていることなどが挙げられます。しかし、女性の昇進意欲の低さや責務に対する消極的な姿勢、男

女平等についての女性の問題意識の低さも格差の原因になっていることを知っておくべきでしょう。

　差別や偏見、不平等と同じように、男女の賃金格差も社会規範を根本から変えなければ改善は難しく、そのためには一人ひとりがもつ固定観念を解消することが重要です。人間は幼児期にさまざまな固定観念が作られる傾向が強いため、その段階から地道に軌道修正していけば少しずつ社会規範が変化し、男女間賃金格差も解消されるのかもしれません。

According to the Organization for Economic Cooperation and Development (OECD), Japan ranked third worst among the 42 countries and regions surveyed, behind South Korea and Israel. The above graph of the wage gap between men and women in the seven major countries shows the gap between men's wages and women's wages; the larger the percentage is, the wider the gap. Japan's wage gap between men and women is 22.5 percent, whereas the average for OECD member countries is 11.6 percent. This means that the wage gap between men and women in Japan is considerably higher than that of the other seven countries.

The causes of the wage gap include the persistence of customs and traditions regarding the division of roles between men and women in society, the lack of adequate systems and services for childcare and nursing care, and the lack of a system to properly evaluate female employees. However, it should be noted that women's low motivation in regard to promotion, their reluctance to take on responsibility and their low awareness of issues regarding gender equality are also causes of disparities.

Like discrimination, prejudice and inequality, the wage gap between men and women is difficult to reduce without fundamentally changing social norms, and for this reason, it is important to eliminate stereotypes held by individuals. Since people tend to form various stereotypes in their early childhood, if we can steadily correct the course from that stage, social norms will gradually change, and the gender wage gap may be eliminated.

Answer　　① Italy　② United Kingdom　③ Canada　④ Japan

UNHCRとは？

　UNHCRは正式名称を the Office of the United Nations High Commissioner for Refugees、日本語では国連難民高等弁務官事務所と言い、文字通り難民問題に関する国連機関です。難民や国内避難民、無国籍者の保護を行っています。

　難民とは、民族・人種・宗教・国籍・戦争・紛争・思想的弾圧・政治的迫害・経済的困窮・自然災害などさまざまな理由によって国境を越えて他国に逃れた人々のことをさします。国境を越えずに避難生活を行っている人々は国内避難民と呼ばれています。2021年時点での紛争や迫害によって移動を強いられたのは8,930万人で、難民2,710万人、国内避難民5,320万人、庇護希望者460万人、ベネズエラ国外避難民440万人という内訳になっています。南米のベネズエラは、情勢不安や社会経済の混乱、食糧不足などの理由から、多くの人々が近隣諸国へ避難を強いられている国です。2011年から内戦が続くシリアに次いで2番目に難民の多い国としてUNHCRが支援活動を積極的に行っています。

　難民になって国外へ逃れる人の出身国は、1位シリア、2位ベネスエラ、3位アフガニスタン、4位南スーダン、5位ミャンマーで、この5カ国が全体の3分の2以上、69パーセントを占めています。難民がいるということは受け入れる国もあるということですが、最大の受け入れ国はトルコで380万人を受け入れています（2位以降は順にコロンビア、ウガンダ、パキスタン、ドイツです）。しかし、受け入れ国もほとんどが開発途上国なので資源やインフラが十分でなく経済的にも余裕がないため、支援の負担が重くのしかかっているのが現状です。

　主に国・国際機関・NGOからの支援によって難民キャンプが作られ難民が受け入れられますが、難民の数が多すぎて常に資金や物資が不足していることが問題になっています。衛生的な水、栄養のある食事、適切な医療、衛生管理が行き届かず、命を落とすこともあるのです。また、難民の8割が女性と子どものため虐待や性暴力が発生したり、教育の欠如なども問題となっています。先進国は難

民キャンプへの資金援助を行っており、日本も2019年にはUNHCRに約133億8,000万円の資金援助を行い、アメリカ、EU、ドイツ、スウェーデンに次いで世界第5位の資金援助国として難民を支援しました。

The UNHCR, officially known as the Office of the United Nations High Commissioner for Refugees, is the United Nations agency responsible for refugee issues. It provides assistance and protection to refugees and internally displaced persons.

Refugees are people who have fled across national borders to other countries for various reasons, including ethnicity, race, religion, nationality, war, conflict, ideological oppression, political persecution, economic hardship and natural disasters. Those who are displaced without crossing borders are called internally displaced persons (IDPs). As of 2021, 89.3 million people were forced to move due to conflict and persecution, including 27.1 million refugees, 53.2 million internally displaced persons, 4.6 million asylum seekers and 4.4 million Venezuelans who are internally displaced. Venezuela is a South American country where many people have been forced to relocate due to the unstable situation, socioeconomic turmoil and food shortages, etc. The UNHCR has been actively engaged in assistance activities as Venezuela is the country with the second-largest number of refugees after Syria, where civil war has been ongoing since 2011.

The countries of origin of refugees are Syria (1st), Venezuela (2nd), Afghanistan (3rd), South Sudan (4th), and Myanmar (5th). These five countries account for more than two-thirds of the total, or 69 percent. The largest host country is Turkey, with 3.8 million refugees (followed by Colombia, Uganda, Pakistan and Germany). However, since most of the recipient countries are also developing nations, they do not have sufficient resources or infrastructure, and they are not economically well off, so the burden of assistance is heavy.

Refugee camps are created and refugees are accepted mainly with support from national governments, international organizations and NGOs, but the problem is that the number of refugees is so large that there is always a shortage of funds and supplies. Lack of sanitary water, nutritious food, proper medical care, and hygiene can cost lives. Abuse and sexual violence occur because 80 percent of the refugees are women and children, and lack of education is also a problem. Developed countries provide financial assistance to refugee camps, and Japan provided approximately 13.38 billion yen to the UNHCR in 2019, making it the world's fifth-largest donor to refugees after the United States, EU, Germany and Sweden.

Answer　① 難民

221

最低所得保障

「政府がすべての人に無条件に一定のお金を定期的に支給する」制度のこと
を英語で何と言いますか？

① Dream Money　　② Basic Income　　③ Special Dispensation

　基本と所得という言葉を組み合わせたベーシックインカムは「最低所得保障」
と訳されることもあります。生きていくために必要な最低限のお金を無条件にす
べての人に配るというシステムです。この考え方は16世紀にイギリスの思想家ト
マス・モアが書いた『ユートピア』という本に記されているようですが、その後
18世紀末にイギリスの哲学者トマス・ペインとトマス・スペンスの2人がベーシ
ックインカムの構想を提唱したと言われています。

　新型コロナウイルスの流行によって雇用不安定や景気悪化で生活困窮者が増え
た中、2020年に一律10万円が支給された特別定額給付金は記憶に新しいでしょ
う。1回のみの政策でしたが、このように誰もが同じ額を受け取れる制度はベー
シックインカムに通じるところがあります。日本で言うと、長引く不況を改善し
て景気を活性化することができること、本当に困っている人の手に確実にお金が
渡ること、生活水準が向上してワーキングプアがなくなるなどのメリットがある
ため、ベーシックインカム導入に前向きな推進派がいます。世界規模で考えた場
合にも、ベーシックインカムの導入によって貧困や経済格差が解消されるため、
試験的に導入や検討を考えている国があるようです。しかし、ベーシックインカ
ムを実現することで、増税が必要になること、労働意欲が低下する可能性や衰退
する企業が出てくること、社会福祉制度が廃止される可能性があることなどのデ
メリットやクリアすべき課題が多いため、導入実現はまだ難しいようです。

　"Basic income" is sometimes translated as *saitei shotoku hoshō* in Japanese
and is a system that unconditionally distributes the minimum amount of
money necessary to live to all people. This idea seems to be described in a
book titled *Utopia*, which was written by the English thinker Thomas More

in the 16th century, and later, at the end of the 18th century, two English philosophers, Thomas Paine and Thomas Spence, are said to have proposed the concept of a basic income.

As the number of people in need increased due to unstable employment and economic deterioration due to the coronavirus epidemic, a special fixed benefit, in which 100,000 yen was paid uniformly to citizens in 2020, will be fresh in our memory. It was a one-time policy, but this system in which everyone can receive the same amount is similar to basic income. In Japan, some people are proponents of a basic income system because it would help to stimulate the economy by ending the prolonged recession, ensure that money gets into the hands of those who are truly in need and eliminate the working poor by improving the standard of living. Looking at basic income on a global scale, its introduction would eliminate poverty and economic disparities, so it seems that some countries are considering introducing it or thinking about using it on a trial basis. However, it still seems difficult to realize the introduction of basic income because there are many disadvantages and issues to be overcome, such as the need to raise taxes, a potential decrease in work ethic, the risk of some companies being harmed by it, and the possibility of the abolition of social welfare systems.

Answer ② Basic Income

物が顧客に届くまで

下の図はチョコレートが消費者に届くまでに関わる活動のそれぞれの占める割合を表したものです。日本語を参考に、空欄に当てはまる言葉を下の語群から選んでください。

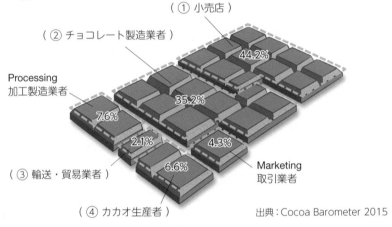

(① 小売店)

(② チョコレート製造業者)

Processing
加工製造業者

7.6%

2.1%

35.2%

44.2%

4.3%

6.6%

Marketing
取引業者

(③ 輸送・貿易業者)

(④ カカオ生産者)

出典：Cocoa Barometer 2015

・Cocoa Farmers 　・Transportation & Traders

・Retailer 　・Chocolate Manufacturer

　物は、さまざまな人の手を経て商品となり顧客の元に届きます。図のように、チョコレートはカカオ豆を栽培する農業従事者から始まり、カカオ豆の加工業者、加工されたものをチョコレートにする製造業者があり、取引業者を経て小売店から商品を購入します。

　カカオ豆の生産地は主にアフリカや南米など開発途上国が多く、カカオ生産者が受け取る利益はチョコレートの価格のわずか6.6パーセントしかありません（2015年のデータ）。これは材料を購入するのが先進国の企業のため、立場の弱い途上国の生産者が不利な取引をさせられてしまうためです。過酷な労働を強いられるうえに低価格で取引されるのでは当然貧困は解消しません。この不公平な貿易の構造を改善する取り組みがフェアトレードです。公正な貿易という意味で、

世界フェアトレード連盟（WFTO）やフェアトレード団体がフェアトレードの基準・原則を設けて開発途上国の生産者への不利な取引をなくすとともに生産者の生活改善と自立を促進しています。また、生産段階で強制労働や児童労働が行われていないか、差別が行われていないか、環境に配慮されて作られているかなど、さまざまな側面から公平な貿易が行われるように働きかけています。

Things become products and reach customers through the hands of various people. As shown in the figure, chocolate begins with farmers who grow cacao beans. Then there are processors of cacao beans and manufacturers who turn the processed products into chocolate. Finally, the products are purchased by retailers via brokers.

Cacao beans are mainly produced in developing countries, mostly in Africa and South America, where cacao producers receive only 6.6 percent of the price of chocolate (data from 2015). This is because companies from developed countries purchase the ingredients, which puts producers in developing countries, who are in a weaker position, at a disadvantage. Poverty will not be eliminated if producers are forced to do hard labor and chocolate is traded at low prices. Fair trade is an effort to improve this unfair trade structure. In terms of fair trade, the World Fair Trade Organization (WFTO) and other groups have established fair trade standards and principles to eliminate unfair trade practices that disadvantage producers in developing countries and to promote the improvement of producers' lives and independence. They also work to ensure fair trade in various aspects, such as the absence of forced labor, child labor, discrimination and environmental considerations in the production process.

Answer
① Retailer
② Chocolate Manufacturer
③ Transportation & Traders
④ Cocoa Farmers

平等と公平

下のイラストは「平等」（equality）と「公平」（equity）の考えを、異なる
3人の状況で表したものです。それぞれのイラストが equality と equity の
どちらに当てはまると思いますか。

①　　　　　　　　　　　②

　不平等をなくすためには「平等」であるべきだと考えられますが、実は「公平」
でなくてはなりません。上のイラストはその違いをよく表したものです。背の高
い大人、子ども、車椅子の人がサッカーの試合を観戦していますが、目の前には
高い壁があります。左のイラストは、3人の置かれた状況を考慮せず平等に同じ
高さの箱を与えています。箱のおかげで背の高い大人と真ん中の子どもは試合を
見ることができますが、車椅子の人は箱に乗ることができないため試合を見るこ
とができません。右のイラストは3人それぞれの状況に合わせて箱の数を調整し
たり、車椅子でも登れるようにスロープ状にしたりして全員が公平に試合を見る
ことができています。
　この公平が不平等をなくすカギとなっています。すべての人に同じ条件や機会
を提供したとしても、それぞれのバックグラウンド（年齢、性別、民族、宗教、

障がいの有無、性自認、性的指向、教育、国籍など）が異なるため不平等は解決されず、むしろ社会的分断や差別、格差を助長してしまう恐れがあります。バックグラウンドの多様性を尊重し、認め合い、共に１つの大きな社会の中に参加できるようにすることが本当の意味での「不平等をなくす」ということになります。

One would think that in order to eliminate inequality, one must be "equal," but in fact one must be "fair." The illustration above is a good example of the difference. A tall adult, a child, and a person in a wheelchair are watching a soccer game, but there is a high wall in front of them. In the illustration on the left, the three people are treated equally and given a box of the same height without considering their situation. Thanks to the boxes, the tall adult and the child in the middle can watch the game, but the person in the wheelchair cannot watch the game because she cannot get on the box. The illustration on the right shows how the number of boxes can be adjusted to suit the situation of each of the three people, and how the boxes can be made into a ramp so that wheelchairs can climb them so that everyone can watch the game fairly. This fairness is the key to eliminating inequality. Providing the same conditions and opportunities to all people will not solve inequality because of their different backgrounds (age, gender, ethnicity, religion, disability, gender identity, sexual orientation, education, nationality, etc.). It may instead foster social divisions, discrimination, and disparities. The real meaning of "diversity" is to respect and recognize diversity of backgrounds and to enable people to participate in society together. In the true sense of the word, "eliminating inequality" means respecting and acknowledging the diversity of people's backgrounds and enabling them to participate together in the society.

Answer   ① equality ② equity

「人や国の不平等をなくそう」
──そのためにあなたは何ができると思いますか？
What can you do to "reduce inequalities"?

　人種の違いによる差別をなくすために、1965年に多国間で「あらゆる形態の人種差別の撤廃に関する国際条約」（ICERD）が締結され、日本も1995年に加入しました。公平や女性の権利を目的に女性差別撤廃を定めた「女性差別撤廃条約」（CEDAW、1981年）もあり、多くの国で差別撤廃に向けて努力が進められています。日本では2016年に、障がいの有無にかかわらず互いに認め合って共に生きる社会を作ることを目的とする「障害者差別解消法」や、差別的言動の解消に向けた「ヘイトスピーチ解消法」が施行されました。しかし、いくら条約が結ばれても、そう簡単には差別や偏見、不平等の解消にはつながりません。

　「あの人、黒人なのにバスケがヘタだね」「男の子なのに料理が上手だね」「マスクしてない人には近づかないほうがいいよ」──このように、その人のバックグラウンドを考えず、科学的根拠もないままつい主観的に言ってしまったり思ったりした経験はないでしょうか。何気なく言ったひと言が相手への差別・偏見となってしまうことがあります。自分の価値観や思い込みで人を判断したり、無意識による偏見や考え方をしてしまわないために、いろいろな角度から知識や情報を得て自分以外の視点を増やすことです。さまざまな人と会って話をすることも、多様な考え方・価値観を知り、自分の考えの幅を広げるためにも重要です。1回では改善されませんが、地道に意識して取り組めば、着実に変化をもたらすことができるはずです。

In 1965, the multilateral International Convention on the Elimination of All Forms of Racial Discrimination (ICERD) was concluded to eliminate discrimination based on racial differences. Japan joined in 1995. There is also the 1981 Convention on the Elimination of All Forms of Discrimination against Women (CEDAW), which stipulates the elimination of discrimination against women for the purpose of fairness and women's rights, and many countries are making efforts toward the elimination of these problems. In Japan, the "Law for the Elimination of Discrimination against Persons with Disabilities," which aims to create a society where people can accept each other and live together regardless of whether they have disabilities, and the "Law for the Elimination of Hate Speech" were enacted in 2016 to eliminate discriminatory words and actions. However, no matter how many treaties are concluded, they will not easily lead to the elimination of discrimination, prejudice and inequality.

"He's Black, but he's a terrible basketball player," "He's a boy, but he's a good cook," "You should stay away from people who don't wear masks."— Have you ever said or thought such things subjectively without considering the person's background and without evidence? A casual remark may turn out to be discriminatory or prejudicial toward the other person. To avoid judging people based on your own values and assumptions, and to avoid unconscious prejudice and thinking, it is important to gain knowledge and information from various angles and increase your own perspectives. It is also important to meet and talk with a variety of people to learn about diverse ideas and values and to broaden your own thinking.

Goal 11
住み続けられるまちづくりを
Sustainable Cities and Communities

包摂的で安全かつ強靭（レジリエント）で持続可能な
都市と人間居住を実現する。

*Make cities and human settlements inclusive, safe,
resilient and sustainable.*

　世界では、人口の半分以上の55パーセントが都市部に暮らし
ています。日本においても人口の51.8パーセントが東京圏、大
阪圏、名古屋圏の3大都市圏に集中しています。都市は経済・
文化の中心で、たくさんの会社や商業施設、公共施設があり、
生活基盤が整って住みやすい場所です。しかし、快適に暮らす
ことでさまざまな問題——排気ガス問題、水の汚染、大量のゴミ
問題、途上国のスラム街問題——があります。また、都市の人口
が増加することで、人口が減って過疎化した地域は経済・社会
活動が停滞し、ますます住みにくくなってしまいます。都市部
とその周りの地域が経済的・社会的・環境的にうまくつながり
合えるような関係を築くにはどうしたらいいのでしょうか。

参照：World Urbanization Prospects 2018
総務省（2020年）

都市部の人口動態

現在、世界の人口の半分以上が都市部に暮らしていますが、2050年には世界人口の何パーセントが都市部に住むようになると思いますか？

① 68パーセント　　② 78パーセント　　③ 88パーセント

　世界都市人口予想の2018年の調査によると、世界の人口の55パーセントが都市部に暮らしています。1950年には30パーセントに過ぎなかった都市部の人口は、2050年には倍以上の68パーセントに達すると予測されています。人口が集中すると、行政や企業も集中するため、サービスや商取引が容易になったり、労働市場が多様化したりします。また、都市のブランド力が向上することで、世界から注目されるようにもなるでしょう。

　しかし、メリットがあればデメリットも存在します。都市部以外の地域での過疎化が深刻化し、政治・経済・行政・情報通信などの中枢機関が1カ所に集中する中で大規模災害が起こった場合には、国全体の機能が麻痺してしまうかもしれません。快適な都市での暮らしを維持していくためには、災害に備えた、安全で回復力のある町づくりが必要です。

　According to a 2018 study by World Urbanization Prospects, 55 percent of the world's population lives in urban areas. The urban population, which was only 30 percent of the total in 1950, is expected to more than double to 68 percent by 2050. Concentration of population also concentrates government and business, facilitating services and commerce and diversifying the labor market. It will also improve the "brand power" of the city, making it more attractive to the rest of the world.

　However, if there are merits, there are also demerits. Depopulation in non-urban areas is becoming more serious, and if a large-scale disaster were to occur while the core institutions of politics, economy, administration, and information and communication are concentrated in one place, the entire country could be paralyzed. In order to maintain a comfortable city life, it is necessary to create a safe and resilient city that is prepared for disasters.

Answer ▶ ① 68パーセント

農村と過疎化に関する用語

次の単語とその意味を線で結んでください。

① rural area   ・   ・ 過疎化

② urban area   ・   ・ 貧民街、スラム街

③ depopulation   ・   ・ 農村部

④ settlements   ・   ・ 都市部

⑤ slum   ・   ・ 居住地域

　農村部は、人口減少と高齢化が問題になっています。農業は気候に左右されやすい不安定な産業であり、農作物の価格が高くないこともあって、より安定した高収入を得られる仕事を求めて農村部から都市部へ人が流れています。

　そうして都市部では人口が増加し、過密化が起こると、大気汚染の問題が深刻化します。車の需要が増えるため、それに比例して排ガスの量が増えますし、産業が活発になれば工場なども増えるため、有害物質を含む煙が大量に排出されて大気が汚染されます。

　過疎化の主な原因は、若者が都市部へ移住することです。そのため、過疎地に住む人の多くは高齢者です。一極集中によって地方が過疎化すると、交通機関の整備も不十分になるため、高齢者は買い物や病院通いなどを含む日常生活を営むうえで、不便な状況に陥ってしまいます。

　貧民街、スラム街は、都市部にある貧しい人々が住む地区のことです。仕事を求めて都市部に来ても、十分な賃金を得られる仕事に就けず貧困に陥ってしまう人がいます。こうした人々が、スラム街のような衛生や安全が十分確保されていない非公式居住区に住まざるを得なくなってしまうのです。

　Rural areas are facing declining and aging populations. Agriculture is an unstable industry that is easily affected by climate, and people are flowing from rural areas to urban areas in search of more-stable, higher-income jobs, partly because crop prices are not high.

Thus, as the population increases in urban areas and overcrowding occurs, the problem of air pollution becomes more serious. As the demand for cars increases, the amount of exhaust gas emissions rises proportionately. As industry becomes more active, the number of factories and other facilities also increases, and these emit large amounts of smoke containing toxic substances and pollute the air.

The main cause of depopulation is the migration of young people to urban areas. As a result, most people living in depopulated areas are elderly. When rural areas become depopulated due to the concentration of people in one area, transportation systems become inadequate, making it inconvenient for the elderly to live their daily lives, including shopping and going to the hospital.

Poor neighborhoods and slums are areas in urban areas where poor people live. Some people come to urban areas in search of work but end up in poverty because they cannot find a job that pays enough. However, they are forced to live in informal settlements that lack adequate sanitation and safety.

Point

　④は複数形にすることで「居住地域」という意味になります。単数形の settlement には、「落ち着くこと、安定すること」や「解決、合意」という意味があります。また、動詞の settle は「（一定の場所に）定住する、住み着く、落ち着く」「解決する、まとまる」「沈殿する」などの意味を表します。

Answer

① rural area ＝ 農村部

② urban area ＝ 都市部

③ depopulation ＝ 過疎化

④ settlements ＝ 居住地域

⑤ slum ＝ 貧民街、スラム街

世界のスラム街事情

開発途上国を中心にスラム街が増加しています。世界のスラム人口はおよそどのくらいだと思いますか？

① 10万人
② 100万人
③ 10億人

　2018年の国連の調査によると、世界のスラム人口は推定10億人以上で、その80パーセントが東アジア・東南アジア（約3億7,000万人）、サハラ以南のアフリカ（約2億3,800万人）、中央アジア・南アジア（約2億2,700万人）の3つの地域に集中しています。人口増加や都市化が、手頃な価格の住宅を建てるスピードをはるかにしのぐ勢いで進んだ場所で、スラム居住者の数も一気に増加しました。都市の中に川や道を隔てて、裕福な人々が住む地域と貧しいスラム居住地が並存する場所があったり、富裕層が使うゴルフコースに隣接してトタン屋根の住居が建ち並んでいたりと、住民の貧富の差が一目でわかります。スラム街が拡大すれば、治安の悪化や衛生環境の低下、教育や医療サービスの不足など、さまざまな問題が起こることが懸念されています。

　世界のスラム居住者の数は、2030年までに30億人以上になると推計されています。多様性を受け入れてすべての人が安全かつ公平に人間らしい暮らしを送るためには、手頃な価格の住宅や基本的なサービスの提供、貧困層の雇用促進などを行う必要があるでしょう。

　According to a 2018 United Nations study, the global slum population is estimated at more than 1 billion, with 80 percent concentrated in three regions: East and Southeast Asia (about 370 million), Sub-Saharan Africa (about 238 million) and Central and South Asia (about 227 million). The number of slum dwellers has grown quickly in these places, where population growth and urbanization have far outpaced the rate at which affordable housing is being built. In some places in cities, the wealthy and the poor live side by side, separated by rivers and roads, and tin-roofed houses stand next to golf courses used by the wealthy. The difference between the rich and the poor can be seen at a glance. If slums expand, there is concern that they will cause a variety of problems, including worsening public safety, poor sanitation and a lack of education and medical services.

It is estimated that the number of slum dwellers worldwide will reach more than 3 billion by 2030. In order to embrace diversity and ensure that all people lead safe and equitable lives, it will be necessary to provide affordable housing and basic services, and to promote employment for the poor.

Answer ③ 10 億人

大気汚染の原因

大気汚染の原因の一つと言われる超微小粒子は何と言いますか？

① PL2.5
② PM2.5
③ PN2.5

　都市の大気汚染の原因は、主に自動車の排ガスや、大量のごみの焼却などに伴って排出される煙です。煙に含まれる化学物質は光化学スモッグやPM2.5、酸性雨などを引き起こします。近年特に問題になっているのはPM2.5という化学物質です。PMは微粒子物質の略で、PM2.5は直径がおよそ2.5マイクロメートル（1マイクロメートル＝1ミリメートルの1,000分の1）以下の超微小粒子のことです。髪の毛の太さの30分の1程度しかないため、肺の奥深くにまで入り込み、喘息や気管支炎を引き起こしたり、肺がんなどのリスクを高めたりする恐れがあります。

　北京などの中国の大都市ではPM2.5による大気汚染が深刻化しており、薄茶色の濃霧が立ち込めて視界が悪化し、高速道路などが封鎖されることもあります。PM2.5の影響で、世界では年間約300万人が死亡しており、日本にも同様の死亡者が年間で約1万7,000人いると言われています。自動車や工場の数が増える一方であるのに対して、化石燃料に代わるエネルギーを使うなどの取り組みは進められていますが、早期解決には厳しい状況です。

Urban air pollution is mainly caused by smoke emitted from vehicle exhaust and from the incineration of large amounts of waste. Chemicals in the smoke cause photochemical smog, PM2.5, acid rain, etc. One chemical that has become a particular problem in recent years is PM2.5. PM stands for particulate matter, and PM2.5 is an ultrafine particle with a diameter of approximately 2.5 micrometers (1 micrometer = 1/1,000 of a millimeter) or less. Because it is only 1/30th the thickness of a hair, it can penetrate deep into the lungs, causing asthma and bronchitis and increasing the risk of lung cancer and other diseases.

Air pollution caused by PM2.5 is becoming more serious in Beijing and other large Chinese cities, causing a thick, light-brown fog that worsens visibility and sometimes blocks highways and other roads. PM2.5 causes about 3 million deaths a year worldwide, and it is estimated that there are about 17,000 similar deaths in Japan each year. While the number of automobiles and factories is increasing, efforts are being made to use alternative energy sources instead of fossil fuels, but the situation is tough to solve quickly.

Answer　② PM2.5

世界遺産

世界遺産（World Heritage sites）を説明した文があります。日本語を参考にしながら、空欄に当てはまる単語を下から選んで文を完成させてください。

World Heritage sites are (　①　) landmarks or areas that have been put on the lists by (　②　). They are (　③　) and preserved as cultural and natural (　④　) sites around the world that are considered to be of high value to (　⑤　).

世界遺産とは、ユネスコのリストに登録される歴史的建造物や地区のことです。人類にとって高い価値をもつと見なされる、世界中の文化および自然遺産として、保護・保存されています。

・protected 　　・UNESCO 　　・heritage

・historic 　　・humanity

　Goal 11には「世界の文化遺産や自然遺産を保護・維持していく努力を強化する」というターゲットも含まれています。世界遺産には主に文化遺産と自然遺産、文化・自然両方を併せもつ複合遺産の3つがあります。日本で言えば、法隆寺地域の仏教建築物（1993年登録）や原爆ドーム（1996年登録）などは文化遺産で、屋久島（1993年登録）や小笠原諸島（2011年登録）などは自然遺産です。ちなみに富士山は信仰の対象と芸術の源泉として文化遺産と見なされています。

　世界には1,154の世界遺産があり、内訳は文化遺産が897、自然遺産が218、複合遺産が39です。そのうちの52が危機遺産とされています。危機に陥っている主な原因は、地球温暖化による自然災害、武力紛争、都市開発、観光開発、大規模工事、商業的密猟などで、世界遺産としての保護・保存が危ぶまれています。世界遺産委員会によって危機遺産と認定された場所は、危機遺産リストに登録され、脅威が去ればリストから外されますが、世界遺産としての価値が失われたと判断される場合には世界遺産リスト自体から削除されてしまいます。

例えば、アメリカのエバーグレーズ国立公園は水生生物の生態の悪化が原因で危機遺産に登録されています。シリアにある６つの文化遺産は内戦により遺跡の状態が悪化しました。オーストリアの文化遺産であるウイーン歴史地区は、都市開発で景観が損なわれたため危機遺産になりました。

生活に快適さを求めて住みやすいまちづくりをすることで、世界遺産のみならず私たちの周りにある後世に残る貴重なものをも危機的状況に陥っている可能性があることを理解し、脅威や危険から守っていくことが重要です。

Goal 11 also includes the target to "strengthen efforts to protect and maintain the world's cultural and natural heritage." There are three main types of World Heritage: cultural heritage, natural heritage, and composite heritage, which is both cultural and natural. In Japan, Buddhist architecture in the Horyu-ji Temple area (registered in 1993) and the Atomic Bomb Dome (registered in 1996) are cultural heritage sites, while Yakushima Island (registered in 1993) and the Ogasawara Islands (registered in 2011) are natural heritage sites. Incidentally, Mt. Fuji is considered a cultural heritage as an object of faith and a source of art.

There are 1,154 World Heritage sites in the world, of which 897 are cultural, 218 are natural and 39 are combined. Fifty-two of these are considered to be in crisis. The main causes of the crisis are natural disasters due to global warming, armed conflicts, urban development, tourism development, large-scale construction, commercial poaching, etc., all of which threaten their protection and preservation as World Heritage sites. Sites identified as critically endangered by the World Heritage Committee are placed on the List of World Heritage in Danger and are removed from the list once the threat has passed, or removed from the World Heritage List itself if their value as a World Heritage site is deemed to have been lost.

For example, Everglades National Park in the United States is listed as a Critically Endangered Heritage Site due to the deterioration of its aquatic ecology. Six cultural heritage sites in Syria have deteriorated due to civil war, which has worsened the condition of the sites. The Historic Centre of Vienna, a cultural heritage site in Austria, became a Crisis Site because urban development has damaged the landscape.

It is important to understand that by making our cities more comfortable to live in, we may be endangering not only World Heritage sites but also the precious things around us that will be preserved for future generations, and it is important to protect them from threats and dangers.

Answer   ① historic   ② UNESCO   ③ protected   ④ heritage   ⑤ humanity

防災グッズ

災害時には、インフラが機能しなくなることが考えられるため、自分で自分の身を守れるよう備えておく必要があります。下の図の中から災害時を想定して備えておくべきものを選んでください。

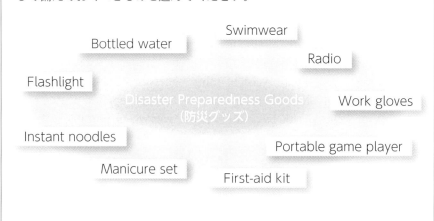

Swimwear

Bottled water

Radio

Flashlight

Disaster Preparedness Goods
（防災グッズ）

Work gloves

Instant noodles

Portable game player

Manicure set

First-aid kit

　災害時に壊滅的な被害を受けた場合、インフラが機能しなくなることがあるでしょう。それを避けるために、災害に強く復旧しやすいインフラ整備が求められていますが、一方で、一人ひとりが最低限の備えをして自分自身を守ることも重要です。

　最も重要な備蓄品は水と食料です。ペットボトルの水やインスタント麺、缶詰食品、レトルト食品などは非常食として必需品です。湯を沸かしたり、食品を温めたりしたいときにはカセットコンロとガスボンベがあると便利です。また、安全面から、ろうそくよりも懐中電灯やランタンを用意したほうがいいでしょう。さらに、災害時の情報収集にラジオは欠かせません。手回し充電ラジオなら電池がなくても使えます。

　その他、現金や健康保険証などの貴重品、衣類、救急用具、軍手、多機能ナイフ、ビニール袋、トイレットペーパー、ウェットティッシュ、携帯トイレや衛生用品など、必要なものはリストアップして用意しておくといいでしょう。

図の中の水着やマニキュア、ポケットゲーム機は災害時の必需品ではありません。

In the event of a catastrophic disaster, infrastructure may cease to function. To avoid this, it is necessary to develop infrastructure that is resistant to disasters and easy to restore, but at the same time, it is also important for each individual to protect themself with a minimum level of preparedness.

The most important stockpiles are water and food. Bottled water, instant noodles, canned food, and retort foods are essential emergency rations. A portable stove and gas cylinder are useful for boiling water and heating food. Also, for safety reasons, it is better to prepare flashlights or lanterns rather than candles. Furthermore, a radio is indispensable for gathering information during a disaster. A hand-cranked radio can be used even without batteries.

You should also prepare a list of other necessities, such as cash, health insurance cards and other valuables, clothing, first aid supplies, work gloves, a multi-function knife, plastic bags, toilet paper, wet wipes, portable toilets and hygiene items.

Swimwear, a manicure set, and portable game consoles in the diagram above are not disaster essentials.

Answer ▶ Bottled water ／ Radio ／ Work gloves ／
First-aid kit ／ Instant noodles ／ Flashlight

242

シンボルマークを覚えよう

下のシンボルは日本でよく見かける障がい者に関するシンボルマークです。
各シンボルとその意味を線で結んでください。

① ・　　　　　・ 耳マーク

② ・　　　　　・ 障がい者のための国際シンボルマーク

③ ・　　　　　・ オストメイトマーク

④ ・　　　　　・ 盲人のための国際シンボルマーク

⑤ ・　　　　　・ ヘルプマーク

　安心して暮らせる町づくりをするには、健常者だけでなく障がい者にとっても利用しやすい環境を整えなければなりません。障がい者は社会の中で、(1)移動面で困難をもたらす物理的バリア、(2)社会のルールで機会の均等が奪われる制度的バリア、(3)必要な情報が得られない文化・情報面のバリア、(4)周囲からの無関心、差別、偏見による意識上のバリア、の4つに直面しています。これらのバリアをなくすために、公共交通機関や公共施設などに、障がい者が利用できることを示すためのシンボルマークをつけて周知します。

　①のマークはオストメイト（人工肛門や人工膀胱を造設している人）のための設備があることを示します。

　②と⑤はともに世界共通のシンボルマークです。②は車椅子の利用者だけを表していると思われがちですが、実はすべての障がい者のためのマークです。⑤の杖をついている人のマークは、視覚障がい者に配慮した施設や機器に付けられて

います。信号や音声案内装置、国際点字郵便物などに使われています。

　③のヘルプマークは人工関節を持つ人や難病を抱える人など、外見からは障がい者だとわからない人が周囲に理解してもらうためのマークです。かばんなどにつけることで周囲に配慮を必要としていることを伝えやすくする目的をもっています。

　④は聴覚障がい者が耳の不自由さを示すとともに、聴覚障がい者への配慮を表すときに使用されます。主に病院や行政機関、図書館、駅などで使用されています。

In order to create a community where people can live with peace of mind, we must create an environment that is accessible not only to able-bodied people but also to people with disabilities. People with disabilities face four barriers in society: (1) physical barriers that cause difficulties in terms of mobility; (2) institutional barriers that deprive them of equal opportunities due to social rules; (3) cultural and informational barriers that prevent them from obtaining necessary information; and (4) awareness barriers caused by indifference, discrimination and prejudice in their surroundings. In order to eliminate these barriers, public transportation and public facilities are marked with symbols to indicate that they are accessible to people with disabilities.

The symbol ① indicates that facilities are available for ostomates (people with a colostomy or artificial bladder).

Both ② and ⑤ are universal symbols. While ② is often thought to represent only wheelchair users, it actually represents all people with disabilities. The symbol of a person with a cane ⑤ is attached to facilities and equipment that are designed for the visually impaired. It is used on traffic signals, voice guidance devices, international Braille mail, etc.

The Help Mark ③ is for people with artificial joints, people with intractable diseases and others who are not recognizable from the outside as disabled so that they can be identified by those around them. The purpose of this symbol is to make it easier to let people around you know that you are in need of consideration by attaching it to your bag or other items.

④ is used to indicate a hearing impairment as well as to show consideration for the hearing impaired. It is mainly used in hospitals, government agencies, libraries, train stations, etc.

Answer　① オストメイトマーク　② 障がい者のための国際シンボルマーク
③ ヘルプマーク　④ 耳マーク　⑤ 盲人のための国際シンボルマーク

環境設定のためのマーク

年齢や性別、障がいの有無などにかかわらず、誰もがわかりやすく使いやすいデザインのことを英語で何と言いますか？

① barrier free
② universal design
③ pictogram
④ good design

　ユニバーサルデザインはそれぞれの単語の頭文字をとってUDと呼ばれることもあります。①は階段の隣に設けられた緩やかなスロープやノンステップバスのように、障壁をなくすことで、誰もが過ごしやすい環境を整えることを表しており、UDの目的の一つです。③のピクトグラムは、非常口のサインやエレベーターのマークなど、誰もが一目でその意味がわかる絵文字のことで、UDの一つです。

　その他、シャンプーの容器の突起、センサー式蛇口、歩道に設置された黄色い点字ブロック、自動ドア、音声機能付きの歩行者用信号機など、私たちの身近にUDを適用して作られたものがあります。UDはアメリカのロナルド・メイス博士によって1980年代に提唱された考えで、次ページの7つの原則をできるだけ取り入れながらデザインすることが求められています。

　高齢者や子ども、妊婦、ベビーカーを使っている人、障がい者など、さまざまな事情を抱えて暮らす人々がいます。災害に備えた施設や環境の整備だけでなく、日常的に誰もが安全に安心して暮らせる町づくりも重要です。だからこそ、UDはより多くの人の不便を便利にするために必要なものなのです。

　Universal design is sometimes referred to using the acronym UD. ① represents the creation of a comfortable environment for everyone by eliminating barriers, such as adding a gentle slope next to stairs or making a low-floor bus, and is one of the purposes of UD. Pictograms in ③ are things like emergency exit signs and elevator symbols, whose meaning everyone can recognize at a glance, and are one of the objectives of UD.

Other items made by applying UD are all around us, such as protrusions on shampoo containers, sensor faucets, yellow Braille blocks on sidewalks, automatic doors and pedestrian signals with voice functions. UD is an idea proposed in the 1980s by Dr. Ronald Mace of the United States, which calls for design that incorporates as many of the seven principles as possible.

There are people living in various circumstances, such as the elderly, children, pregnant women, people using baby strollers and people with disabilities. It is important not only to improve facilities and environments in preparation for disasters, but also to create communities where everyone can live safely and securely on a daily basis. That is why UD is necessary to make inconvenient things more convenient for more people.

	The 7 Principles of UD	UD の 7 原則
Principle 1	Equitable use	誰でも公平に利用できること
Principle 2	Flexibility in use	使う上で自由度が高いこと
Principle 3	Simple and intuitive use	使い方が簡単で直感的にわかること
Principle 4	Perceptible information	欲しい情報がすぐにわかること
Principle 5	Tolerance for error	ミスや危険がなく安全なこと
Principle 6	Low physical effort	身体へ負担をかけずに楽に使用できること
Principle 7	Size and space for approach and use	アクセスしやすく使いやすい広さや大きさ

Answer　② universal design

人口の集中問題

下の英文は、日本において、都市部に人口が集中することによって地方で生じる問題を説明するものです。この英語が意味する事柄を選択肢から選んでください。

Rural communities where more than half of the population is over 65 years of age

① 限界集落
② 幽霊都市
③ 地方自治体

　総務省の発表によると、2020年4月の時点で限界集落は全国で2万372カ所に上りました。限界集落の特徴は、元々の人口が50人未満であったことに加え、繁華街や役場から10キロメートル以上離れた山間部にあることです。生活に不便なため、出ていく人のほうが多く、人口が増えなくなっています。空き家が増加し、建物が老朽化して災害時に倒壊しやすくなったり、周辺での治安が悪化したり、ごみの不法投棄などで不衛生になったり、景観が損なわれたりします。また、独居老人が増え、認知症をわずらう人や、孤独死を迎える人が増えるなどの問題も出てきます。

　このような問題の解決策として、「空き家バンク」というサービスを行っている自治体や民間企業があります。移住目的で不動産物件を探している人や、観光目的で短期・長期滞在先を探している人に向けたマッチング事業です。空き家を利用する人が増えれば、店やサービスも増えて産業が活発になり、集落の活性化につながるでしょう。

　According to the Ministry of Internal Affairs and Communications, as of April 2020, there were 20,372 marginal villages nationwide. Marginal villages are characterized by things like an original population of fewer than

50 people, and being located in mountainous areas more than 10 kilometers away from downtown areas and town halls. Due to the inconvenience of living in the areas, more people are leaving and the population is no longer growing. The number of vacant houses increases, buildings become dilapidated and more likely to collapse in the event of a disaster, public safety deteriorates in the neighborhood and illegal dumping of garbage leads to unsanitary conditions and spoils the landscape. In addition, the number of elderly people living alone increases and the number of people suffering from dementia and those who die alone also rises.

As a solution to this problem, some municipalities and private companies offer a service called a "vacant house bank." This is a matching project for those who are looking for real estate properties for relocation and for those who are looking for a place to stay short or long term for tourism purposes. The more people who use vacant houses, the more stores and services will be available, and the more active the industry will be, leading to the revitalization of the village.

Point

　問いの英文は「65歳以上の人口が半分以上を占める地方のコミュニティー」という意味で、①の限界集落（marginal village）のことです。marginal は「（生活の程度が）最低限の、ギリギリの、限界の」、village は「村、村落」という意味です。aging and depopulated village などと言い換えることも可能です。

　②の幽霊都市は別名ゴーストタウン（ghost town）で、都市や集落が廃墟化して建物などの痕跡だけが残っている場所のことです。

　③の地方自治体（local government）は県や市町村などの行政単位のことで、その地域に住んでいる人の生活をサポートするためにさまざまな行政サービスを提供する役割があります。

Answer　① 限界集落

持続可能な町づくり

「生活のあらゆる機能を身近なところに集めた、効率的で持続可能な町づくり」のことを何と言いますか？

① Smart city
② Woven city
③ Compact city

　地方都市では郊外に大型店舗やショッピングセンターが作られ、中心市街地が衰退していくことが問題となっています。多くの人が自動車を所有して郊外に住みますが、高齢化が進み、自動車を使わない人は不便な生活を強いられることになります。

　③のコンパクトシティは、自動車を使わないで移動できるコンパクトな範囲に、住宅や公共・福祉・商業施設など生活に必要な機能を集約した都市を造り、超高齢化社会や自動車依存社会を改善する試みです。都市部のような利便性の向上やインフラ整備の負担の軽減、環境保護など、持続可能な社会づくりが実現できると期待されています。

　①のスマートシティはAIやビッグデータなどICT技術を活用して都市や地域の機能を最適化し、環境に配慮しながら生活する人の利便性や快適性の向上を目指す町づくりのことです。

　② ウーブンシティは、トヨタ自動車が静岡県裾野市に東京ドーム15個分の広大な敷地に開発した実験都市の名称です。スマートシティの一つで、自動運転車やロボット、AI、スマートホーム（スマホアプリや音声であらゆる住宅設備の操作が可能な住宅）などの最先端技術を人々の生活環境に導入した都市です。

　The problem in cities in outlying areas is that large stores and shopping centers are being built in the suburbs, causing the central areas to decline. Many people own automobiles and live in the suburbs, but as the population ages, those who do not use cars are forced to live in ways that are inconvenient.

③ A compact city is an attempt to improve a super-aging society and automobile-dependent society by building a city that concentrates the functions necessary for daily life, such as housing, public and welfare services, and commercial facilities, within a compact area that can be traveled without the use of a car. It is expected that it will be possible to create a sustainable society by improving the convenience of urban areas, reducing the burden of infrastructure development and protecting the environment.

① A smart city is a town development that aims to optimize urban and regional functions using ICT technologies, such as AI and big data, to improve convenience and comfort for people living in the city while taking the environment into consideration.

② Woven City is the name of an experimental city developed by Toyota Motor Corporation in Susono, Shizuoka Prefecture, on a vast site the size of 15 Tokyo Domes. It is a smart city where cutting-edge technologies, such as self-driving cars, robots, AI and smart homes (homes where all housing facilities can be operated by smartphone apps or voice) are introduced into people's living environment.

Answer ③ Compact city

「住み続けられる町づくりを」
──そのためにあなたは何ができると思いますか？

What can you do to promote the creation of "sustainable cities and communities"?

　自分が住んでいる町を、長く住み続けられる快適な町にするために何ができるでしょうか。まずは住んでいる町をよく知ることから始めましょう。自分の住んでいる町の自治体がどんな町づくりに取り組んでいるか、公共交通機関は安全で誰もが使いやすいか、災害時の避難場所や防災設備が整っているかなど、知っておきたいことはたくさんあります。その中で、自分が参加できる地域の取り組みがあれば実際に参加し、問題を解決したり地域を盛り上げたりしながら、自分からより良い町づくりに関われば達成感を得られるでしょう。

　防災については、一人ひとりが家庭で備蓄品をそろえたり、家族と避難場所を確認したりすることで、大規模災害が起きても迅速に対処できるよう準備を進めましょう。また、日頃から地域の人と関わることで、災害時に助け合える関係が生まれるはずです。

　さらに、自分の住む町だけでなく、観光プロモーションを行っている地域や町おこしを積極的に行っている場所に足を運んでみてください。その土地の活性化につながるだけでなく、自分の住む町をより良くするヒントを与えてくれるかもしれません。

What can you do to make your town a pleasant place to live in for a long time? Let's start by getting to know the town you live in. There are many things you need to know, such as what kind of community development efforts the local government is making in your town, whether the public transportation system is safe and easy for everyone to use and whether evacuation sites and disaster prevention facilities are in place in case of a disaster. If there is a local initiative that you can participate in, actually take part in it and get involved in making your town a better place by solving problems and helping to make the community livelier.

In terms of disaster prevention, each of us should prepare for a prompt response in the event of a large-scale disaster by stocking up on supplies at home and confirming evacuation sites with family members. In addition, by getting involved with people in your community on a regular basis, you will be able to build relationships that will allow you to help each other in the event of a disaster.

In addition, try to visit not only your own town but also other areas that are actively promoting tourism or revitalizing their towns. Not only will this help to revitalize the area, but it may also give you hints on how to improve your own community.

Goal 12

つくる責任 つかう責任
Responsible Consumption and Production

持続可能な生産消費形態を確保する。
Ensure sustainable consumption and production patterns.

　　大量生産、大量消費が地球環境に良くないことはよく知られていることでしょう。良くないことはわかっているけれど、どの程度良くないのか知っているでしょうか。着るものや食べるもの、日常生活で使うものなど、すべてのものは地球上のあらゆる資源からできています。しかし、１年間に生み出すことができる資源の量よりも全人類が１年間に生活するために消費する資源の量のほうが多い状態がここ50年ほど続いているのが現状です。地球で１年間に資源が作られる量の74パーセント超過、およそ地球1.75個分以上の資源を使っていることになります。資源を使いすぎることは、さまざまな環境問題に影響を及ぼします。資源を使ってものをつくる側とそれをつかう側が責任をもってこの問題の解決策を考えていかなければならないでしょう。

参照：Global Footprint Network: Earth Overshoot Day 2022

生産と消費に関する用語

次の語句とその意味を線で結んでください。

① use-by date　　　　　　　　・　　　　　　・　大量生産

② mass consumption　　　　・　　　　　　・　賞味期限

③ best-before date　　　　　・　　　　　　・　無駄にする

④ waste　　　　　　　　　　・　　　　　　・　大量消費

⑤ mass production　　　　　・　　　　　　・　消費期限

　消費期限とは、定められた方法にしたがって保存されている食品を、安全に飲食できる期限という意味です。サンドイッチや弁当など、傷みやすい食品に表示されていることが多く、消費期限を過ぎた食品は口にしないほうがいいでしょう。

　大量消費は、頻繁に商品を買い替えたり、余計なものを買ったりすることで生じ、大量廃棄にもつながります。食べ物の場合、注文した量が多すぎて食べ切れないと、残った分を廃棄することになり、食品ロスにつながります。現在では大量生産・大量消費・大量廃棄を見直し、地球環境や社会、地域に配慮して、作られたものを必要な分だけ購入するエシカル消費が実践されつつあります。

　賞味期限は、定められた方法にしたがって保存されている食品を、品質が維持されたままおいしく飲食できる期限という意味です。カップ麺や缶詰など、比較的傷みにくい食品に表示されています。賞味期限を過ぎた食品は味が落ちるだけで、飲食できないというわけではありません。ただし、一度開封した食品は早めに消費したほうがいいでしょう。最近では、非常食用として長期保存可能な食品も売られています。

　大量生産は、産業革命以降、猛スピードで産業が発展し、科学技術が進歩した結果とも言えるでしょう。しかし、大量にものが作られることで多くの天然資源が消費され、枯渇の危機にさらされています。大量生産が大量消費を促し、さらに大量廃棄という問題にまで発展しています。

"Expiration date" means the date until which a food can be safely eaten or consumed if it is stored according to the established methods. It is often indicated on perishable foods, such as sandwiches and boxed lunches, etc. Foods past the expiration date should not be consumed.

Mass consumption is caused by frequent replacement of products and buying extra items, which also leads to mass waste. In the case of food, if the quantity ordered is too much to eat, the remaining portion is discarded, leading to food waste. Today, mass production, mass consumption and mass disposal are being reconsidered, and ethical consumption is being practiced by purchasing only the necessary amount of products that are made in consideration of the global environment, society and local communities.

The best-before date means the period during which food stored according to the prescribed method can be eaten while maintaining its taste and quality. It is displayed on foods that are relatively resistant to spoilage, such as instant noodles and canned foods. Food that has passed its expiration date just loses some of its flavor, and that does not mean you cannot eat or drink it. However, once the food is opened, it is better to consume it as soon as possible. These days, food that can be stored for a long time is also being sold as emergency food.

Mass production can be said to be a result of the breakneck pace of industrial development and advances in science and technology since the Industrial Revolution. However, the mass production of goods has consumed many natural resources, putting them in danger of depletion. Today, mass production encourages mass consumption, which in turn leads to the problem of mass waste.

Point

use-by date は、expiration date（exp. date）とほぼ同じ意味です。
waste は、物品についてもお金や時間についても使うことができる万能な言葉です。

Answer

① use-by date ＝ 消費期限
② mass consumption ＝ 大量消費
③ best-before date ＝ 賞味期限
④ waste ＝ 無駄にする
⑤ mass production ＝ 大量生産

食品廃棄の量

世界の食品廃棄（food waste）の量は年間で10トントラック何台分だと
思いますか？

① 約5,310万台
② 約7,310万台
③ 約9,310万台

　国連環境計画（UNEP）のUNEP Food Waste Index Report 2021によると、
この年、家庭やレストラン、店で販売された食品のうち約9億3,100万トンがご
みとして捨てられました。これは、10トントラックに換算すると9,310万台分。
生産・流通過程で失われた食品も合わせると、全体で生産量の3分の1が消費さ
れることなく廃棄されています。食品が廃棄されるということは、食品が作られ
る過程で使われた土地や水、燃料なども無駄になっているということで、環境・
社会・経済への影響につながっていきます。実際に、世界の温室効果ガス排出量
の8～10パーセントが、廃棄された食品に関連しているということです。
　日本の状況はどうでしょうか。2021年に農林水産省が発表した2018年の食品
廃棄量は、家庭系・事業系を合わせると約600万トンで、国民1人当たりに換算
すると1日約130g、茶碗1杯分ほどのご飯の量に相当します。なんと、アジア圏
でワースト1位という現状です。ごみの量が多いということは、ごみ処理の際に
も余計にコストがかかっていることになります。その額は2,200億～2,300億円
にのぼり、費用には私たちの税金が使われています。また、食料自給率が低い日
本は多くの食料を海外から輸入しているため、輸入コストもかかります。食料輸
入コスト、食品加工・製造コスト、そして無駄になった食品の処理コストを考え
ると、かなりのお金が無駄になっていることになります。食べられるものを食べ
られる分だけ買い、食べ残さないといったことを、少しずつ実行していくことが
大切です。

According to the UNEP Food Waste Index Report 2021 of the United Nations Environment Programme (UNEP), approximately 931 million tons of food sold at homes, restaurants and stores was thrown away as garbage this year. This is equivalent to 93.1 million 10-ton trucks. Including food lost in the production and distribution process, one-third of all food produced is discarded without being consumed. When food is wasted, it means that the land, water, fuel and other resources used in the food production process are also wasted, leading to environmental, social and economic impacts. In fact, 8 to 10 percent of global greenhouse gas emissions are related to food waste.

What about the situation in Japan? In 2021, the Ministry of Agriculture, Forestry and Fisheries (MAFF) announced that the total amount of food waste in 2018, including household and business waste, was about 6 million tons, which, when converted to a per capita measurement, is equivalent to about 130 grams of rice per day, or about one bowl. The current situation is the worst in the Asian region. The large volume of waste means that extra costs are incurred in waste disposal. The cost amounts to 220 to 230 billion yen, which is paid for by our taxes. In addition, Japan has a low food self-sufficiency rate and imports much of its food from overseas, which also incurs import costs. Considering the cost of food imports, food processing and manufacturing costs, and the cost of disposing of wasted food, a great deal of money is wasted. It is important that little by little, we start buying only what we can eat and not leave any food uneaten.

Answer ③ 約 9,310 万台

日本の消費資源量は？

現在、人間が消費する地球上の資源の量は1年間に地球が生産する資源の量を上回り、世界平均で年間地球約1.75個分の消費を続けています。もし世界が日本と同じ生活をする場合、1年間に消費する資源量はおよそ地球何個分だと思いますか？

① 約0.8個
② 約2.9個
③ 約5.1個

　国際的な非営利団体のグローバル・フットプリント・ネットワーク（GFN）によると、2022年時点で、もし世界中の人が日本に住む人と同じような暮らしをしたら、2.9個分の地球が必要になります。人間の活動が地球にどのくらいの負荷をかけているかを示す指標に、エコロジカルフットプリントがあります。これは国や地域の経済活動の規模を地球の表面積で表した指標です。国別に見ると、アメリカ、カナダ、アラブ首長国連邦は地球約5.1個分、ロシアは約3.4個分、インドは約0.8個分となっています。

　またGFNは毎年、エコロジカルフットプリントが、1年間に地球が生産する資源量を上回る、地球の「限界日」を計算して割り出しています。この地球の「限界日」はアース・オーバーシュート・デーと呼ばれ、世界平均をもとに算出された2022年の日付は7月28日でした。日本のアース・オーバーシュート・デーは、これよりも2カ月半早い5月6日。1年分の資源を5月6日で使い切り、12月31日までは将来の分を先取りして使うことになるのです。

　国によって経済・産業などの豊かさが異なるため、消費する資源量にも違いが表れます。アース・オーバーシュート・デーを限りなく12月31日に近い日まで遅らせる、つまり環境に負荷の少ない国に水準を合わせる必要がありますが、非現実的です。ちなみに、2022年で最も12月31日に近い国はアフリカ・ベニン共和国の12月26日です。

According to the Global Footprint Network (GFN), an international non-profit organization, if everyone in the world lived like residents in Japan as of 2022, we would need 2.9 Earths. The Ecological Footprint is an indicator of how much burden human activities place on the Earth. It expresses the scale of economic activities of a country or region in terms of the surface area of the Earth. By country, the United States, Canada and the United Arab Emirates have an ecological footprint equivalent to about 5.1 Earths, Russia has an ecological footprint equivalent to about 3.4 Earths, and India has an ecological footprint equivalent to about 0.8 Earths.

Each year, GFN also calculates and determines the Earth's "critical day" when the Ecological Footprint exceeds the amount of resources produced by the Earth in a year. This is called Earth Overshoot Day, and the date for 2022, calculated based on the global average, was July 28. Japan's Earth Overshoot Day is May 6, two and a half months earlier than this date, meaning that one year's worth of resources will be used up on May 6, and future resources will be used ahead of time until December 31.

Different countries have different economies, industries and other forms of affluence, and this will show differences in the amount of resources consumed. It is necessary to delay Earth Overshoot Day to as close to December 31 as possible, i.e., to adjust the level to that of countries with less environmental impact, but this is unrealistic. Incidentally, the country closest to December 31 in 2022 is the African Republic of Benin, with a December 26 overshoot date.

Answer ② 約 2.9 個

ごみの取り扱い

下の図は、ごみの取り扱いについての優先度を逆ピラミッドで表したものです。各階層の説明文を参考にしながら、①〜⑤の空欄に当てはまる言葉を下から選んでください。

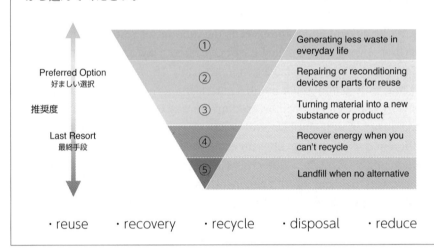

・reuse　・recovery　・recycle　・disposal　・reduce

　なるべくごみを出さないに越したことはありませんが、ごみが出た場合、捨てる前に「これはまだ使えるかな」「何かの代用にならないかな」などと考えて「使い切る」努力をすることが重要です。

　よく知られている3Rの1つであるreduceは「減らす」という意味で、「ごみの量を減らす」ということ。必要なもの以外は買わない、エコバッグを使う、などがリデュースに向けた行動です。

　reuseは「再利用（する）」という意味です。「ものを繰り返し使う」ということで、壊れた物を修理して使ったり、容器を繰り返し使えるように詰め替え商品を買ったりすることが、リユースに向けた行動です。

　recycleは「再生利用する」という意味です。reuseと似ていますが、リサイクルは分別されたごみを一度資源に戻してから新たなものとして再利用することです。新聞紙がトイレットペーパーになったり、ペットボトルがフリース生地にな

ったりして、消費者がそれらを購入することで再利用という構造が生まれます。

recoveryは「回収」という意味です。リサイクルできない廃棄物を単に焼却処分せず、焼却時に発生する熱エネルギーの一部を回収・利用するリサイクル方法のことです。サーマルリサイクルとも呼ばれ、ごみの焼却熱を利用した温水プールがその例として挙げられます。

そして、代替手段がないごみは、最終的に廃棄の工程を経て埋立地などへ向かうことになります。

It is best to generate as little waste as possible, but when waste is generated, it is important to make an effort to "use it up" by thinking "is this still usable?" or "can it be used in place of something else?" before discarding it.

Herasu, one of the well-known 3Rs, means "reduce," as in reducing the amount of garbage. Buying only what you need, using eco-friendly bags, etc. are actions toward reducing.

Sairiyō suru means "reuse." This can be done by using things over and over again, repairing broken items and buying refillable products so that containers can be used again.

Saisei riyō suru means "recycling" and is similar to reusing. Recycling is the process of turning separated garbage back into resources and then reusing them as something new. Newspapers are turned into toilet paper, plastic bottles into fleece fabric and so on, and a pattern of reuse is created when consumers purchase these items.

Kaishū means "recovery." It refers to a recycling method in which non-recyclable waste is not simply incinerated, but rather a portion of the thermal energy generated during incineration is recovered and utilized. Also called thermal recycling, an example is a heated swimming pool that uses the heat from waste incineration.

When there is no other alternative, waste will eventually go through the disposal process to a landfill or other site.

Answer ① reduce ② reuse ③ recycle ④ recovery ⑤ disposal

Goal 12

3R+1 に向けた行動

次の英文は、それぞれ reduce、reuse、recycle、recovery へ向けた行動を表しています。それぞれに当てはまるものを空欄に書いてください。

① I sometimes sell my clothes at an online flea market. （　　　）
② I always wash milk cartons before taking out the trash. （　　　）
③ I usually carry a water bottle. （　　　）
④ Waste heat is used in this facility's heating system. （　　　）

Point

　①は「私はときどきオンラインのフリマで自分の服を売ります」という意味です。不要になった服を捨てずに、必要としている人に譲るという行動はreuseにあたります。

　②は「私はいつも、牛乳パックをごみとして出す前に洗います」という意味で、recycleの行動です。牛乳パックは古紙からリサイクル処理されたリサイクルパルプではなく、安全面や衛生面を考慮して製造されたバージンパルプから作られています。リサイクル処理するためには必ず中身を洗ってパックを開き、平らにして乾かします。その後、リサイクル工場でトイレットペーパーやティッシュとして生まれ変わります。

　③は「私はいつも水筒を持ってきます」という意味です。出先でそのつどペットボトルの水を買うと、飲み終えた後にごみが出ますが、水筒を持ち歩けばごみが減ります。この行動はreduceにあたります。

　④は「この施設の暖房システムには廃熱が使われています」という意味です。waste heatはheat produced by waste disposalと言い換えることもできます。廃棄物を燃やすときに作られる熱を回収して別の用途に利用する仕組みを指しているのでrecoveryです。

Answer　　① reuse　② recycle　③ reduce　④ recovery

衣服の処分量

日本人が1年間に処分する衣服は1人あたり約何着だと思いますか？

① 約12着
② 約18着
③ 約25着

　トレンド感のある衣服が短いサイクルでぞくぞく店に入荷し、低価格で販売されるファストファッション。UNIQLOやGU（日本）、H&M（スウェーデン）、ZARA（スペイン）、GAP（アメリカ）などのブランドがその代表格です。短期間で商品が入れ替わり、しかも低価格というのは消費者の満足度を高める効果がありますが、そのためには製造過程でコストを下げて大量生産しなければなりません。その結果、消費者には安い商品を大量に購入する機会が増えました。しかし、低価格品をたくさん買うと一着一着に愛着が生まれにくくなるため、消費者はすぐに衣類を処分しかねません。環境省の調査によると、日本人が1年間に購入する衣服は1人あたり約18着、処分する衣服は約12着、1年間に一度も着なかった衣服は約25着だそうです。処分する数よりも購入数のほうが多く、しかも一度も着なかった衣服が処分する衣服の2倍もあるのです。処分方法で一番多いのは、ごみとしての廃棄で68パーセント。その理由は、処分に時間や労力、費用がかからないからということです。1年間に一度も着なかった衣服を翌年に着る可能性は低く、そのまま処分されがちであることを考えると、確実に大量廃棄につながるでしょう。

　大量生産の裏側には、劣悪な労働環境の問題や、有害物質による環境破壊や健康被害、低品質による大量廃棄など多くの問題があります。使う側にとって「より安くより多く」は魅力的ですが、製品が作られた背景を考え、ごみにならないように先のことを考えて必要なものだけを購入し、長く大切に着ることを心がける必要があるでしょう。

In fast fashion, trendy clothes arrive in stores in short cycles and are sold at low prices. Brands such as UNIQLO and GU (Japan), H&M (Sweden), ZARA (Spain) and GAP (US) are typical examples. The rapid turnover of products and low prices have the effect of increasing consumer satisfaction, but this requires mass production at lower costs in the manufacturing process. As a result, consumers have more opportunities to purchase inexpensive items in large quantities. However, they may quickly dispose of clothing because buying a large number of low-priced items makes it difficult to develop a love for each one. According to a survey by the Ministry of the Environment, each Japanese person buys about 18 items of clothing per year, discards about 12 items, and about 25 are not worn during the year. The number of clothes purchased is larger than the number disposed of, and the number of clothes never worn is twice as large as the number disposed of. The most common method is disposal as garbage, at 68 percent. The reason is that it does not take time, effort and money to dispose of them. Considering that clothes that have not been worn once in a year are unlikely to be worn in the following year and tend to be discarded as they are, it will surely lead to mass disposal.

Behind the scenes of mass production, there are many problems, such as poor working environments, environmental destruction and health damage due to harmful substances and mass disposal due to low quality. "Cheaper and more" is attractive for the consumer, but it is important to think about the background behind the product's creation, to purchase only what is necessary to prevent it from becoming waste, and to wear it carefully for a long time.

Answer ① 約12着

循環型経済システムの流れ

下の図は大量生産・大量消費の経済システムと廃棄物ゼロを目指す循環型経済システムの流れを表したものです。それぞれに「〜 economy」という名称が与えられています。①②に当てはまる言葉を選んでください。

① (　　　　) economy　　　② (　　　　) economy

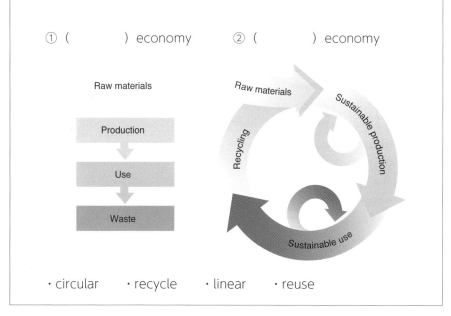

・circular　　・recycle　　・linear　　・reuse

　産業革命以降、近年まで続いた単一方向型の経済システムのことをリニアエコノミー（直線型経済）と言います。地球の資源やエネルギーを大量消費して製品を大量に生産し、使い終えたら廃棄するというやり方です。左側の図①のように、原材料（地球資源）を使ってものを作り、消費者が使い、廃棄するという直線的な流れです。この経済システムを続けた結果、環境破壊やエネルギー不足、資源の枯渇、気候変動などの問題を招くことになりました。その後、廃棄物を減らすことを目指す３Ｒ（reduce、reuse、recycle）が進められ、リサイクルエコノミーという経済システムの流れに変わりましたが、ここでも最終的には廃棄物が出てしまいます。

そこで近年、右側の図②のように、円を描くような循環型経済という経済システムが提唱されるようになりました。サーキュラーエコノミーの特徴は、①サスティナブルプロダクション（作る側が廃棄物・汚染などを出さない設計をすること）、②サスティナブルユーズ（製品や資源を使い続けること）、③リサイクル（廃棄せずに再生可能資源の活用や土壌への養分還元などをすること）です。作る側と使う側が地球に残された貴重な資源を無駄にすることなく循環させながら経済を成長させることが目標です。身近な例として、コンポストを使って生ごみを堆肥に変えて家庭菜園で使う、ものや場所などを共有・交換するシェアリングサービスを利用する、といったものがあります。

The unidirectional economic system that has existed since the Industrial Revolution until recently is called a linear economy. It is a way of mass-producing products by consuming large amounts of the earth's resources and energy and then disposing of the products when they are finished with. As shown in the figure ① on the left, the flow is linear: raw materials (earth resources) are used to make products, consumers use the products, and then they are disposed of. The continuation of this economic system has resulted in environmental destruction, energy shortages, resource depletion, climate change and other problems. Subsequently, the 3Rs (reduce, reuse, recycle) were promoted, aiming to reduce waste, and the economic system was changed to a recycling economy, but even here, waste is still generated in the end.

In recent years, therefore, an economic system called a circular economy has been proposed, as shown in the figure ② on the right. The circular economy is characterized by ① sustainable production (designing products so that they do not produce waste or pollution), ② sustainable use (continuing to use products and resources), and ③ recycling (using renewable resources and returning nutrients to the soil without discarding them). The goal is to grow the economy while allowing both the producer and the user to circulate the precious resources left on the earth without wasting them. Familiar examples include using composting to turn food scraps into compost for use in vegetable gardens, and using sharing services to share and exchange things and places.

Answer   ① linear   ② circular

アップサイクルについて

3R とは異なる２つの新しい概念があります。廃棄物や、使わなくなった資源・製品にデザインやアイデアなどの付加価値をつけてグレードアップさせるアップサイクル（upcycle）と、使わなくなった資源や製品を、付加価値は低いながらももう一度使用可能なものにするダウンサイクル（downcycle）です。次のそれぞれに、upcycle / downcycle のどちらかを当てはめてください。

① 廃消防ホースから作ったかばん　　　　　　　　　　（　　　　）
② 廃棄炊飯米から作ったビール　　　　　　　　　　　（　　　　）
③ 着古したＴシャツから作った雑巾　　　　　　　　　（　　　　）
④ 廃棄野菜から作ったクレヨン　　　　　　　　　　　（　　　　）
⑤ 古新聞から作った生ごみ袋　　　　　　　　　　　　（　　　　）

　アップサイクルもダウンサイクルもリサイクルの一種です。アップサイクルには、より創造性とデザイン性に富んだものにするイメージがあります。①の廃消防ホースから作ったカバンはアップサイクルです。ビルや公共施設に備えられた消防ホースの９割が使われることなく破棄されるため、未使用の消防ホースを使ってかばんが作られています。

　②の廃棄炊飯米から作ったビールもアップサイクルの例です。廃棄炊飯米が出ることに悩んでいたカレー店の店主が、フードテック企業の技術提供を受け、炊いたご飯を原材料とするクラフトビールを完成させました。このビールはカレー店でも販売されているということなので、アップサイクルとサーキュラーエコノミーを両立させた良い例と言えます。

　③の着古したＴシャツから作った雑巾と、⑤の古新聞から作った生ごみ袋はダウンサイクルの例です。ごみとして捨てられるものに手を加えて別のものとして役立てるリサイクルとしては良いアイデアでしょう。

　④の廃棄野菜から作ったクレヨンはアップサイクルです。収穫の際に捨てられてしまう野菜と、米ぬかから採れる米油、ライスワックスを原材料として作られ

ているため、万が一子どもが口に入れても安全ということです。

Both upcycling and downcycling are types of recycling. Upcycling has the image of creativity and design-rich products. Fire horse bags made from waste fire hoses in ① are an example of upcycling. Since 90 percent of fire hoses installed in buildings and public facilities are discarded without being used, the bags are made from unused fire hoses.

② Beer made from discarded rice is another example of upcycling. The owner of a curry shop who was concerned about the amount of waste rice being produced, developed a craft beer made from cooked rice with the help of a food tech company. This beer is now being sold at the curry shop, so this is a good example of both upcycling and the circular economy.

Dust cloths made from used T-shirts ③ and food waste bags made from old newspapers ⑤ are examples of downcycling. It is a good idea to recycle something that would otherwise be thrown away as garbage by modifying it to make it useful as something else.

Vegetable crayons made from discarded vegetables in ④ are an example of upcycling. They are made from vegetables that are thrown away during harvest, rice oil from rice bran and rice bran wax, which means that they are safe even if children put them in their mouths.

Answer ① upcycle ② upcycle ③ downcycle ④ upcycle ⑤ downcycle

環境マークを覚えよう

下のマークは、どれも人や社会・環境などに配慮した製品についているものです。それぞれのマークとその意味を線で結んでください。

①   ・　　　・ 森林を守るマーク

② ・　　　・ オーガニック繊維製品のマーク

③ ・　　　・ 障がい者が農林水産業に携わったマーク

④ ・　　　・ 持続可能な農園産のものにつけるマーク

⑤   ・　　　・ 環境に配慮した商品のマーク

　国内外を問わず、人・社会・地域・環境などに配慮した製品につけられる第三者認証マークが数多くあります。マークを発行する機関とは別の第三者機関が、そのマークの基準が守られているかを厳しくチェックし認証します。

　地域の活性化や雇用などを含む、人・社会・地域・環境に配慮した消費行動をエシカル消費と言います。第三者認証マークがついた商品を意識的に買うことはエシカル消費につながり、消費者それぞれのスタンスで何ができるのかを考えてみたり、社会的課題の解決に取り組む生産者や企業を応援したりすることになります。

　①は「レインフォレスト・アライアンス認証」です。国際NPOのレインフォレスト・アライアンスが運営機関で、劣悪な労働環境と低賃金問題をクリアしたより持続可能な農業を行う農園産の原料、製品であることを示すマークです。主に、コーヒーや紅茶、バナナなどについています。

②は日本農林規格の「ノウフクJAS」です。障がい者が生産工程に携わった生鮮食品・加工食品であることを認証するマークです。

③はおなじみの「エコマーク」です。日本環境協会が運営者で、生産から廃棄までのサイクルで環境負荷が少なく環境保全に役立つと認証された商品につけられます。食品だけでなく、日用品や文具、制服など幅広い商品についています。

④は森林管理協議会が運営する「FSC認証」です。森や動植物、林業を営む人などに配慮し、適切に管理された森林の木材を使用したことを認証するマークです。紙パックやトイレットペーパー、コピー用紙などについています。

⑤は「GOTS認証」です。GOTSとはオーガニックテキスタイル世界基準の略で、布などの繊維製品分野のオーガニックに関する世界基準のことです。コットンやウール、麻、絹などの原材料が環境や社会に配慮したオーガニック繊維製品であることを認証するマークです。製品の原料の70パーセント以上がオーガニックであることを保証するものです。

There are a number of third-party certification marks, both domestic and international, that can be applied to products that are friendly to people, society, the community and the environment. A third-party organization, separate from the organization issuing the symbol, rigorously checks and certifies that the standards of the mark are being followed.

Ethical consumption refers to human-, social-, community- and environmentally-conscious consumption behavior that includes local revitalization and employment. Consciously buying products with a third-party certification mark leads to ethical consumption, which encourages each consumer to consider what they can do based on their own stance toward the environment and to support producers and companies that are working to solve social issues.

① is the Rainforest Alliance Certification. The Rainforest Alliance, an international NPO, is the governing body for this mark, which indicates that the raw materials and products are from farms with more sustainable farming practices that have cleared the problems of poor labor conditions and low wages. It is mainly used for coffee, tea, bananas, etc.

② is "Nofuku JAS," a Japanese Agricultural Standard. This certifies that people with disabilities have been involved in the process of producing fresh and processed foods.

③ is the well-known "Eco Mark." Operated by the Japan Environment Association, it is attached to products that have been certified as contributing to environmental conservation with little environmental impact in the cycle from production to disposal. It is attached to a wide range of products, not only food, but also daily necessities, stationery and uniforms.

④ is the FSC certification operated by The Forest Stewardship Council. This mark certifies that wood from properly managed forests is used in consideration of forests, animals, plants and forestry workers. It is found on paper cartons, toilet paper, copy paper, etc.

⑤ is the GOTS certification, which stands for the Global Organic Textile Standard, a global standard for organic textile products, such as cloth. The mark certifies that raw materials, such as cotton, wool, hemp and silk are organic textile products that are environmentally and socially friendly. It guarantees that at least 70 percent of the raw materials in the product are organic.

Goal 12

Answer

① 持続可能な農園産のものにつけるマーク

② 障害者が農林水産業に携わったマーク

③ 環境に配慮した商品のマーク

④ 森林を守るマーク

⑤ オーガニック繊維製品のマーク

フードマイレージ

次の英語は、作る人と使う人の両方にとってメリットのある考え方を表したものです。日本語で何と言いますか？

locally grown and locally consumed

　フードマイレージという言葉を知っているでしょうか。直訳すると「食料の輸送距離」となり、食料の生産地から消費者のもとに届くまでにかかった輸送距離を「食料の重さ×距離」で表したものです。遠く離れた生産地から届く食料は、石油などの輸送コスト、食料を保管するためのコストなど多くのエネルギーが使われているのでフードマイレージが大きく、関連する二酸化炭素などの排出量が多いために環境に負荷がかかります。食料自給率が低い日本は、自国で生産できる食料が少なく、他国からの輸入に依存しています。そのため、日本で消費される食料はフードマイレージが高くなっています。

　そこで今、見直されているのが、フードマイレージを減らすことができる地産地消という考え方です。地元の生産者が栽培した野菜や果物、地元産の加工品などを地元の産直販売所やスーパーなどで購入すれば、輸送コストが低く新鮮で安全な食材を手に入れることができます。生産者にとっても、直接販売することで収益の増加を見込めたり、規格外品や不ぞろい品などの販売が可能になることで廃棄処分を抑えたりするメリットもあります。さらに、地元産の食材を学校給食や地域の飲食店で利用すれば、食料生産の増加や地域の活性化を促すことにもなるでしょう。人や地域社会、環境に配慮した地産地消の取り組みは、エシカル消費の一つだと考えることもできます。

　Have you ever heard the term "food mileage?" It refers to the distance it takes for food to reach the consumer from the place of production, expressed as the weight of the food multiplied by the distance. Food delivered from distant production sites has a high food mileage because a lot of energy is used, including transportation costs, such as oil and the cost of storing food, and the related carbon dioxide and other emissions are high, which places a burden on the environment. With a low food self-sufficiency rate, Japan produces little food for itself and is dependent on imports from other countries. As a result, food consumed in Japan often has a high food mileage.

This is why the concept of local production for local consumption, which can reduce food mileage, is now being reevaluated. If you buy vegetables and fruits grown by local producers and local processed products at farmers' markets and supermarkets in your area, you can get fresh and safe ingredients with low transportation costs. Producers can also benefit from increased revenues from direct sales and reduced waste by being able to sell non-standard products. Furthermore, the use of locally grown food in school lunches and local restaurants would encourage increased food production and community revitalization. Initiatives for local production for local consumption that take into consideration people, local communities and the environment can be considered a form of ethical consumption.

Goal 12

Point

locally は「地元で、その地域で」という意味、grown は grow「育つ、栽培する」の過去分詞で「育てられた、栽培された」、consumed は「消費された、購入された」という意味です。local production for local consumption と言うこともできます。

Answer　地産地消

「作る責任、使う責任」
——そのためにあなたは何ができると思いますか？
What can you do for "responsible consumption and production"?

　持続可能な消費と生産を実現するために、生産と消費のバランスの確保や環境・地域・社会・人への配慮など、さまざまな取り組みが必要です。私たちに求められるのは主に「使う責任」の部分です。とても身近なことなので、取り組めることはたくさんあるのではないでしょうか。

　まず、必要なものを必要な分だけ買って無駄にしないこと。ものを購入するときは、エシカル消費を実践してみましょう。人・社会・地域・環境などに配慮したフェアトレード製品を選ぶ、地産地消を心がける、障がい者支援につながる商品を選ぶ、エコバッグを使うなど、どれもエシカルな行動です。また第三者認証マークを見つけたら、その製造工程を想像したり、背景にある問題を考えてみるといいでしょう。

　ごみは分別するのが前提ですが、まずは捨てる前に、リユースやリサイクルを考えて「使い切る」ことを意識してみてください。作る側がなるべくごみの出ないような製品を、資源を大切にしながら必要な分だけ造り、廃棄物をそのまま捨てることなく再生可能資源として活用すれば、おのずと使う側もごみを減らすために長く大切に使ったり、食品ロスをなくしたりすることができるのではないでしょうか。自分にできることを、楽しみながら少しずつ実行し、生活の一部にしてみてください。

In order to achieve sustainable consumption and production, we need to ensure a balance between production and consumption and consider the environment, community, society and people. Most importantly, we have to keep in mind our "responsibility to use" food products. There are many things that we can work on in our everyday lives.

First of all, we should buy only what we need and not waste it.

274

When purchasing things, try to practice ethical consumption. Choosing fair trade products that are considerate of people, society, community and the environment, making an effort to locally produce things for local consumption, choosing products that support the disabled and using eco bags are all ethical actions. Also, when you find a third-party certification mark, try to imagine the production process and consider the issues behind it.

Although garbage is supposed to be separated, first try to "use it up" by thinking about reuse and recycling before throwing something away. If the manufacturers can make products that generate as little waste as possible, and only as much as is needed while conserving resources, and if waste is used as a renewable resource instead of being thrown away as is, then naturally the users will be able to use the products carefully for longer periods of time to reduce waste and eliminate food loss. Please try to do what you can, little by little, while having fun, and make it a part of your daily life.

Goal 13
気候変動に具体的な対策を
Climate Action

気候変動とその影響を軽減するための緊急対策を講じる。
Take urgent action to combat climate change and its impacts.

　日本には春夏秋冬の4つの四季があります。それぞれの季節にはそれぞれの特徴があり私たちを楽しませてくれます。季節の変化は地球の傾きと太陽との距離が関係していて、幸運なことに日本はちょうど良いあたりに位置しているため4つの季節をはっきり感じることができるのです。しかし近年では穏やかな気候の春が短く感じられたり、夏には強烈な暑さが長く続いたりと気温の上昇や四季の変化があいまいになっています。暑さだけでなく台風やゲリラ豪雨、水不足が起こることも増えています。これは日本だけの問題でなく世界各地でも起きていて、人間の生活や生態系にも影響を及ぼしています。気候変動を理解し、現在起きている被害を軽減させながら、将来起こりうる自然災害を防ぐために私たちに何ができるのか考えてみましょう。

気候変動のリスク

「グローバル気候リスク指数 2021」（Global Climate Risk Index 2021）
で、日本の気候変動のリスクの高さは世界で何番目にランクインされたと思
いますか？

① 1 位
② 4 位
③ 7 位
④ 10 位

　ドイツの環境 NGO ジャーマンウォッチが発表した「グローバル気候リスク指
数 2021」によると、2020 年の調査において、日本は気候変動のリスクが世界 180
カ国中 4 番目に高い国とランク付けされました。グローバル気候リスク指数とは、
国や地域がどの程度、気候変動の影響を受けているかを分析・数値化したもので
す。前年の気象災害事象が反映されるため順位は毎年異なりますが、日本は 2017
年に 36 位、2019 年に 1 位、2020 年に 4 位という結果なので、上位にランク付け
されているのは必ずしも偶然とは言えないでしょう。日本の順位を決めている主
な要因は水害で、夏から秋にかけての台風や集中豪雨などが影響しています。
　ワースト 10 カ国を見てみると、1 位がモザンビーク、2 位がジンバブエ、3 位が
バハマです。4 位の日本以降は順に、マラウイ、アフガニスタン、インド、南ス
ーダン、ナイジェリア、ボリビアと続きます。気づいた読者もいると思いますが、
先進国ランクインしているのは日本だけです。また、この年の日本の自然災害に
よる死者数は 290 人と少ないにもかかわらず、経済損失額が約 290 億ドルで、イ
ンドの約 690 億ドルに次ぐ規模です。一般的に自然災害の影響を受けやすいのは
途上国ですが、日本のような先進国でも年々異常気象が深刻化し、それによる災
害の影響を受けやすくなっているため、災害に強く復旧しやすい環境を整備する
ことが重要な課題となっています。

According to the "Global Climate Risk Index 2021" released by the German environmental NGO Germanwatch, in a 2020 survey, Japan was ranked as having the 4th highest risk from climate change among 180 countries in the world. The Global Climate Risk Index analyzes and quantifies the extent to which countries and regions are affected by climate change. The rankings vary each year because they reflect weather-related disasters from the previous one, but Japan's high ranking is not necessarily a coincidence, as it was ranked 36th in 2017, 1st in 2019 and 4th in 2020. The main factor that determines Japan's ranking is flood damage, which is affected by typhoons and torrential rains from summer to autumn.

Looking at the bottom-10 countries, Mozambique is No. 1, Zimbabwe is No. 2, and the Bahamas is No. 3, followed by Japan at No. 4, then Malawi, Afghanistan, India, South Sudan, Nigeria, and Bolivia, in that order. As some readers may have noticed, Japan is the only developed country near the top of the rankings. And even though the number of deaths from natural disasters in Japan this year was only 290, the country's economic loss was about $29 billion, second only to India's $69 billion. In general, developing countries are more vulnerable to the effects of natural disasters, but even developed countries like Japan are becoming more susceptible to disasters due to weather conditions that become more extreme year by year, making it an important issue to ensure that the country is protected against disasters and can recover from them easily.

Answer ② 4位

自然災害

次の英文を日本語に訳してみましょう。

① More than 600 people in the US are killed by extreme heat every year.
② Localized heavy rain occurs with greater frequency in Japan.
③ There are five types of floods—river floods, coastal floods, storm surges, inland floods and flash floods.
④ 80 to 90 percent of natural disasters in the last 10 years have been caused by floods, droughts, tropical cyclones, heat waves and severe storms.

① アメリカのCDC（アメリカ疾病予防管理センター）によると、毎年600人以上のアメリカ人が熱中症などの猛暑が原因で死亡しています。アメリカでは6月中旬頃から熱波が発生します。熱波とは通常2日以上続く異常に高温な空気が覆う天候のことで、各州で40℃を超える高温日が続き、これによる山火事も深刻な問題となっています。CDCでは涼しくして水分をとり、最新の情報を入手できるようにしましょうと呼びかけています。

② ゲリラ豪雨は集中豪雨の一種で、突発的・局地的大雨のことです。

③ 通常の洪水は、大雨で河川の水位や流量が急激に増大したり氾濫したりする状況を指します。沿岸洪水は、温暖化に伴って海水の量が増えることで、満潮時や暴風雨などで海岸地域が洪水の影響を受ける状況のことです。高潮浸水は、台風などで海面が上昇し、低地などが浸水することです。内水氾濫は、大雨に伴って下水道の雨水排水処理ができなくなることが原因で氾濫が起きることです。鉄砲水は、急に河川の水量が増して一気に下流へ流れ出る現象で、大量の土砂と水が時速数十キロメートルで流れ下りる現象を土石流と言います。

④ WHOによると、世界で毎年、約5,500万人が干ばつの影響を受けていて、2030年までに干ばつによる深刻な水不足のため約7億人が避難民となる恐れがあるといいます。

① According to the Centers for Disease Control and Prevention (CDC), more than 600 Americans die each year from heatstroke and other heat-related causes. Heat waves occur in the US starting around mid-June. A heatwave is a period of unusually hot air that usually lasts for two or more days, with high temperatures exceeding 40°C (104°F) in each state. Wildfires caused by this are also a serious problem. The CDC urges people to stay cool, stay hydrated and stay up-to-date on the latest information.

② A guerrilla downpour is a type of torrential downpour that occurs suddenly and locally.

③ Ordinary floods refer to situations in which the water level or discharge of a river suddenly increases or there is an overflow due to heavy rain. Coastal flooding is a situation in which areas near the sea are affected by flooding during high tides and storms due to the increased volume of seawater caused by global warming. Storm-surge flooding occurs when the sea level rises due to typhoons, etc., and low-lying areas are inundated. Inland flooding occurs when heavy rainfall causes the sewage system to lose its ability to handle rainwater drainage. A flash flood is a phenomenon in which the volume of water in a river suddenly increases and flows downstream at once. A mudslide is a phenomenon in which a large amount of sediment and water flows downstream at a speed of tens of kilometers per hour.

④ According to the WHO, about 55 million people worldwide are affected by drought each year, and about 700 million people could be displaced by 2030 due to severe water shortages caused by drought.

Goal 13

Point

localizedは「局部的な」という意味で、代わりにisolated「独立した、単独の」を使うことも可能です。heavy rainはdownpour「豪雨、土砂降り」に置き換えることができます。

Answer

① アメリカでは毎年600人以上が猛暑で亡くなっています。

② ゲリラ豪雨は日本でかなり高い頻度で発生します。

③ 洪水には５種類あります——河川氾濫、沿岸洪水、高潮浸水、内水氾濫、鉄砲水です。

④ 過去10年間の自然災害の80〜90パーセントは洪水、干ばつ、熱帯低気圧、熱波、そして暴風雨によるものです。

地球温暖化による気温上昇

地球温暖化によって 2100 年までに上昇すると予想されている平均気温は、最大何℃だと思いますか？

① 2.7℃
② 4.7℃
③ 5.7℃

　地球温暖化によって、ゲリラ豪雨などの異常気象やハリケーン、大規模火災などが頻発しています。IPCC（気候変動に関する政府間パネル）第6次評価報告書によると、2020年の世界平均気温は1850年と比べると1.09℃上昇しており、このまま新たな対策を取らずにいると今世紀末までに2.7℃上昇するとの見通しで、予想最高気温は最大で5.7℃まで上昇するということです。

　温暖化防止には温室効果ガス排出量を抑えなければならず、2015年に採択された「パリ協定」で日本は、2050年までに排出量を80パーセント削減するという目標を掲げました。現実には80パーセント削減は厳しいかもしれませんが、私たちが日々行える取り組みで可能となるかもしれません。例えば、地産地消で二酸化炭素排出量を90パーセント削減したり、灯油暖房ではなくエアコン暖房を使用すれば35パーセントの削減ができます。白熱灯をLED電球に替えれば電力消費量を80パーセント削減できるのです。生活の質を落とすことなく、日々のちょっとした行動で対策に貢献するといいでしょう。

　Global warming has led to the frequent occurrence of extreme weather events such as heavy downpours, hurricanes, and large-scale fires. According to the Sixth Assessment Report of the Intergovernmental Panel on Climate Change (IPCC), the global average temperature in 2020 will be 1.09°C higher than in 1850, and if no new measures are taken, it is projected to warm by 2.7°C by the end of the century, with the projected maximum temperature rising to a maximum of 5.7°C.

In order to prevent global warming, greenhouse gas emissions must be curbed, and in the Paris Agreement adopted in 2015, Japan set a goal of reducing emissions by 80 percent by 2050. In reality, an 80 percent reduction may be difficult to achieve, but it might be possible through actions we can take on a daily basis. For example, we can reduce our carbon footprint by 90 percent through local production for local consumption, or by 35 percent by using air conditioning instead of kerosene heating. Switching from incandescent to LED bulbs can reduce electricity consumption by 80 percent. It is a good idea to contribute to these measures through small daily actions without compromising the quality of life.

Answer ③ 5.7℃

気温上昇と熱帯夜

2050年に世界の平均気温が2℃上昇した場合、日本では熱帯夜が何日発生することになると思いますか？

① 50日
② 60日
③ 70日

熱帯夜は、夕方から翌朝までの気温が25℃以上になる夜のことです。IPCC（気候変動に関する政府間パネル）第6次評価報告書のデータを元にした2050年の日本の天気予報によると、もしも地球温暖化への対策を何もとらずに2050年に世界の平均気温が2℃上昇した場合、日本の熱帯夜は60日になる可能性があるといいます。気温が上昇することで、夏の平均気温は35℃前後となり、真夏の最高気温が40.8℃、真夏日が連続して50日という状況が10月上旬まで続きます。それによって熱中症で死亡する人が6,500人以上になる可能性が出てきます。また、熱波の影響で四季もずれてしまい、京都の紅葉の見頃がクリスマス頃になると予想されています。海面水温の上昇と大量の水蒸気によって大型台風が頻発し、海面水位の上昇とともに5〜10メートルにも及ぶ高潮のリスクも大きくなります。夏の気温の上昇は、現在でも体感されていることで、2050年の予想が現実味を帯びてきています。

A sweltering night is one when the temperature is above 25°C from evening until the next morning. According to a weather forecast for Japan in 2050 based on data from the IPCC (Intergovernmental Panel on Climate Change) 6th Assessment Report, if no action is taken against global warming and the global average temperature rises by 2°C, there could be 60 tropical nights per year in Japan. As the temperature rises, the average summer temperature will be around 35°C, and the maximum temperature in midsummer will be 40.8°C, with 50 consecutive days of extreme heat continuing until early October. More than 6,500 people could die from heatstroke. In addition, due to the effects of the heat wave, the four seasons will be shifted, and it is expected that the best time to see the autumn leaves in Kyoto will be around Christmas. Rising surface temperatures in the ocean and large amounts of water vapor will cause frequent large typhoons, and along with rising sea levels, there will be a greater risk of storm surges as high as 5 to 10 meters. Increasing summer temperatures are still being experienced today, and forecasts for 2050 are beginning to become a reality.

Answer ② 60日

Goal 13

国内避難民

下の世界地図は、自然災害による国内避難民（IDPs: Internally Displaced Persons）の数を国ごとに色分けして示したものです。次の各英文に、内容が合っていれば T を、間違っていれば F をつけてください。

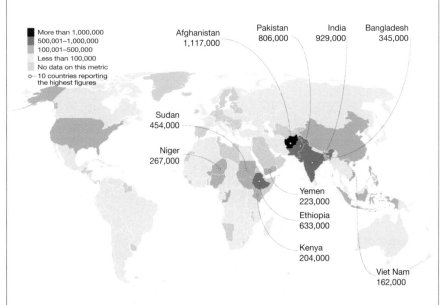

出典：IDMC—Total number of IDPs by disasters as of 31 December 2020

① The total number of IDPs in Sudan is larger than the number in Bangladesh. (　　)

② The total number of IDPs in Afghanistan is the highest in the world. (　　)

③ There are between 100,001 and 500,000 IDPs in Australia. (　　)

④ There is no data on IDPs available for Saudi Arabia. (　　)

気候変動やそれに伴う災害で避難を余儀なくされた人々のことを気候変動避難民などと呼びます。避難を強いられた人々は自国内の他の場所へ避難することになります。そのような人々のことを国内避難民と呼んでいます。

　国内避難民監視センター（IDMC）が104の国・地域の国内避難民状況を調査した結果、2020年12月末時点で約3,070万人が新たに国内避難民になり、そのうちの約3,000万人が気象関連の出来事による避難民でした。地図で国名が示されているところは、104の国・地域の中で最も国内避難民の数が多かったところです。問題となっているのは、国内避難民は国際条約で保護されていないうえ、難民キャンプ以外の場所に身を寄せていることが多いため、人道支援が行き届かないことです。自然災害が原因の国内避難民は2050年までに少なくとも12億人にのぼる可能性があると言われています。気候変動による国内避難民の定義を明確にし、保護・支援することが急務となっています。

People displaced by climate change and related disasters are called climate change refugees. Those who are displaced will be evacuated to other parts of their country. Such people are called internally displaced persons.

The IDMC (Internally Displaced Persons Monitoring Center) surveyed the status of internally displaced persons in 104 countries and territories and found that approximately 30.7 million people were newly internally displaced as of the end of December 2020, of which 30 million were displaced due to weather-related events. The countries indicated on the map are those with the highest number of internally displaced persons among the 104 countries/regions. The problem is that internally displaced persons are not protected by international treaties and are often located outside of refugee camps, making them inaccessible to humanitarian assistance. It is estimated that by 2050, at least 1.2 billion people will be internally displaced due to natural disasters. There is an urgent need to clarify the definition of internally displaced persons due to climate change, and to protect and support them.

Point

　気候変動避難民は、climate change refugees や climate migrants、climate displaced people などの言い方があります。

　①は「スーダンの（国内避難民の）人数はバングラデシュのそれより多い」という意味です。地図からスーダンの人数（45万4,000人）とバングラデシュの人数（34万

5,000人）を比較すれば、正しいことがわかります。

②は「アフガニスタンの（国内避難民の）人数は世界で一番多い」。アフガニスタンは他の国よりも濃い色で塗られています。左上の凡例を確認するとMore than 1,000,000（100万人以上）となっているため、国内避難民の数が一番多いことがわかります。

③は「オーストラリアの国内避難民は10万1人から50万人の間である」という意味です。オーストラリアを探して色を確認すると、Less than 100,000（10万人未満）なので間違いです。

④は「サウジアラビアの利用可能なデータはない」という意味です。サウジアラビアはYemen（イエメン）の北に位置しています。グレーで塗られており、No data on this metric（測定基準データなし）なので、英文は合っています。

Answer ① T ② T ③ F ④ T

地球温暖化による生活への影響

地球温暖化による異常気象・自然災害が私たちの暮らしにどのような影響を
与えるでしょうか。それぞれの事象とその影響を線で結んでください。

① Drought ・ ・ⓐ
- Facing water shortage and power supply threat
- Poor harvest

② Sea level rise ・ ・ⓑ
- Facing serious food shortage
- Poor harvest

③ Heat wave ・ ・ⓒ
- Changing marine ecosystems
- Fish and other seafood shortage

　地球温暖化の影響にはさまざまなものがあります。対策をとらずにそのままにしておくと、自然や野生生物、私たちの暮らしに大きな影響を与えてしまうと言われています。

　干ばつにより農地開拓が難しくなり、農作物の不作が起こるほか、水不足や水力発電によるエネルギーの供給も困難になります。また、気温上昇で南極やグリーンランドを覆う陸上氷河やヒマラヤなどの山岳氷河から氷が溶け出すと、海面上昇が起こります。海水温度の上昇で深海の栄養分が海面付近へ行きわたらなくなると、魚の餌となる藻類やプランクトンが激減し、魚の生息域が変化したり、魚の種や個体数が減少したりして、将来海産物がとれなくなる可能性が生じます。熱波もさらに頻発し、農作物や自然環境に影響を及ぼして、多くの人が食糧難に陥ることになります。熱中症で死亡するリスクもさらに高まります。人間が経済活動の中で出す二酸化炭素が地球温暖化の主な原因とされているため、私たちは、暮らしの中で二酸化炭素を出さない工夫をしていくことを心がけなければなりません。

There are various effects of global warming. It is said that if left untreated, it will have a major impact on nature, wildlife and our lives.

Droughts make it difficult to cultivate farmland, resulting in crop failures, as well as water shortages and difficulties in supplying energy through hydroelectric power generation. In addition, rising temperatures will cause sea level rise as ice melts from land glaciers covering Antarctica and Greenland, and from mountain glaciers in the Himalayas and elsewhere. If, due to rising sea temperatures, nutrients in the deep sea are not distributed near the surface, then the amount of algae and plankton, which are food for fish, will decrease dramatically, resulting in changes in fish habitats and a decrease in fish species and populations, possibly leading to a loss of seafood products in the future. Heat waves will become more frequent, affecting crops and the natural environment, and causing food shortages for many people. The risk of death from heatstroke will also increase. Since carbon dioxide emitted by humans in the course of economic activities is considered the main cause of global warming, we must try to reduce carbon dioxide emissions in our daily lives.

 Answer ① = ⓐ ② = ⓒ ③ = ⓑ

炭素サイクル

下の図は、炭素が地球上のさまざまな生物の間を循環する「炭素サイクル」（carbon cycle）を示したものです。日本語を参考にしながら、①～⑤に当てはまる英語を下の語群から選んでください。

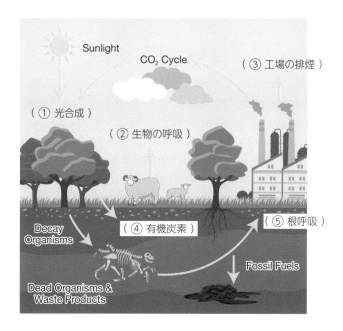

- factory emissions
- organic carbon
- photosynthesis
- animal respiration
- root respiration

炭素は地球上の大気、陸上生物、海洋、堆積物、水などの間でバランスよく排出と吸収を繰り返し、循環過程に応じて、二酸化炭素、有機物、化石燃料などの形に変化します。たとえば、図のように、植物は太陽光と大気中の二酸化炭素を取り込んで光合成を行い、有機炭素として生物に取り込まれ、生物の呼吸によって二酸化炭素が大気に排出されます。土壌に蓄積した植物由来の腐敗物や生物の死骸・廃棄物などの堆積物が、年月を経て化石燃料となり、自動車や工場に使用されて二酸化炭素などとして大気に排出されます。

18世紀の産業革命以前には、大気中に存在する二酸化炭素の量とそれ以外の炭素量のバランスが保たれていましたが、産業革命以後そのバランスは崩れ、人間の経済活動によって排出される二酸化炭素が大気中に滞留し、炭素サイクルも崩れ始めました。炭素サイクルが崩れると地球環境にさまざまな影響が及ぼされるため、世界では脱炭素の取り組みが進められています。

Carbon is repeatedly emitted and absorbed in a well-balanced manner among the earth's atmosphere, terrestrial organisms, oceans, sediments, water, etc., and it changes into forms such as carbon dioxide, organic matter and fossil fuels through the circulation process. For example, as shown in the figure, plants take in sunlight and atmospheric carbon dioxide through photosynthesis, and they are incorporated into organisms as organic carbon. Also, carbon dioxide is emitted into the atmosphere through the respiration of organisms. Over the years, plant-derived decaying matter, dead organisms, waste and other sediments that accumulate in the soil become fossil fuels, which are used in automobiles and factories and emitted into the atmosphere as carbon dioxide and other gases.

Before the Industrial Revolution in the 18th century, the balance between the amount of carbon dioxide in the atmosphere and the amount of other carbon was maintained, but after it, that balance was disrupted, and the carbon cycle also began to be disrupted as carbon dioxide emitted by human economic activities became retained in the atmosphere. The collapse of the carbon cycle has various effects on the global environment, and decarbonization efforts are being promoted around the world.

Answer ① photosynthesis ② animal respiration ③ factory emissions
④ organic carbon ⑤ root respiration

絶滅危惧種

Goal 13

生物が絶滅の危機に瀕する原因のひとつに、地球温暖化による気温上昇や気候変動があります。気温の上昇で生物の生息域が変わったり、気候変動による洪水や豪雨などで地形が変わり、動植物の生息域が奪われたりすることもあります。

国際自然保護連合（IUCN）が2021年12月に情報を更新した「絶滅のおそれのある野生生物の種のリスト（レッドリスト）」では、4万84種の野生生物が絶滅危惧種とされています。2000年時点では1万1,000種ほどだったので、20年間で4倍近く増加したことになります。レッドリストの中で気候変動が要因の絶滅危惧種は5,775種でした。生息環境の変化、干ばつ、暴風雨・洪水、極端な気温の変化などが、この20年で野生生物にも深刻な脅威をもたらしていることが明らかになっています。

野生生物の絶滅危機の要因は、人間の活動が原因の気候変動と根底でつながっています。その関係性を理解し、多種多様な生物の問題と気候変動の問題を1つのものとして捉えて一緒に解決していくことが必要でしょう。

One of the reasons that organisms are on the verge of extinction is temperature rise and climate change due to global warming. Rising temperatures can change the habitats of organisms, and floods and heavy rains caused by climate change can change landforms and deprive plants and animals of their habitats.

The International Union for Conservation of Nature (IUCN) updated its "List of Threatened Wildlife Species (Red List)" in December 2021, listing 40,084 species of wildlife as endangered, up from about 11,000 in 2000, a nearly fourfold increase in 20 years. There are 5,775 threatened species on the Red List due to climate change. It is clear that habitat change, drought, storms/floods and extreme temperatures have also posed serious threats to wildlife over the past 20 years.

The factors contributing to the wildlife extinction crisis are fundamentally linked to climate change caused by human activities. We need to understand the relationship between these two issues, and to see the problems of various species and climate change as one and work together to solve them.

Answer   ① threatened species

気候変動への対策

気候変動への対策が2つあります。1つは原因を低減する「緩和」(mitigation)。
もう一つは何だと思いますか?

① 抑制 (restraint)
② 適応 (adaptation)
③ 受容 (acceptance)

　気候変動への対策には、「緩和」と「適応」の2つがあります。「緩和」は気候変動によるさまざまな影響を回避するために、二酸化炭素などの温室効果ガスの排出を削減して気候変動を抑える対策のことです。節電や省エネ、再生可能エネルギーの利用、森林を増やすなどが緩和策の例です。
　一方、気候変動を「緩和」させるだけでなく、気候変動の悪影響を軽減しつつその変化に「適応」していくことも不可欠です。豪雨や洪水などの災害に備えるハザードマップの作成、高温でも育つ作物の品種開発、高潮・高波対策の強化や観光地での災害情報の多言語化など、変化する環境の中でよりよく暮らしていけるように対策します。より必要な対策は「緩和」ですが、緩和策の効果が現れるには長い時間がかかることが予想されているため、並行して適応策を進めていくことも必要なのです。

　There are two types of measures to address climate change: "mitigation" and "adaptation." "Mitigation" refers to measures to reduce climate change by reducing emissions of carbon dioxide and other greenhouse gases in order to avoid the various impacts of climate change. Examples of mitigation measures include saving electricity, conserving energy, using renewable energy and increasing forests.

　On the other hand, it is essential not only to "mitigate" climate change, but also to "adapt" to it while reducing its negative impacts. Measures to help people live better in a changing environment include creating hazard maps to prepare for disasters, such as heavy rains and floods, developing crop varieties that can grow even in high temperatures, strengthening storm surge and tidal wave countermeasures and making disaster information available in multiple languages at tourist destinations. A more necessary measure is "mitigation," but since it is expected to take a long time for the effects of mitigation measures to appear, it is also necessary to proceed with adaptation measures at the same time.

Answer ② 適応 (adaptation)

気候変動に対する考え

下の英文が示す「気候変動に対する考え」を日本語で何と言いますか？

It refers to 'denial' or 'unwarranted doubt' of the scientific 'consensus' on global warming, its importance or its connection to 'human behavior'.

① 気候変動肯定論
② 気候変動中立論
③ 気候変動懐疑論

refer to ～ ～と言う　　denial 拒否　　unwarranted doubt 根拠のない疑い
consensus 意見　　connection to ～ ～とのつながり

　気候変動の問題の解決策が求められる一方で、気候変動（地球温暖化）に対する懐疑論や否定論があることも事実です。気候変動懐疑論や気候変動否定論は、いずれも地球温暖化の深刻さや人為的要因に懐疑的（または否定的）なものとして、ほぼ同じ意味と捉えられています。特にアメリカでは、共和党支持者に懐疑論者が多いようです。

　懐疑論・否定論の中でよく聞かれる主張には、次のようなものがあります。気候変動は10万年の長期スケールで見れば自然のサイクルで今が気温の上昇期である、過去にもかつてないほどのスピードで地球の気温が上昇する時期があった、人間の活動が地球温暖化の原因ではなく活発化した太陽が気温の上昇に影響を与えているのだ、歴史的に見れば現在の地球温暖化の農業・健康・環境への影響は悪化しておらず、むしろ1560～1660年の気候変動による寒冷化（小氷期）のほうが食糧不足や伝染病・自然災害を顕著に引き起こした、などです。

　確かに、医学誌 *The Lancet Planetary Health* で発表された2000～2019年の地球の平均気温と超過死亡の関係に関する調査結果によると、全世界で毎年

508万人の超過死亡があり、そのうち寒さによる死亡が459万人（全死者の9.43パーセント）、暑さによる死亡が49万人（全死者の0.91パーセント）でした。この20年間で気温の上昇は確実に起こっており、寒さによる死者は大幅に減り暑さによる死者はやや増えましたが、それでもなお全体としては温暖化のほうが寒冷化よりも死者を減少させる傾向があるとのことです。

　懐疑論者・否定論者はやみくもに「気候変動はうそだ！」と言っているわけではなく、科学を理解し正確なデータを読み解いた上で確信をもって主張している人も多くいます。一辺倒な考えにとらわれると思考が停止してしまうので、別の考えも知識として受け入れられる柔軟さがあるといいのではないでしょうか。

While solutions to the problem of climate change are being sought, it is also true that there is skepticism and denial about climate change (global warming). Climate change skepticism and climate change denial are both viewed as meaning roughly the same thing: skepticism (or denial) about the severity of global warming and anthropogenic factors. In the United States, in particular, skeptics seem to be more common among supporters of the Republican Party.

Some of the most commonly heard claims of skepticism and denialism include the following: climate change is a natural cycle on a long-term scale of 100,000 years, and we are in a period of rising temperatures; there have been periods in the past when global temperatures rose at unprecedented rates; human activity is not the cause of global warming, but, rather, an increasingly active sun is causing rising temperatures; historically speaking, the current global effects of global warming on agriculture, health and the environment have not worsened; the cooling (Little Ice Age) caused by climate change from 1560 to 1660 caused more-pronounced food shortages, epidemics and natural disasters.

Indeed, according to a study published in the medical journal *The Lancet Planetary Health* on the relationship between average global temperature and excess deaths during 2000–2019, there were 5.08 million excess deaths worldwide each year, of which 4.59 million (9.43 percent of all deaths) were due to cold and 490,000 (0.91 percent of all deaths) were due to heat. Although temperatures have risen steadily over the past two decades, resulting in significantly fewer deaths from cold and slightly more deaths from heat, overall warming still tends to cause fewer deaths than cold, according to the report.

Skeptics and deniers are not blindly saying, "Climate change is a lie!" There are many people who are convinced by their understanding of the science and accurate data. It is good to be flexible enough to accept other ideas as knowledge, because if you are stuck in one way of thinking, you will stop thinking.

Answer　③ 気候変動懐疑論

Goal 13

「気候変動に具体的な対策を」
──そのためにあなたは何ができると思いますか？
What can you do to promote "climate action"?

　気候変動への具体的な対策は、SDGsの他の目標と深く関係しています。再生可能エネルギーや太陽光発電などのクリーンエネルギーを積極的に利用することは、Goal 7「エネルギーをみんなに、そしてクリーンに」の取り組みと同じです。LED照明に代えたり、地産地消を進めたり、二酸化炭素排出量の少ない商品を選んだりすることは、Goal 12「つくる責任 つかう責任」の取り組みと同じです。気候変動への対策で最も重要なのは、やはり二酸化炭素の排出量をなるべく減らすことです（緩和策）。電気をつけっぱなしにしない、プラスチックごみを減らす、徒歩や自転車で行ける距離に自動車を使わないなど、ふだんの生活を通して実践できることがたくさんあり、意識せずに行っていることもあるのではないでしょうか。また、気候変動の影響による自然災害時の避難対策や熱中症予防策など、適応策も個人で取り組めるはずです。目の前の小さなことから無理のない範囲で進めてみましょう。

　Specific measures to address climate change are closely related to the other goals of the SDGs. Actively using renewable energy, solar power and other clean energy sources is in line with Goal 7, "Affordable and Clean Energy"; replacing regular lights with LEDs, promoting local production for local consumption and choosing products with low carbon footprints are in line with Goal 12, "Responsible Consumption and Production." The most important measure to combat climate change is still to reduce carbon dioxide emissions as much as possible (mitigation measures). There are many things we can do in our daily lives, such as not leaving the lights on, reducing plastic waste, and not driving cars within walking or bicycling distance, which we may be doing without even being aware of it. Individuals should also be able to take measures to adapt to the effects of climate change, such as evacuation measures in the event of natural disasters and measures to prevent heatstroke. Let's start with the small things in front of us and proceed within a reasonable scope.

Goal 14
海の豊かさを守ろう
Life Below Water

持続可能な開発のために、海洋・海洋資源を保全し、
持続可能な形で利用する。

**Conserve and sustainably use the oceans, seas and
marine resources for sustainable development.**

　90パーセント、80パーセント、70パーセント、60パーセント、50パーセント──これは、それぞれ胎児、新生児、子ども、成人、高齢者の体のおよその水分量です。人間の体はほとんど水でできていて、水なしでは生きることができません。人間に限らず水はすべての生き物、特に海の生き物には必要不可欠です。しかし、その海が私たちが出す大量のゴミや排水で汚れてしまったら、海の生き物はどうなるのでしょうか。私たちが生きるために水産物を獲りすぎてしまったら、海洋生態系や環境はどうなるのでしょうか。海には総量1億トン以上のプラスチックごみがあると言われています。細かい破片になったプラスチックを魚が食べ、その魚を人間が食べる……。海にも海洋生物にも人間にも悪影響をもたらすことは明らかでしょう。多様な海の生き物とその美しい環境を守るためにできることを考える必要があります。

環境問題に使われる単語

次の語句とその意味を線で結んでください。

① drift　　　　　・　　　　　・　消滅する

② pollute　　　　・　　　　　・　破壊する

③ disappear　　・　　　　　・　保全する

④ damage　　　・　　　　　・　蓄積する

⑤ conserve　　・　　　　　・　汚染する

Point

　①の drift は、There are millions and millions of tons of plastic drifting in the ocean. のように「たまる、停滞する」という意味で使われます。同様に accumulate も「蓄積する、堆積する、たまる」という意味でよく使われます。

　②の pollute の名詞形は pollution です。海洋汚染（marine pollution）の原因は、人間が出す大量のごみや工場などからの排水、タンカーの事故で流出した石油などです。さまざまな有害物質、プラスチックなどが海洋生物（marine life）に悪影響をもたらし、その影響は最後に人間に戻ってくることになります。

　③の disappear は「消える、なくなる」などの意味で最もよく使われる単語です。vanish や cease to exist、perish なども似た意味を表しますが、disappear には「完全に消えてなくなる、絶滅する」というやや強いニュアンスがあります。サンゴ礁（coral reef）には海洋生物の約25パーセントが生息していると言われますが、海水の温暖化や酸性化（ocean acidification）、異常気象による巨大台風などによって、このサンゴ礁が急激に減少しています。サンゴ礁が消滅すると海の生態系が崩れ、漁場もなくなってしまうでしょう。

　④の damage や harm は「修復可能な程度に破壊する」、destroy や devastate は「修復不可能な状態まで破壊する」というニュアンスを持った語です。

　⑤の conserve は、自然や文化的価値のあるものを「保全する、保護する、保存する」という意味で、「現状を維持する、守る」というニュアンスがあります。preserve

も同様に「保存する、保護する」という意味ですが、「保存・保護するためにアクション
を起こす」ニュアンスがあります。「ジャム」のことをpreserveと呼ぶことがあり
ます。これは、果物を貯蔵するために砂糖を加えて煮詰めることから来ています。

Answer ① drift ＝ 蓄積する

② pollute ＝ 汚染する

③ disappear ＝ 消滅する

④ damage ＝ 破壊する

⑤ conserve ＝ 保全する

Goal 14

魚の乱獲

「魚の乱獲」を英語で何と言いますか？

① overfishing　　② fisheries　　③ fishing ban

　世界の海で、水産物の違法な漁が問題になっています。主に、中国、インドネシア、ベトナムなどのアジア諸国の漁獲量が増大していて、中国は世界の15パーセントを占めています。持続可能なレベルで水産物を利用できるようにするには、世界全体で漁獲量の管理を行うのはもちろんのこと、途上国などで漁業中心の生活をしている人たちの生活をサポートしたり、海洋環境を悪化させずに養殖漁業を増やす仕組みを考えたりなど、国際的な協力が必要です。

　Illegal fishing of marine products is a growing problem in the world's oceans. Generally, Asian countries, such as China, Indonesia and Vietnam, are increasing their catches, with China accounting for 15 percent of the world's total. In order to make marine products available at a sustainable level, international cooperation is needed not only to manage fish catches on a global scale, but also to support the livelihoods of people in developing nations and other countries where people's livelihoods are centered on fishing, and to develop mechanisms to increase aquaculture without degrading the marine environment.

Point

　「魚の乱獲」は、英語でoverfishingあるいはindiscriminate fishingと言います。indiscriminateは「無差別の、見境のない」という意味です。over- は量などを「超えて、上回って」などの意味をもつ接頭辞で、ほかにovereating（食べ過ぎ）、oversleep（寝過ごす）、overdose（薬剤・麻薬などの過剰摂取）などの語を構成しています。

Answer　① overfishing

海洋マイクロプラスチックの発生源

下のグラフは海洋マイクロプラスチックの発生源とその割合を示したものです。各空欄に当てはまる言葉を下の語群から選んでください。

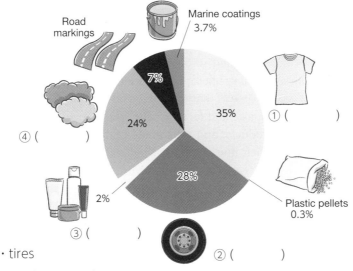

Where Do the Microplastics in the Oceans Come from?

by source (in %)

Road markings

Marine coatings 3.7%

7%

35%

① (　　　　　　)

24%

④ (　　　　　)

28%

2%

Plastic pellets 0.3%

③ (　　　　　)

② (　　　　　)

· tires
· synthetic textiles
· personal care products
· city dust

Goal 14

　マイクロプラスチックは発生源の違いによって、一次マイクロプラスチックと二次マイクロプラスチックに分けられます。一次マイクロプラスチックは製造時点ですでに微小のプラスチック片になっているもので、歯磨き粉やスクラブ洗顔料などのパーソナルケア製品に含まれるマイクロビーズや、プラスチック製品を

作るときの粒状の原料ペレット、道路に残留するタイヤくずなどです。製品原料として使われるものなので粒が細かく、回収が難しいことが特徴です。

　一方、二次マイクロプラスチックはペットボトルやビニール袋などが劣化して細かい破片となったものです。もともとのプラスチックは大きいので、ごみとして廃棄するときの量や出し方などを工夫すれば、ある程度マイクロプラスチックになるのを抑制できます。

　円グラフ中では市中のほこりの割合が、衣服などの合成繊維、タイヤに次いで大きいことがわかります。これは、埋立地などで劣化した二次マイクロプラスチックやタイヤの摩擦によって出る細かな粒子、着用する衣服から出る合成繊維などがほこりとなって大気中を舞い、雪や雨に混ざって海へ降り注ぐためです。マイクロプラスチック繊維は生分解されないため、海中でマイクロプラスチックになって微生物に「だけ」分解してもらえるわけではなく、ほかの生物にも食べられてしまうリスクがあります。結局のところ、プラスチックへの依存を減らして生産量を減少させていくことが賢明なのです。

Microplastics can be divided into primary and secondary microplastics, based on their source. Primary microplastics are those that are already in tiny plastic fragments at the time of manufacture, such as microbeads in personal care products, like toothpaste and facial scrubs, granular raw material pellets used to make plastic products, and tires made of synthetic rubber. They are often characterized by their fine granularity and can be difficult to recover.

Secondary microplastics, on the other hand, are the fine fragments of plastic bottles and plastic bags that have deteriorated. Since the original plastic is large, it is possible to reduce the amount of microplastics to a certain extent if the amount and method of disposing of waste are carefully controlled.

The pie chart shows that the percentage of dust in the city is the second-largest after synthetic fibers like clothing and tires. This is because the secondary microplastics degraded in landfill sites, the fine particles produced by the friction of tires, and the synthetic fibers from the people's clothing all form dust in the air. Since microplastic fibers are not biodegradable, they do not become microplastics in the sea and microorganisms are not the only thing that decompose them. There is a risk that they will be eaten by other organisms. Ultimately, it makes sense to reduce our reliance on plastic and reduce production.

Answer　① synthetic textiles　② tires
　③ personal care products　④ city dust

食物に含まれる海洋マイクロプラスチック

私たちの食べ物の中にもマイクロプラスチック（microplastic）が含まれています。1週間にクレジットカード何枚分を食べていると思いますか？

① 0.5枚
② 1枚
③ 2枚

　有害物質が付着した海洋マイクロプラスチックを小魚や海鳥が食べ、その小魚をより大きな魚などの動物が食べ、そして私たち人間は、それらの生き物を食べることで無意識にプラスチックを摂取しています。その量は、1人あたり1週間で約5グラム、クレジットカード1枚分に相当します。1カ月でレゴブロック1個分、1年でヘルメット1個分にもなるのです。

　プラスチック製品は私たちの生活に欠かせないものですが、使えば使うほど海を汚染し人体にも悪影響をもたらします。例えば、マイクロビーズ（微小プラスチック粒）が入っているスクラブ洗顔料は、洗面所から排出されて海に流れ込みます。プラスチック繊維でできた軽くて暖かいフリースは、洗濯するたびに数十万本の繊維が抜け落ちて洗濯排水と一緒に流れ出ていきます。ペットボトルやプラスチック容器などは、海洋上で細かい破片（マイクロプラスチック）になり蓄積されます。

　マイクロプラスチックは5ミリ以下の微小なプラスチックで、スポンジのように海中の有害物質を表面に付着させる性質があるため、魚も人間も、プラスチックにもともと含まれる環境ホルモンなどの有害物質と海中の有害物質の両方を摂取することになるのです。また、食物連鎖の上位に進むにつれて、蓄積される有害物質の濃度が濃くなる生物濃縮という現象が起こるため、将来的に人間の健康被害につながる可能性は否定できません。

Small fish and seabirds eat marine microplastics with toxic substances attached to them, and are then eaten by larger fish and other animals, so we humans unknowingly ingest plastic by eating these animals. That's about 5 grams per person per week, or the equivalent of one credit card; that's the equivalent of one Lego block per month, or one helmet per year.

Plastic products are an essential part of our lives, but the more we use them, the more they pollute the oceans and harm the human body. For example, facial scrubs containing microbeads (microscopic plastic particles) are discharged from washrooms and end up in the ocean. Lightweight, warm fleece made of plastic fibers loses hundreds of thousands of fibers each time it is washed, and these are washed out with the laundry wastewater. Plastic bottles and plastic containers accumulate in the ocean as tiny pieces (microplastics).

Microplastics are tiny pieces of plastic less than 5 mm in diameter, and like sponges, they have the property of adhering to the surface of toxic substances in the ocean, so fish and humans ingest both the environmental hormones and other toxic substances originally contained in the plastic and those in the ocean. In addition, as one moves up the food chain, the concentration of accumulated toxic substances becomes higher due to a phenomenon known as bioaccumulation, and the possibility that this could lead to health problems for humans in the future is undeniable.

Answer ② 1 枚

日本の漁獲量

世界の漁獲量は養殖を含めて増加傾向にありますが、日本の漁獲量は年々減少しています。その理由は何だと思いますか？

① 地球温暖化で水温が上昇したから。
② 水産資源の管理が行き届いていないから。
③ クジラが漁場の魚を食べてしまうから。
④ マイワシが減少しているから。

　魚が生育し個体数が増加するペースと、漁獲量のバランスを調整していけば、持続可能なレベルで魚を獲ることができます。世界の漁獲量が増加傾向にあるということは「獲りすぎ」ではないかと思われますが、実は、北欧、北米、オセアニアなどでは実際に漁獲できる数量よりも大幅に漁獲量を制限しています。これは、1977年に各国が200カイリ（約370キロ）の排他的経済水域（EEZ）体制に移行して、限られた海域で持続的に利益が得られるように、科学的に漁獲量を算出するなどして水産資源の管理を始めたからです。日本はEEZ体制に移行したものの、各国のような厳しい水産資源管理が行われていないのが現状です。魚の種類によって漁獲量の上限を設定する法律はありますが、他国に比べて規制が甘いため、漁獲量の上限が設定されているのはたったの8魚種（アメリカでは約500魚種）で、乱獲につながっています。

　2020年にSDGsに関する最新の評価結果（Sustainable Development Report 2020）が発表されました。持続可能な開発目標の達成期限は2030年ですが、Goal 14のうち、水産資源管理に関わる目標の達成期限は2020年でした。そしてその評価は、過剰漁業による水産資源の崩壊の割合が70.8パーセントで、悪化が進んでいるという厳しいものでした。国として水産資源管理の制度をしっかり整え、資源を回復させることが急務となっています。

　By balancing the rate at which fish grow and increase in population with the amount of fish that are caught, we can achieve sustainable levels of fish catch. The fact that global catches are on the rise would seem to indicate that we are "overfishing," but in fact, countries in Northern Europe, North America, Oceania and elsewhere are limiting their catches so that they take in much less than they can actually could. This is because in 1977, each country shifted to a 200 nautical mile (approximately 370 km) exclusive economic zone (EEZ) system and began to manage fishery resources by scientifically calculating the amount of fish caught so that profits could be made sustainably in the limited ocean area. Although Japan has moved to an EEZ regime, it has not yet implemented the same strict management of fishery resources as other countries. Although there are laws that set catch limits for different species of fish, regulations are less stringent than in other countries, and only 8 species (compared with about 500 species in the US) have catch limits, leading to overfishing.

The latest assessment on the SDGs (Sustainable Development Report 2020) was released in 2020. The deadline for achieving the Sustainable Development Goals is 2030, but the deadline for achieving Goal 14, which is related to fisheries resource management, was 2020. The assessment was grim, showing that 70.8 percent of fisheries resources were collapsing due to overfishing, and the situation is worsening. There is an urgent need for the government to establish a solid system for fisheries management and to restore the resources.

Point

①は理由としてありえますが、世界で漁獲量が増加しているのに、日本の海だけ温暖化の影響下にあるとは考えにくいでしょう。③については、クジラの生育域が日本周辺ではないので、理由にはならないでしょう。④については、実際には2011年以降、マイワシの漁獲量が大幅に増加しています。

Answer ② 水産資源の管理が行き届いていないから。

限りある水産資源

下のマークは持続可能な漁業で獲られた天然の水産物につけられる認証ラベルです。このラベルの通称は何だと思いますか？　空欄に入る文字を選んでください。

(　　　　　　　)

① 海洋エコラベル
② 天然魚ラベル
③ 海のエコラベル

　「海のエコラベル」は、水産資源と海洋の自然環境に配慮し管理された天然の水産物の証です。英語圏ではCertified Sustainable Seafoodと表記されています。世界では適切な量の漁獲が行われているのは60パーセントですが、獲りすぎているのは34パーセントで十分な水産資源量があるのはわずか6パーセントほどです。このまま魚の成長以上に獲るスピードが速い状態が続けば、魚の個体数は減少してしまいます。また、乱獲によって周囲の生態系が崩れることも懸念されています。その問題を解決するために、海洋管理協議会（MSC）が海のエコラベルを作りました。MSC認証では、①持続可能な水産資源か、②漁業によって生態系が破壊されていないか、③国際ルールや国内法など漁業管理システムが有効に管理されているか、を第三者機関が厳しくチェックした結果、MSC認証を取得できた漁業の下で獲られたサスティナブルな水産物に、このラベルが付けられます。認証水産物と非認証水産物が混ざらないようにする仕組み「MSC CoC：加工・流通過程の管理認証」もあり、MSC CoC認証を取得した卸売り・加工・最終包装業者が責任をもって消費者へ水産物を届ける流れになっています。

　The "MSC Ecolabel" is a certification of natural marine products that are managed with consideration for marine resources and the natural marine environment. In English-speaking countries, the label is used for Certified Sustainable Seafood. In the world, while 58 percent of fish are caught in

313

suitable quantities, 34 percent are overfished and only about 6 percent have sufficient fisheries resources. If we continue to catch fish faster than they can grow, fish populations will decline. There is also concern that overfishing will disrupt the surrounding ecosystem. In order to solve this problem, the Marine Stewardship Council (MSC) created the Marine Ecolabel, a certification system that requires third-party organizations to strictly check ① whether fishery resources are sustainable, ② that ecosystems are not being destroyed by fishing and ③ whether fishery management systems, including international rules and national laws, are effectively managed. The label is applied to sustainable marine products caught in fisheries that have achieved MSC certification as a result of rigorous checks by a third-party organization to ensure that the fishery management system is effectively managed in accordance with international rules and national laws. MSC CoC (Chain of Custody) certification, a system that prevents certified and non-certified marine products from being mixed, is also in place, and wholesalers, processors and final packers who have obtained MSC CoC certification are responsible for delivering marine products to consumers.

Answer ③ 海のエコラベル

海洋酸性化

海洋酸性度は、産業革命以前との比較で何パーセント上昇したと思いますか？

① 26 パーセント　　② 46 パーセント　　③ 16 パーセント

　炭素サイクルの中で、海は人間が生産する二酸化炭素の約30パーセントを吸収して大気中の二酸化炭素の濃度を調整し、熱の吸収などを行って地球の温暖化を緩和しています。しかし、大気中の二酸化炭素濃度が増すことで、海に吸収される二酸化炭素の量も多くなり、海水の成分が酸性化する海洋酸性化が問題となっています。海の生物は弱アルカリ性の海で暮らしており、酸性化が進むと、サンゴや貝類が死んでしまったり、育たなくなってしまったりします。そうなると、サンゴ礁を生息域にしていた海の生き物や貝類を食べる魚も減ってしまい、生態系が崩れてしまいます。いったん海洋酸性化が進むと、元の弱アルカリ性の海に戻すことは困難なので、二酸化炭素の排出量を減らすといった地球温暖化を防止する対策が必要になります。

　In the carbon cycle, the oceans absorb about 30 percent of the carbon dioxide produced by humans, adjusting the concentration of carbon dioxide in the atmosphere and absorbing heat, thereby mitigating global warming. However, as the concentration of carbon dioxide in the atmosphere increases, the amount of carbon dioxide absorbed by the sea also goes up, causing ocean acidification, which is the acidification of seawater components. Marine organisms live in weakly alkaline seas, and as acidification progresses, coral and shellfish die or are unable to grow. As a result, the number of marine organisms that use coral reefs as habitats and the number of fish that eat shellfish will also decrease, and the ecosystem will collapse. Once ocean acidification has progressed, it is difficult to return the oceans to their original slightly alkaline state, so measures to prevent global warming, such as reducing carbon dioxide emissions, are necessary.

Answer　① 26 パーセント

海洋ごみ

海洋ごみ（marine debris）には、「漂着ごみ」「漂流ごみ」「海底ごみ」の３種類あります。それぞれの日本語と英語を線で結んでください。

①漂着ごみ　・　　　　　　　　・　underwater litter

②漂流ごみ　・　　　　　　　　・　stranded marine debris

③海底ごみ　・　　　　　　　　・　floating marine litter

　漂流していた海洋ごみが海岸に打ち上げられたものを「漂着ごみ」と言います。材木やペットボトル、釣具などさまざまなものが海岸に打ち上げられます。2011年の東日本大震災で発生した津波によって、アメリカ西海岸に大量のごみが流れ着いたことはよく知られています。

　ポイ捨てや雨風などが原因で川に流れ落ちたごみは、海へ流れ着いて海洋ごみとなります。水面や水中に浮遊する海洋ごみのことを「漂流ごみ」と言います。漂流ごみのうち、プラスチックごみが水面や水中で波の衝撃や太陽光などにより細かく砕かれることでマイクロプラスチックになります。また、捨てられた釣り糸や網なども漂流ごみで、これらが体に巻き付き、ウミガメや魚、アザラシなどが身動きできなくなったり、プラスチック片を食べてしまったりして死に至ることもあり、海洋生態系や環境に影響を及ぼしています。

　海底ごみは、ビンや缶をはじめとする重たいものが、海を浮遊せずに海底に沈んだ場合の呼び名です。

Marine debris that is washed ashore is called "stranded marine debris." Lumber, plastic bottles, fishing tackle, and various other items are washed up on the beach. It is well known that a large amount of litter washed up on the West Coast of the United States as a result of the tsunami generated by the 2011 Great East Japan Earthquake.

Litter washed into rivers due to littering, wind and rain, etc., ends up in the ocean and becomes marine debris. Marine debris floating on the surface of the water or in the water is called "drifting debris." Among drifting debris, plastic debris becomes microplastics when it is broken into small pieces by the impact of waves and sunlight on the surface of the water and under the water. Discarded fishing lines and nets are also drifting debris, which can become wrapped around the bodies of sea turtles, fish, seals and other animals, causing them to become immobile, and creatures even die from eating pieces of plastic, so debris has a significant impact on the marine ecosystem and the environment.

Marine debris is the name given to bottles, cans and other heavy objects that sink to the seafloor instead of floating in the ocean.

Point

①の stranded は「（海岸などに）打ち上げられた」という意味です。debris は「破片、がれき」という意味で、litter という語でも言い換えが可能です。

②の floating は「浮遊している」という意味で、drifting と言い換えることもできます。

Answer ①漂着ごみ＝ stranded marine debris
②漂流ごみ＝ floating marine litter
③海底ごみ＝ underwater litter

巨大ごみ海域

太平洋上にある巨大ごみ海域を何と言うでしょう？

① Great Pacific Garbage Patch
② Pacific Belt Zone
③ Pacific Ocean Waste Landfill

海のごみが大きな潮の流れによって大量に集められる場所があります。太平洋ごみベルトと呼ばれる海域で、北太平洋の中央に位置し、その面積は日本の国土面積の4倍以上もあると言われています。太平洋ごみベルトの存在は、1988年にアメリカ海洋大気庁が公表した文書で予測されていましたが、オランダのNPOオーシャン・クリーンアップが上空から確認した結果、実在していることがわかりました。

オーシャン・クリーンアップは2013年、当時18歳だったボイヤン・スラットが創設したNPOで、クリーンエネルギーを使った回収装置を開発し、2021年には9,000キログラム、2022年には10万キログラム以上の海洋ごみを回収することに成功しています。太平洋ごみベルトは世界最大の海洋プラスチックごみの渦で、1兆8,000億個以上もあると言われていますが、同NPOは最新の装置を駆使して、この海洋プラスチックごみを一掃することを目指しています。

There is a place where marine debris is collected in large quantities by large tidal currents. It is called the Great Pacific Garbage Patch. It is located in the middle of the North Pacific Ocean and is said to be more than four times the size of Japan. The existence of the Great Pacific Garbage Patch was predicted in a document published by the US National Oceanic and Atmospheric Administration in 1988, and the Dutch NPO Ocean Cleanup confirmed from the sky that it does exist.

Ocean Cleanup is a non-profit organization founded in 2013 by Boyan Slat, who was 18 years old at the time, and has developed a clean energy recovery device that had successfully recovered 9,000 kg of marine debris by 2021 and over 100,000 kg by 2022. The Great Pacific Garbage Patch is the world's largest vortex of marine plastic debris, estimated to contain over 1.8 trillion pieces, and the NPO aims to clean up this marine plastic debris using the latest equipment.

Answer　① Great Pacific Garbage Patch

Goal 14

プラスチックごみの悪影響

日本語を参考に、カッコの中の英語を正しい順に並べ替えて文を完成させてください。

By 2050, there (fish / plastic / more / will / than / be) in the ocean.
2050年までに、海には魚よりもプラスチックが多くなるでしょう。

　世界では年間、少なくとも800万トンのプラスチックごみが海に流れ込んでいると言われています。その量は東京スカイツリー222基分になります。これほどの量のプラスチックが毎年流れ込むと、海はどうなるでしょうか。エレン・マッカーサー財団と世界経済フォーラム（WEF）の共同報告書によると、2050年には少なくとも9億3,700万トンのプラスチックごみと8億9,500万トンの魚が海にいる状態になるということで、海中のすべての魚の重量よりもプラスチックの重量ほうが大きくなると予測されています。また、プラスチックの原料は石油なので、プラスチックの製造には大量の化石燃料を消費し、製造工程で二酸化炭素を排出します。2050年には、プラスチックが世界の石油消費量の20パーセントを、カーボンバジェット（温室効果ガスの累計排出量）の15パーセントを占めると予想されています。世界のプラスチック生産量の増加の主な要因は、包装や梱包に使う袋や容器の需要にあります。食料品の容器やペットボトル、ビニール袋、発泡スチロールや気泡緩衝材などが、プラスチックの生産量全体の42パーセントを占めています。そして、そのほとんどが使い捨てなので、これらの海への流出を防ぐには、いかに私たちの生活で脱プラスチックを実行できるかが鍵になるでしょう。

　It is said that at least 8 million tons of plastic waste is washed into the oceans each year worldwide. This amount is equivalent to 222 Tokyo Skytrees. What will happen to the oceans if this much plastic continues to flow into them every year? According to a joint report by the Ellen MacArthur Foundation and the World Economic Forum (WEF), by 2050 there will be at least 937 million tons of plastic waste and 895 million tons of fish in the ocean, so the weight of plastic will be greater than the weight of all fish. In addition, since the raw material for plastics is petroleum, the production of plastics consumes large amounts of fossil fuels and emits carbon dioxide during the manufacturing process. In 2050, plastics will account for 20 percent of global petroleum consumption and 15 percent of the global carbon budget. The growth in global plastic production is primarily driven by demand for bags and containers used for packaging and wrapping. Food containers, plastic bottles, plastic bags, Styrofoam and bubble cushioning materials account for 42 percent of total plastic production. And since most of them are disposable, the key to preventing these from entering the ocean will be how we can implement de-plasticization in our lives.

Answer   By 2050, there (will be more plastic than fish) in the ocean.

Goal 14

「海の豊かさを守ろう」

——そのためにあなたは何ができると思いますか？

What can you do to help "life below water"?

　豊かな海と共存するために、私たちが生活の中でできることはたくさんあります。水産物の乱獲を防いで海の環境を守るために、MSC「海のエコラベル」がついた商品を選んで購入してみましょう。スーパーなどへ行ってエコラベルがついた商品を探したり、サイズの小さな水産物が売られていたら、乱獲が原因ではないのかと考えてみたりしてください。小さなことですが、意識して観察することはとても大切です。

　また、海洋汚染については、プラスチックを含むごみを減らす努力をするといいでしょう。エコバッグやマイボトルを持ち歩いたり、簡易包装の商品を選んだり、リユースやリサイクルを積極的に行ったりしてみましょう。家庭からの排水がそのまま海へ流れ出ることを考えて、皿やフライパンを洗うときには油をそのまま流さずに一度キッチンペーパーなどで拭き取ったり、界面活性剤が含まれる食器洗剤や洗濯洗剤、シャンプーやリンスなどを見直して、人にも環境にもやさしい製品を選んだりするのもいいでしょう。さらに、町や観光地でのごみ拾い活動に参加するのもいいでしょう。実際に行動することで、どのくらいのごみが捨てられているのか、どんなごみがあるのかなどを知ることができるので、環境への意識が深まります。

There are many things we can do in our daily lives to coexist with the abundant oceans. To prevent overfishing of marine products and protect the marine environment, try to select and purchase products with the "MSC Ecolabel." Go to supermarkets and look for products with eco-labels, and if you see small-sized fishery products being sold, consider whether overfishing is the cause. It is a small thing, but it is very important to be aware of and observe.

Regarding marine pollution, you should also make an effort to reduce the amount of garbage that contains plastic. Try carrying eco-bags or your own bottle, choose products with simple packaging and actively reuse and recycle. Considering that household wastewater flows directly into the ocean, it is also a good idea to wipe up oil with paper towels when washing dishes and pans instead of pouring it directly into the sink, and to review dishwashing detergents, laundry detergents, shampoos and conditioners that contain surfactants, and to choose products that are friendly to both people and the environment. In addition, it is a good idea to participate in trash pickup activities in towns and tourist areas. By actually taking action, you can learn how much trash is being thrown away and what kind of trash there is, which will deepen your awareness of the environment.

Goal 14

Goal 15
陸の豊かさも守ろう
Life on Land

陸域生態系の保護、回復、持続可能な利用の推進、持続可能な森林の経営、砂漠化への対応、ならびに土地の劣化の阻止・回復と生物多様性の損失を阻止する。

Protect, restore and promote sustainable use of terrestrial ecosystems, sustainably manage forests, combat desertification, and halt and reverse land degradation and halt biodiversity loss.

　世界には美しい海、森、山、川といった自然があり、自然界に棲む生き物は生態系を保ちながら生きてきました。しかし、人間による産業や文明の発達で自然環境が破壊され、生き物たちの生息地が奪われたり、絶滅の危機に瀕している生き物もいます。現在4万84種の野生生物が絶滅危惧種と指定され、この20年で4倍近く増加しています。野生生物だけでなく植物も育たなくなれば私たちの食料も不足することになるでしょう。

　地球温暖化や森林伐採によってあと100年もすれば地球上の森林は消えると予想されています。自然の中に暮らす動植物を守り、バランスの取れた自然環境を保ちながら、私たちが暮らしていくためには何ができるのかを考えてみましょう。

参照：国際自然保護連合（IUCN）2022
国連食糧農業機関（FAO）

生物多様性

「生物多様性」を英語で何と言いますか？

① biomechanical
② bioactive
③ biodiversity

　生物多様性とは、地球上に生きるさまざまな動植物と自然が関わり合いながら生命を育んでいる状態のことです。1995年5月に策定された「生物多様性条約」では、生態系の多様性、種の多様性、遺伝子の多様性の3つがあるとされています。生態系の多様性は、海・川・森・山などの生物が暮らす環境の多様性のこと、種の多様性は人間・動物・植物・細菌・微生物などすべての生物の多様性のこと、遺伝子の多様性は同じ種でも遺伝子の違いによって外観や生態が異なるような遺伝子レベルの多様性のことです。

　これら3つのレベルの多様性は、バランスを保ちながら共存していましたが、人間の経済・産業の発達で環境汚染や森林伐採、地球温暖化などが起こり、そのバランスが崩れてきていることが問題となっています。

Biodiversity refers to the state in which nature nurtures life through interactions between the various plants and animals living on the earth. The Convention on Biological Diversity, formulated in May 1995, identifies three types of biodiversity: ecosystem diversity, species diversity and genetic diversity. Ecosystem diversity refers to the diversity of environments in which organisms live, such as oceans, rivers, forests and mountains; species diversity refers to the diversity of all organisms, including humans, animals, plants, bacteria and microorganisms; and genetic diversity refers to diversity at the genetic level, where the same species may differ in appearance and ecology depending on its genetic makeup.

These three levels of diversity used to coexist in balance, but the problem is that things are becoming increasingly unstable due to environmental pollution, deforestation, global warming and other factors caused by human economic and industrial development.

bio- は「生、生物、生物学の」、diversity は「多様性、さまざまな種類」という意味です。bio- がつく言葉は biology（生物学）、biography（伝記）、biotechnology（バイオテクノロジー）、antibiotic（抗生物質）などいろいろあります。

Answer　③ biodiversity

Goal 15

樹木の伐採に関する用語

次の単語とその意味を線で結んでください。

① deforestation　　　　　・　　　　　・　土地の劣化

② desertification　　　　　・　　　　　・　植生

③ vegetation　　　　　　・　　　　　・　森林破壊

④ ecological devastation　・　　　　　・　砂漠化

⑤ land degradation　　　　・　　　　　・　環境破壊

　世界の人口の25パーセントにあたる16億の人たちが木材や燃料を調達したり、食料や飼料を採取したりするために森林を必要としています。一方で、樹木の伐採によって気候変動や砂漠化、土地の劣化、作物の不育などさまざまな問題が引き起こされています。

　「砂漠化」とは、森林の減少によって、もともと緑が多かった土地の4分の1で、植物などが育ちにくくなることです。乾燥して人が住める環境にない「砂漠」とは状況が異なります。

　「植生」とは、地球の陸地のあらゆる場所に生育している植物すべてのことです。大きくは、森林、草原、荒原の3つに分かれます。

　「土地の劣化」は、森林伐採や農地の使いすぎ（過耕作）、あるいは家畜が多すぎて牧草が食べ尽くされ、地面が踏み固められてしまうこと（過放牧）などが原因で、土地が荒れると、植物や樹木が育たなくなってしまいます。

　Twenty-five percent of the world's population, or 1.6 billion people, need forests for timber, fuel and the extraction of food and fodder. On the other hand, deforestation causes a variety of problems, including climate change, desertification, land degradation and crop failure.

　"Desertification" refers to the fact that deforestation has made it difficult for plants and other vegetation to grow on one-fourth of the land that was originally green. The situation differs from that of "deserts," which are arid and uninhabitable.

"Vegetation" refers to all the plants that grow everywhere on the earth's land areas. There are three main categories: forests, grasslands and wastelands.

"Land degradation" is caused by deforestation, overuse of farmland (overcultivation) or too many livestock that eat up all the grass and trample the ground (overgrazing), which results in the land becoming too rough for plants and trees to grow.

Point

　「砂漠」は desert、「〜化すること」は -fication です。④は ecological [environmental] destruction と言うこともできます。⑤ degradation の動詞形 degrade は、「分解させる、退化させる」という意味です。

Answer

① deforestation ＝ 森林破壊

② desertification ＝ 砂漠化

③ vegetation ＝ 植生

④ ecological devastation ＝ 環境破壊

⑤ land degradation ＝ 土地の劣化

Goal 15

森林の陸地面積

森林は地球の陸地面積の何パーセントを占めると思いますか？

① 31 パーセント
② 35 パーセント
③ 46 パーセント

　地球の海と陸の割合は7対3で、陸地面積の31パーセントを占めるのが森林です。森林の面積は約41億ヘクタールあり、地表面積全体の約1割にあたります。地域の面積に占める森林面積の割合を見ると、南米が51パーセントと最も高く、次いでヨーロッパ（46パーセント）、北・中米（26パーセント）となります。国別に見ると、1位がフィンランドで73.9パーセント、2位が日本で68.2パーセント、3位がスウェーデンで66.9パーセントとなっていて、日本がいかに森林の占める割合の高い国かがわかります。

　一方で、毎年地球上で1,370万ヘクタールの森林が失われていると推測されています。日本の森林面積が約2,500万ヘクタールなので、そのおよそ半分が毎年消失していることになります。森林には原生林、天然林、人工林の3種類があり、アマゾン川流域の熱帯林には原生林が含まれます。原生林は手付かずの森林で、多種多様な動植物が生育していますが、アマゾン川流域、インドネシア、ロシア、アラスカ、カナダなどにわずかに残る程度です。そんな豊かな生態系を育む森林が、農業用地や産業用地の確保のための伐採や、自然災害などが原因で大幅に減少してきました。特にアマゾン川流域やインドネシアの熱帯雨林は1990年代に大規模に伐採され、ブラジルでは年間290万ヘクタール、インドネシアでは年間190万ヘクタールもの熱帯雨林を消失していました。森林が広範囲にわたって消失すると、温暖化や砂漠化、酸性雨につながる恐れがあるほか、大規模な洪水や土砂崩れ、地滑りなどが頻発しやすくなるといった影響もあり、各国で植林による緑化計画が進められています。

The ratio of the Earth's oceans to land is 7 to 3. Forests cover 31 percent of the land area. Forests cover approximately 4.1 billion hectares, or about 10 percent of the total land surface area. South America has the highest forested area as a percentage of the region's total area (51 percent), followed by Europe (46 percent) and North and Central America (26 percent). By country, Finland is in first place with 73.9 percent, followed by Japan with 68.2 percent and Sweden with 66.9 percent. This shows that Japan is a country with a high percentage of forests.

On the other hand, it is estimated that 13.7 million hectares of forest are lost every year on our planet. Since Japan's forest area is about 25 million hectares, this means that about half of that area is lost every year. There are three types of forests: primary forests, natural forests and planted forests. Primary forests are pristine forests where a wide variety of plants and animals grow, but only a few remain in the Amazon River basin, Indonesia, Russia, Alaska, Canada and other areas. The forests that nurture such rich ecosystems have been drastically reduced due to logging to secure land for agriculture and industry, as well as natural disasters. In particular, tropical rainforests in the Amazon River Basin and Indonesia were extensively logged in the 1990s, resulting in the loss of 2.9 million hectares of rainforest per year in Brazil and 1.9 million hectares per year in Indonesia. Widespread loss of forests can lead to global warming, desertification and acid rain, as well as increasing the frequency of large-scale floods and landslides, and countries are now promoting greening programs involving afforestation.

Answer ① 31 パーセント

Goal 15

生物多様性ホットスポット

下の世界地図は、多様な生態系が存在する地域を示した「生物多様性ホットスポット」(biodiversity hotspots) です。次の各文の内容が正しければ T を、間違っていれば F をつけてください。

① 北欧のバルト海沿岸には、広範囲にわたって生物多様性ホット　　（　　　）
　トスポットがある。
② 東メラネシア諸島は生物多様性ホットスポットである。　　　　　（　　　）
③「アフリカの角」と呼ばれる一帯には生物多様性ホットス　　　　（　　　）
　ポットがある。
④ 南米の東海岸沿いには熱帯アンデスとアトランティック・　　　　（　　　）
　フォレストという 2 つの生物多様性ホットスポットがある。

　2017年時点で世界には36カ所の生物多様性ホットスポットがあります。本来ならば、その土地固有のシダや草木（原生自然）など多様な生態系が数多く存在する地域なのですが、産業革命以降の農地開拓や道路整備、生物の乱獲、鉱山の開

発などによって、それらの自然生態系の70パーセント以上がすでに破壊されてしまいました。生物多様性ホットスポットにある原生自然は、地球の陸地面積の2.4パーセントほどに縮小していますが、そこに生育する固有の動植物は、全世界の植物・両生類・爬虫類・鳥類・哺乳類の30〜60パーセントを占めています。絶滅危惧種も多く生息しているため、迅速な生物多様性の保全・保護が必要です。

As of 2017, there were 36 biodiversity hotspots in the world. Originally, these areas were home to many diverse ecosystems such as ferns, grasses and trees native to the land, but more than 70 percent of these natural ecosystems have already been destroyed by the development of agriculture, road construction, overharvesting of living organisms and mining since the Industrial Revolution. Although the amount of wilderness in biodiversity hotspots has shrunk to about 2.4 percent of the Earth's land area, the endemic plants and animals that grow there account for 30 to 60 percent of the world's plants, amphibians, reptiles, birds and mammals. Many endangered species also inhabit the areas, requiring rapid biodiversity conservation and protection.

Point

①は、北欧のバルト海沿岸（Baltic Basin）ではなく地中海沿岸が広範囲に示されているので、Fです。

②の東メラネシア諸島（East Melanesian Islands）はニューカレドニア（New Caledonia）の北に位置していて、生物多様性ホットスポットに指定されているので、Tです。

③の「アフリカの角」は、アフリカ大陸東端のソマリアとエチオピアの一部を占める尖った形の半島の呼び名です。英語はHorn of Africaと言います。地図上で探してみると生物多様性ホットスポットに指定されているので、Tです。

④は、南米の東海岸沿いに熱帯アンデス（Tropical Andes）とチリ冬季降雨地帯・ヴァルディヴィア森林（Chilean Winter Rainfall Valdivian Forests）があり、アトランティック・フォレスト（Atlantic Forest）は西海岸沿いのブラジル南東部に位置しているため、Fです。

Answer　①F　②T　③T　④F

日本の生物多様性ホットスポット

アジア・太平洋地域には 15 の「生物多様性ホットスポット」(biodiversity hotspots) があり、日本もそのうちの一つです。日本のホットスポットに生息する脊椎動物の種の中で固有種が占める割合はどのくらいだと思いますか?

① 約 4 分の 1
② 約 3 分の 1
③ 約 2 分の 1

生物多様性ホットスポットは生物学者のノーマン・マイヤーズが提唱した概念で、2000年に最初の25の地域が選定された後、日本を含む残りの11地域が指定されました。日本は、南北に変化に富んだ気候帯が広がり、多様な生態系を育んでいます。3,000を超す大小の島々から構成されていること、広大な森林があることなどから、隔離された環境下で、生きた化石として細々と生息する生き物や独自に進化した生き物たちが多く存在する極めて珍しい国です。

日本に生息する脊椎動物の種の4分の1ほどが固有種です。しかし、陸の固有種には絶滅危惧種も相当数含まれます。たとえば、哺乳類ではイリオモテヤマネコやアマミノクロウサギ、爬虫類ではヤクヤモリやミヤコカナヘビ、両生類ではオオサンショウウオやトノサマガエル、鳥類ではコウノトリやライチョウなどです。

日本の生物の多様性を破壊する要因の一つは、都市開発による森林の伐採や干潟の埋め立てです。また、ブラックバスやカミツキガメなどの外来種が持ち込まれ、在来種が食べられたり生息地を奪われたりすることも、大きな影響を及ぼしています。ほかに、人間がペットにしたり剥製にしたり、あるいは毛皮や漢方薬などに使ったりする目的で、珍しい生き物を乱獲・密猟することもあります。日本の固有種を保全・保護することは、地球規模での生物多様性の保全・保護に貢

献することにもなります。人間と、それ以外の生物が共存できる環境作りをしなければなりません。

Biodiversity hotspots are a concept proposed by biologist Norman Myers. After the first 25 areas were selected in 2000, the remaining 11, including Japan, were designated. The country is unique in that it is made up of more than 3,000 islands, large and small, and has vast forests, making it home to many creatures that have evolved in their own unique way and exist in isolation as living fossils.

About a quarter of Japan's vertebrate species are endemic. However, the terrestrial endemic species include a significant number that are endangered. Examples include the Iriomote wildcat and the Amami rabbit among mammals, the Yakushima gecko and the Miyako grass lizard among reptiles, the giant salamander and block-spotted pond frog among amphibians and the stork and grouse among birds.

One of the factors destroying biodiversity in Japan is the logging of forests and reclamation of tidal flats due to urban development. Another major impact is the introduction of non-native species, such as black bass and snapping turtles, which eat or take away habitat from native species. Other examples include the overhunting and poaching of rare creatures by humans for use as pets, taxidermy, fur or herbal medicine. The preservation and protection of Japan's endemic species also contribute to the conservation and protection of biodiversity on a global scale. We must create an environment where humans and other living creatures can coexist.

Answer ① 約 4 分の 1

生態系ピラミッド

次の図は生態系ピラミッド（ecological pyramid）です。各空欄に入る生物の名称を下の語群から2つずつ選んでください。

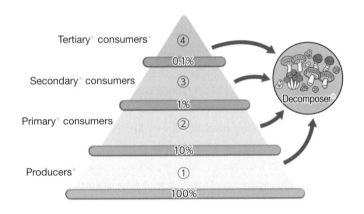

- grasshopper
- pine tree
- lion
- snake
- scorpion
- hawk
- rabbit
- rain tree

* tertiary 第三次の　consumer 消費者　secondary 第二次の　primary 第一次の
producer 生産者　decomposer 分解者

　生態系ピラミッドは、「食う・食われる」の関係を表す食物連鎖を、生物の個体数に応じて積み重ねたものです。微生物や細菌などの分解者は、他の生物の排泄物や死骸を分解して無機物を作り出し、生産者は光合成などを利用して無機物から植物などの有機物を作り出します。そして第一次消費者である草食動物が生産者（植物）を食べ、第二次消費者である肉食動物が草食動物を食べ、最終的に第三次消費者であるより大きな肉食動物が小さな肉食動物を食べます。並行して、それぞれの消費者の排泄物や死骸は土壌に帰って分解生物が分解し、同様のサイクルで循環していきます。

このように、すべての生物は共存関係にあり、この関係をバランスよく保つ状態が生物多様性なのです。逆に言えば、この生態系の中で、1種類の昆虫が減ると、それを食べていた動物も餌がなくなるため次第に数が減少し、全体としてバランスが保てなくなるのです。

The ecological pyramid is a food chain that represents the "eat/eaten" relationship, stacked according to the number of organisms. Decomposers, such as microorganisms and bacteria, break down the excrement and carcasses of other organisms to produce inorganic matter, while producers use photosynthesis and other processes to create organic matter, such as plants, from inorganic matter. Then, herbivores, the primary consumers, eat the producers (plants). Carnivores, the secondary consumers, eat the herbivores, and finally, the tertiary consumers, larger carnivores, eat smaller carnivores. In parallel, the excrement and carcasses of each consumer return to the soil to be decomposed by decomposing organisms, and the cycle continues in a similar manner.

In this way, all living things are in a relationship of coexistence, and biodiversity is the state in which this relationship is maintained in a well-balanced manner. Conversely, if one type of insect in this ecosystem declines, the number of animals that feed on it will also gradually decrease because they will no longer have food, and the overall balance will not be maintained.

Goal 15

Point

　草食動物はherbivoreのほか、planet eaterとも言えます。肉食動物はcarnivoreは、meat-eating animalでも構いません。
　ここにリストアップされた生物の名称は、grasshopper（バッタ）、pine tree（マツ）、lion（ライオン）、snake（ヘビ）、scorpion（サソリ）、hawk（タカ）、rabbit（ウサギ）、rain tree（アメリカネムノキ）です。①には植物が入るので、pine treeとrain treeを選びます。ちなみにrain treeは日立グループによる「この木なんの木」のテレビCMでおなじみの、ハワイ・オアフ島などにある植物の英語名です。②には草食動物のgrasshopperとrabbitが入ります。③には小型肉食動物のsnakeとscorpionが入ります。④には大型肉食動物のlionとhawkが入ります。

Answer　① pine tree ／ rain tree　② grasshopper ／ rabbit
③ snake ／ scorpion　④ lion ／ hawk

世界自然保護基金

WWF（世界自然保護基金）の正式名称は次のどれでしょうか？

① World Wildlife Fund for Nature
② Wildlife World Foundation
③ World-Wide Life Fund for Nature
④ World Natural Life Fund

　世界自然保護基金（WWF）は国際的な環境保全NGOです。1961年にスイスで設立され（現在の本部所在地はアメリカのニューヨーク）、100カ国以上で自然環境・野生生物・森や海を守りながらサスティナブルな社会を作る活動をしています。WWFの最初期の取り組みは、野生生物の取引の監視や密猟の防止など、絶滅の危機に瀕する種の保護活動が中心でした。その当時は世界野生生物基金という名称でしたが、現在でも当時の略称WWFが用いられています。その後、1986年に地球環境分野を視野に入れた活動も行うようになったため、名称がWorld Wildlife Fund for Natureに変わりました。日本では1971年にWWFジャパンが発足し、主に国内の野生生物の保全活動やFSC認証などの国際認証の仕組みを日本に導入する活動、湿地・干潟環境の保全活動、生物多様性の保全活動などに取り組んでいます。

　The World Wide Fund for Nature (WWF) is an international conservation NGO, founded in Switzerland in 1961 (its current headquarters is in New York, USA), that works to create sustainable societies while protecting the natural environment, wildlife, forests and oceans in over 100 countries. In its early years, the WWF's efforts were focused on protecting endangered species by monitoring trade in wildlife and preventing poaching. At that time, the organization was called the World Wildlife Fund, and that name is still used today. Later, in 1986, the name was changed to the World Wildlife Fund for Nature, as it began to take on activities in the global environment field as

338

well. In Japan, WWF Japan was established in 1971, and has been engaged mainly in domestic wildlife conservation activities, activities to introduce international certification schemes such as FSC certification to Japan, wetland and tidal flat environment conservation activities and biodiversity conservation.

Answer   ① World Wildlife Fund for Nature

アマゾン熱帯林

森林は地球上の酸素や二酸化炭素などの循環を調節しています。南米アマゾン川流域の熱帯林は、どのように呼ばれていると思いますか？

① 地球の口
② 地球の目
③ 地球の肺

　地球上で最大の熱帯林であるアマゾン熱帯林は、面積が550万平方キロメートルにも及び、地球上の熱帯林の総面積のおよそ半分を占めています。全長7,000キロのアマゾン川の水が豊かな森を育み、森と川が多種多様な生態系を育んでいます。そんな広大なアマゾン熱帯雨林が「地球の肺」と呼ばれている理由は、地球上の酸素の20パーセントを生産しているからです。酸素や二酸化炭素などの循環を調節する役割を果たしており、人間が放出した二酸化炭素の一部を吸収することで温暖化の促進を防いでくれているというわけです。

　アマゾンでは、7〜10月の乾季の乾燥や落雷が原因で森林火災が起こりやすいうえ、家畜の放牧や耕地開拓のために原生林が人為的に焼かれてしまうことも多いのです。2019年から2020年にかけて、違法な森林伐採などを目的とした、史上最悪の大規模火災が立て続けに起こりました。アマゾンの熱帯林が火災にみまわれると、生態系が基盤から崩れるのはもちろんのこと、そこに住んでいた先住民の生活の基盤や文化、アイデンティティも失われるリスクがあります。そして人為的火災によって大気が汚染されれば、都市に住む人々にも影響が及ぶでしょう。科学雑誌 *Nature* に掲載された研究チームの論文は、このままアマゾンの火災が繰り返され、大気中の二酸化炭素を吸収する役割を持つ森林が奪われると、2035年にはアマゾンの熱帯林が二酸化炭素を発生する側に変わってしまう危険性があると指摘しています。

　The Amazon, the largest tropical forest on earth, covers an area of 5.5 million square kilometers and accounts for about half of the total tropical forest area on the planet. The water from the 7,000-kilometer-long Amazon River nurtures the rich forests, and the forests and rivers nurture a wide variety of ecosystems. The vast Amazon rainforest is called the "lungs of the earth" because it produces 20 percent of the oxygen on the planet. It plays a role in regulating the circulation of oxygen and carbon dioxide, and by absorbing some of the carbon dioxide released by humans, it helps prevent the acceleration of global warming.

The Amazon is prone to forest fires caused by dry weather and lightning strikes during the dry season from July to October, and the native forests are often artificially burned for livestock grazing and arable land cultivation. From 2019 to 2020, the worst large-scale fires in history occurred in quick succession due to illegal deforestation. When tropical Amazonian forests burn, not only are ecosystems destroyed from the ground up, but the livelihoods, cultures and identities of the indigenous peoples who live there are also at risk. And if the air is polluted by human-caused fires, urban dwellers will also be affected. The team's paper, published in *Nature*, points out that if the Amazon fires continue to recur, depriving the forests of their role in absorbing carbon dioxide from the atmosphere, there is a danger that by 2035 the Amazon's tropical forests will be transformed into carbon dioxide generators.

Answer　③ 地球の肺

Goal 15

間伐

間伐（thinning）の意味を説明した英文があります。日本語を参考にしながら、空欄に当てはまる単語を下から選んで書き入れ、文を完成してください。

Thinning: the selective (　①　) of trees to make (　②　) for the (　③　) of the remaining (　④　).
間伐：残っている木々の生育を助けるために木々の密度を調整する間引く伐採のこと。

・room　　・growth　　・removal　　・trees

　間伐は山や林木の生育を守るための伐採方法です。樹木は、互いの間隔が狭いと太陽の光を十分に浴びることができず、育たなくなってしまいます。樹木の足元の土壌まで日光が届かないと土の保水力が下がり、樹木が育たないうえ、土壌付近の植物も育たなくなります。そこで、森を育てるために、特に植林地では間伐による手入れをしなければなりません。適度な間隔になるよう樹木を間引くことで、残った樹木の1本1本に太陽の光が十分行き渡り、成長が促進されます。また、土壌保全能力も高まるため、周囲の植物も生育してバランスのとれた生態系になり、二酸化炭素の吸収量も増加します。日本の森林の40パーセントは人工林ですが、海外からの安価な木材が輸入されていることで国産木材の需要が低下し、森林のほとんどが放置されていることが問題となっています。森林は、管理されないと土壌の水の浸透機能や保水機能が低下するので、台風や集中豪雨による土砂災害が発生しやすくなったり、生物多様性が失われたりする恐れがあります。
　間引かれた木のことを間伐材と言います。間伐材を製品として有効利用する企業があります。そうした企業は、例えば、割り箸やペレットストーブの固形燃料、ペットボトル飲料の代替容器となるカートンの原料として間伐材を利用しています。カートンはプラスチックの削減に、非化石燃料のペレットは地球温暖化対策にも貢献できるでしょう。

Thinning is a logging method to protect the growth of trees in mountains and forests. When trees are spaced too close to one another, they do not get enough sunlight and will not grow. If sunlight does not reach the soil at the foot of the trees, the soil's water retention capacity will decrease, preventing the trees from growing, and this also prevents plants nearby from growing. Therefore, in order to nurture the forest, especially in afforested areas, trees must be thinned for maintenance. By thinning the trees to an appropriate spacing, each remaining tree will receive sufficient sunlight to promote growth. It also increases soil fertility, allowing surrounding plants to grow and creating a balanced ecosystem that absorbs more carbon dioxide. Forty percent of Japan's forests are planted forests, but the demand for domestic timber has declined due to the importation of inexpensive timber from overseas, and most of the forests are neglected. If forests are not managed, the soil's water infiltration and water retention functions will decline, making it more likely that typhoons and torrential rains will cause landslide disasters and biodiversity loss.

Trees that have been thinned are called "thinned wood." Some companies make effective use of it as a product. They use thinned wood, for example, as raw material for disposable chopsticks, solid fuel for pellet stoves and cartons that serve as alternative containers for beverages in plastic bottles. The cartons will help reduce the use of plastics, while the non-fossil fuel pellets will contribute to the fight against global warming.

Answer ① removal ② room ③ growth ④ trees

「陸の豊かさも守ろう」
──そのためにあなたは何ができると思いますか？
What can you do for "life on land"?

　森と野生生物を守る世界の取り組みには、絶滅危惧種の野生動植物の国際的な取引を規制する目的で定められたワシントン条約（CITES）や、生物多様性の保全を目指す生物多様性条約（CBD）などがあります。

　野生生物や絶滅危惧種、森林の減少などは、私たちの日常生活に直接影響がないように感じられるので、ピンとこない人が多いのではないでしょうか。しかし、広い視野の下で考えてみれば、野生生物・森林・人間はつながっていることに気づくはずです。違法伐採・人為的火災による森林の減少、乱獲による野生生物の減少など、人間の都合で自然環境が破壊されれば、生態系のバランスが崩れたり、地球温暖化につながったりして、人間の生活を脅かすことになります。

　外国製の安価な木材は、もしかすると違法伐採によるものかもしれません。違法伐採によらない、認証された森林から生産・調達された木材や、そうした木材を使った製品にはFSC認証ラベルがついているので、製品を選ぶときに確認してみるといいでしょう。また、日本の森林を守り、林業を支えるために、国産の木材を選ぶのもいいでしょう。緑化活動や森林資源の保護活動を行っている団体に寄付をしたり、実際にボランティアとして植林活動に参加したりすることも可能です。

　絶滅危惧種を救うために、団体や企業を通して募金やイベントに参加することもできます。例えば、WWFジャパンのウェブサイトでは、自然や環境関連のイベントやボランティアの情報を入手できます。また、プロ野球チームの埼玉西武ライオンズは、絶滅危惧種であるライオンを救うために「SAVE LIONS（セイブライオンズ）」というプロジェクトを推進しており、ホームランの数に応じた球団からの寄付やファンからの募金を通じた活動を行っています。

　Global efforts to protect forests and wildlife include the Convention on International Trade in Endangered Species of Wild Fauna and Flora (CITES), which was established to regulate international trade in endangered species of wild fauna and flora, and the Convention on Biological Diversity (CBD), which aims to conserve biodiversity.

Wildlife, endangered species and deforestation may not seem to have a direct impact on our daily lives, so many people may not have a clear idea of their significance. However, if you think about it from a broader perspective, you will realize that wildlife, forests and humans are connected. Destruction of the natural environment due to reasons involving humans, such as depletion of forests through illegal logging and human-made fires, and depletion of wildlife due to overfishing, will disrupt the balance of ecosystems and lead to global warming.

Cheap foreign-made lumber may possibly be the result of illegal logging. It is a good idea to check for FSC-certified labels when choosing products, as wood produced and procured from certified forests that are not illegally logged and products made from such wood have FSC-certified labels on them. It is also a good idea to choose domestically produced wood to protect Japan's forests and support the forestry industry. You can also donate to organizations that are engaged in greening activities and forest resource conservation, or actually participate in tree-planting activities as a volunteer.

You can also participate in fundraising and events through organizations and companies to save endangered species. For example, you can visit the WWF Japan's website for information on nature- and environment-related events and volunteer opportunities. The Saitama Seibu Lions, a professional baseball team, is promoting a project called "Save Lions" to save endangered lions through donations from the team based on the number of home runs and donations from fans.

Goal 16

平和と公正をすべての人に
Peace, Justice and Strong Institutions

持続可能な開発のための平和で包摂的な社会を促進し、
すべての人々に司法へのアクセスを提供し、あらゆるレベルにおいて
効果的で説明責任のある包摂的な制度を構築する。

**Promote peaceful and inclusive societies for
sustainable development, provide access to justice for all and
build effective, accountable and inclusive institutions at all levels.**

　紛争や戦争で犠牲になるのはいつも子どもたちです。実に2
億4,600万人が武力紛争の影響を受けている国や地域で暮らし
ています。日本は紛争がなく平和に見えますが、子どもの虐待
やDVなどなかなか表面化されない問題や、投票率の低下、政治
の腐敗などの問題があります。
　平和で公正な世の中にするためには、すべての人々が戦争や
紛争、暴力などによって被害を受けることなく、公正な判断が
下される環境で日常生活を送ることが必要です。非常に難しい
問題ですが、解決するために私たちは何ができるのでしょうか。

参照：UNICEF：UNICEF connect

紛争に関する用語

次の単語とその意味を線で結んでください。

① regional conflict ・　　　　　・ 地域紛争

② ceasefire ・　　　　　・ 内戦

③ terrorism ・　　　　　・ 軍事衝突

④ civil war ・　　　　　・ 停戦

⑤ military confrontation ・　　　　　・ テロ（行為）

Point

　①は特定の地域に限定される紛争のことで、宗教や民族・部族の違い、政治的な問題などによって起こります。長期化することで紛争難民が生まれてしまいます。

　②は戦争や紛争の一時的な停止のことです。cease という動詞には「停止する、やめる」という意味があり、ceasefire で「停戦」です。

　③のテロ行為を行う人（＝テロリスト）は、terrorist と言います。terror も「テロ（行為）」という意味で使われますが、terror には horror と同様に「恐怖」という意味もあります。

　④は、1つの国の中での民族・部族抗争（ethnic violence）や武力紛争（armed conflict）を表します。国家間の紛争は war（戦争）です。

　⑤の military は「軍の、軍事的な」、confrontation は「対立」という意味で、戦争には発展しないまでも軍が介入する紛争を指します。武力紛争（armed conflict）と同じです。military clash と言うこともあります。

Answer

① regional conflict ＝ 地域紛争

② ceasefire ＝ 停戦

③ terrorism ＝ テロ（行為）

④ civil war ＝ 内戦

⑤ military confrontation ＝ 軍事衝突

進行中の紛争・戦争

2022年現在、世界で進行中の紛争・戦争の数はどのくらいだと思いますか？

① 6
② 63
③ 126

　2022年の時点で継続して起こっている武力紛争・戦争は、大規模なものが6つ、小中規模のものを含めると63にもなります。さまざまな紛争・戦争が進行していますが、領土紛争と内戦がほとんどを占めています。また、現在進行中の紛争の80パーセントがアジアとアフリカで起こっています。アメリカの研究機関である外交問題評議会（CFR）では、領土紛争や内戦以外にも、国家間紛争、政情不安、多国籍テロ、宗派間紛争、犯罪的暴力などが紛争として定義されています。

　The number of armed conflicts and wars that are ongoing as of 2022 is as high as 63, including six major and 57 minor and medium-scale ones. While a variety of conflicts and wars are ongoing, territorial disputes and civil wars account for most of them. In addition, 80 percent of all ongoing conflicts take place in Asia and Africa. The Council on Foreign Relations (CFR), an American research organization, defines conflict as not only territorial disputes and civil wars, but also interstate conflict, political instability, transnational terrorism, sectarian conflict and criminal violence.

Goal 16

Answer　② 63

紛争による難民

紛争などが原因で故郷を追われた人は、世界で何人に 1 人いると思いますか？

① 78 人に 1 人
② 148 人に 1 人
③ 218 人に 1 人

　2021年末の時点で紛争や迫害によって移動を強いられた人の数は約8,930万人。難民が2,710万人、国内避難民が5,320万人、庇護希望者が460万人、ベネズエラ国外避難民が440万人という内訳です。そして国連難民高等弁務官事務所（UNHCR）が2022年6月に発表した報告書によると、ウクライナ侵攻などによる人道危機で、その数が1億人を突破しました。世界の78人に1人、全世界人口の1パーセントが難民になっていることになります。中でも特に増加しているのが国内避難民の数で、全体の60パーセントを占めています。国外避難民は国際法の下で保護・支援されますが、国内避難民には国際法が及ばないので、自国の政府に頼るしかありません。しかし、実際には国内避難民を保護する能力やその意志すらない政府が多いのです。国内避難民は、世界の難民の中で最も立場の弱い人たちだと言えるでしょう。

　At the end of 2021, the number of people forced to move due to conflict and persecution was approximately 89.3 million. The breakdown is 27.1 million refugees, 53.2 million internally displaced persons, 4.6 million asylum seekers and 4.4 million Venezuelans internally displaced. And according to a June 2022 report by the United Nations High Commissioner for Refugees (UNHCR), the number has surpassed 100 million due to the humanitarian crisis caused by the invasion of Ukraine and other factors. This means that one out of every 78 people in the world, or 1 percent of the global population, is a refugee. Of these, the number of internally displaced persons is particularly high, accounting for 60 percent of the total. Refugees are protected and assisted under international law, but since international law does not extend to IDPs, they must rely on their own governments. In reality, however, many governments do not have the capacity or even the will to protect IDPs. The IDPs are perhaps the most vulnerable of the world's refugees.

Point

難民は refugee だけでなく、the displaced とも言います。

Answer　① 78 人に 1 人

子ども兵士

世界には、子ども兵士（child soldiers）がどのくらいいると思いますか？

① 約 5 万人
② 約 15 万人
③ 約 30 万人

　国連によると、世界にはおよそ30万人の子ども兵士がいると推定されています。その数は1989年の調査時と変わらぬままだとも言われています。子ども兵士とは、男女を問わず18歳未満の兵隊のことで、戦争や武力紛争で強制動員させられます。子ども兵士のおよそ3分の1以上がアフリカにいます。アジアでは、ミャンマーに数万人います。平均年齢は14歳で、およそ59の武装組織に属して小型の武器を操ったり、後方支援などで戦闘に参加したりしています。男女比は6：4で、少年は主に兵士として戦地で戦い、少女は武装組織の構成員と強制結婚させられたり、自爆テロ要員となったりします。子どもたちは突然誘拐されて兵士にさせられてしまうこともありますが、紛争による貧困に苦しむ子どもたちを武装組織が保護して関係を築いた結果、子どもたち自らが組織に加わるケースもあります。戦闘要員となった子どもたちは、身近な人を殺したり傷つけたりするよう命令されて、人を殺すことへの抵抗感を奪われます。命令に従わない子どもは、体の一部を切り落とされるなどの虐待を受けてしまいます。組織は恐怖心を植えつけて子どもたちをコントロールするほか、アルコールや麻薬を用いて洗脳することもあります。

　UNICEFなどは、武装組織に子ども兵士を解放させたり、子どもの強制動員を廃止したりする取り組みを進め、2017年までに6万5,000人の子どもたちが武装組織から解放されました。しかし、解放された後の精神的ケアや社会的サポートが不十分だと、子どもたちが再び武装組織に戻ってしまうこともあります。長期的に子どもたちを保護・支援することが必要です。

According to the United Nations, there are an estimated 300,000 child soldiers worldwide. This number seems to be unchanged from that of the 1989 survey. Child soldiers are military personnel, both male and female, under the age of 18 who are forcibly mobilized for war or armed conflict. More than one-third of child soldiers are in Africa. In Asia, there are tens of thousands in Myanmar. The average age is 14, and they belong to about 59 armed groups, wielding small arms and participating in combat as logistical support. The male-female ratio is 6:4, with boys fighting mainly as soldiers on the battlefield and girls forced into marriage to members of armed groups or becoming suicide bombers. In some cases, children are suddenly kidnapped and forced to become soldiers, while in other cases, children who are suffering from poverty due to the conflict are protected by armed groups, and as a result of the relationships they build, they join the groups themselves. Children who become combatants are ordered to kill or maim those close to them, depriving them of their resistance to killing. Children who do not follow orders are subjected to abuse, such as having body parts cut off. Organizations control children by instilling fear and may also brainwash them with alcohol and drugs.

UNICEF and other organizations have advanced efforts to force armed groups to release child soldiers and end the forced mobilization of children, and by 2017, 65,000 children had been freed from armed groups. However, inadequate psychological care and social support after release can lead children to return to armed groups. Long-term protection and support for them are needed.

Answer ③ 約30万人

無国籍の問題

下の英文はある集団を説明しています。①〜③のどれを説明していると思いますか？

People who are not considered* to be nationals* by any state* under the operation of its law*

① homeless people
② mindless people
③ stateless people

*consider 認める　national 国民　state（主権をもつ）国家、国　operation of law 法律の運用

　国連難民高等弁務官事務所（UNHCR）によると、世界の無国籍者の数はおよそ430万人だといいます。自国に暮らす無国籍者の数を把握している国は96カ国しかないため、実際の数はさらに多いと推測されます。人種や宗教、民族などの国籍法上の差別があったり、社会情勢・政治情勢の変動で国家が消滅したりすると、無国籍者が生まれます。国籍をもたない人は、政治的・経済的・社会的・文化的に拒否され、学校に通うことも、公的サービスを受けることも、仕事をすることもできません。また、無国籍者の親から生まれる子ども、出生国が適切に出生登録などを行わなければ無国籍になってしまうため、無国籍の負の連鎖が次世代へ続く恐れもあります。実際、無国籍者の子どもの4人に1人が出生登録されずに無国籍のままになっています。

　日本には、2020年の時点で在留資格のある645人が無国籍者として登録されています。日本の国籍法では、日本で生まれ、両親が不明あるいは無国籍者の場合のみ出生と同時に日本国籍が与えられますが、それ以外の人は帰化しなければなりません。

According to the Office of the United Nations High Commissioner for Refugees (UNHCR), there are approximately 4.3 million stateless people in the world. Since only 96 countries know the number of stateless people living in their countries, the actual number is estimated to be even higher. Stateless people are born when there is discrimination under nationality laws based on race, religion or ethnicity, or when a nation ceases to exist due to changes in social or political conditions. People without nationality are politically, economically, socially and culturally rejected and cannot attend school, receive public services or work. In addition, children born to stateless parents, if the country of birth does not properly register births, etc., become stateless, and there is a fear that the negative cycle of statelessness will continue into the next generation. In fact, one in four children of stateless persons remains stateless without birth registration.

In Japan, 645 people with residency status are registered as stateless as of 2020. Under Japan's nationality law, only those born in Japan with unknown or stateless parents are granted Japanese citizenship upon birth; all others must be naturalized.

Point

　英文は「国の法律の運用下で、どの国の国民としても認められていない人々」という意味です。選択肢はそれぞれ、①ホームレスの人々、②思慮のない人々、③無国籍の人々、という意味なので、③が正解です。

Answer　③ stateless people

児童虐待

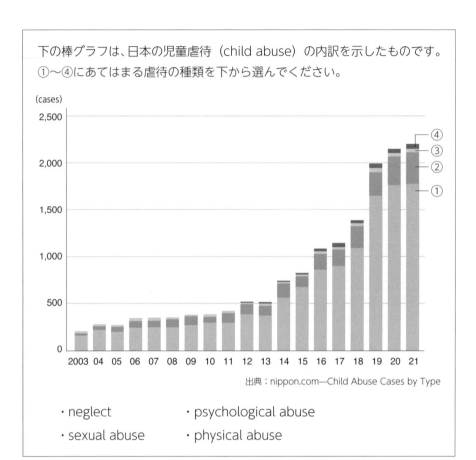

下の棒グラフは、日本の児童虐待（child abuse）の内訳を示したものです。
①〜④にあてはまる虐待の種類を下から選んでください。

(cases)

出典：nippon.com—Child Abuse Cases by Type

・neglect　　　　　・psychological abuse

・sexual abuse　　・physical abuse

　日本の児童虐待の件数は年々増加する一方で、2021年の検挙数は過去最高の
2,174件でした。特に2020〜2021年には新型コロナウイルスの影響で休校やリ
モート授業が増えたり外出が制限されたりしたことから、家庭内で保護者と子ど
もが過ごす時間が長くなり、保護者の育児ストレスや孤立、経済的不安など、さ
まざまな要因で児童虐待が増加しました。
　児童虐待は主に4つの種類に分けられます。①の身体的虐待は、子どもに殴る、
蹴る、叩く、拘束するなどの暴行を加えることです。2021年度の検挙数の中では

これが最多の1,766件で、全体の8割を占めました。

　②性的虐待は、子どもへの性的行為や子どもに性的行為を見せることなどを指します。2021年には339件ありました。

　③ネグレクトは、育児放棄のことです。子どもを世話する責任をもった保護者がその責務を怠ることで、食事を与えなかったり、病気でも放置したり、衛生管理を行わなかったりすると、これに該当します。2021年の検挙件数は21件でした。

　④心理的虐待には、子どもに暴言を吐く、子どもを無視する、きょうだい間で差別する、子どもに家庭内暴力（DV）を見せる、などがあります。2021年の検挙数は48件でした。

The number of cases of child abuse in Japan is increasing every year, with a record 2,174 arrests in 2021. In particular, from 2020 to 2021, the COVID-19 pandemic caused an increase in school closings, remote classes and restrictions on outings, resulting in longer time spent by parents and children in the home, and various factors such as parental stress, isolation and economic insecurity of parents increased the number of child abuse cases.

Child abuse can be divided into four main types. ① Physical abuse refers to assaulting children by hitting, kicking, slapping, restraining, etc. In fiscal year 2021, this was the most common type of abuse, accounting for 1,766 arrests, or 80 percent of all cases.

② Sexual abuse refers to sexual conduct toward a child or exposing a child to sexual acts; there were 339 cases in 2021.

③ Neglect is the abandonment of a child. It includes things not done by a parent or guardian who is responsible for the care of a child, such as not feeding the child, not taking care of children when they are sick or failing to maintain hygiene. Twenty-one arrests were made in 2021.

④ Psychological abuse includes verbally abusing children, neglecting children, discriminating between siblings and letting children witness domestic violence (DV). Forty-eight arrests were made in 2021.

Goal 16

Point

　児童虐待には２つの言い方があり、child abuse 、または child maltreatment でも構いません。

Answer ① physical abuse　② sexual abuse
③ neglect　④ psychological abuse

あきれるような法律

世界には、あきれるような法律（outrageous laws）が存在します。次のうち、本当にあるものはどれだと思いますか？

① フランスの公共プールでは男子のハーフパンツ水着の着用が禁止されている。

② スリランカでは仏像の写真を撮ることが禁止されている。

③ イタリアではイヌの散歩を1日3回以上しないと罰金が課せられる。

④ スイスでは夜10時以降にシャワーを浴びることが禁止されている。

① フランスの公共プールでは、競泳用のようなピッタリ密着した水着を着用しないと入れてもらえません。かつてはトランクス型の下着で泳ぐ人が多く、衛生上良くないという理由と、ハーフパンツの水着のまま街を歩くのが好ましくないという理由から、これが禁止されました。水着に関して言えば、イスラム教徒が着る顔以外の部分をすべて覆った女性用水着「ブルキニ」も、宗教色の強い服装が公の秩序を乱すという理由から、フランスの複数の自治体で着用が禁止されています。

② スリランカでは仏像の写真を撮ることは禁止されていませんが、仏像を背景にした自撮りは禁止されているそうです。自撮りするときに仏像に背を向けることが敬意を欠いた行為とみなされるからです。仏像を指差すことも禁止されています。

③ イタリアのトリノで本当に施行されている法律です。イヌやネコなどのペットが大量に不法投棄された過去があるからだそうで、徒歩で散歩させなければならないなど、決められています。

④ スイスでは、夜中にシャワーを浴びるときの音が騒音公害とみなされるため、主に賃貸住宅などで夜10時以降のシャワーの使用が禁止されています。同様に、トイレの水を流すことも禁止されています。

① Public swimming pools in France will not let you in unless you wear a tight-fitting swimsuit like those used for competitive swimming. In the past, many people used to swim in trunks-type underwear, and this was banned because it was not good for hygiene, and because it was not desirable to walk around town wearing them. As for swimsuits, the burkini, a women's bathing suit worn by Muslims that covers all parts of the body except the face, has also been banned in several French municipalities on the grounds that the strongly religious garments are disruptive to public order.

② In Sri Lanka, taking pictures of Buddha images is not prohibited, but taking selfies with Buddha images in the background is banned. This is because turning your back to the Buddha image when taking a selfie is considered an act of disrespect. Pointing at the Buddha image is also prohibited.

③ This law is actually enforced in Turin, Italy. It is due to a past history of illegal dumping of large numbers of dogs, cats, and other pets, and it has been decided that they must be walked on foot.

④ In Switzerland, the use of showers after 10 p.m. is prohibited in most rented houses because the sound of showering in the middle of the night is considered noise pollution. Similarly, flushing the toilet is also not allowed.

 Answer ① ③ ④

報道されない重要な危機

毎日のようにメディアで取り上げられる紛争がある一方で、報道されない紛争もあります。報道されない重要な問題のことを英語で何と言うと思いますか？

① unknown crisis　　② silent crisis　　③ left-behind crisis

　2022年2月に勃発した、ロシアによるウクライナ侵攻は日本でもメディアを通じて大々的に報道されてきました。もともとウクライナ東部では、侵攻開始の9年前から武力紛争が続いていて、市民らは日常的に銃撃音や警報サイレンの音を聞き、死と隣り合わせの生活をしてきました。その延長上にあるのが今回の大規模な軍事侵攻だったのです。

　メディアからの一方向的な情報だけに頼っていると、あたかもウクライナ侵攻が世界で唯一の紛争と思いがちですが、世界ではほかにも多くの紛争が起きています。マスメディアは最も伝えたいことを連日のように報道して人々の意識を一点に集中させますが、その陰に、報道されないが実はとても重要な人道危機や社会問題が隠れているのです。それを表す言葉がサイレントクライシスです。silentは「静かな、無言の」、crisisは「危機、危機的状況」の意味です。

　70年以上もの間、内戦状態が続くミャンマーでは、軍の治安部隊が市民を大量虐殺したり、80万人以上のロヒンギャ族が無国籍のまま隣国で難民になったりしており、人口の4分の1にあたる人々が支援を必要としています。2010年から10年以上続くシリア内戦では、これまでに1,300万人以上が紛争難民になっています。2015年から続くイエメン内戦では、経済不安から食糧危機が深刻化していて、220万人の子どもたちが飢餓に苦しんでいます。ベネズエラでは政治的混乱と経済危機によって人々が極度の貧困に陥り、600万人以上が国外へ避難しているにもかかわらず、紛争が原因ではないために、適切な支援が行われていません。

　実に世界人口の4分の1が何らかの紛争に巻き込まれています。今この瞬間にも紛争は起きていて、世界中に不安定な情勢の国や地域で暮らしている人がたくさんいるのです。アメリカをはじめ各国のウクライナへの巨額な軍事支援が、ウクライナ侵攻を長引かせる要因になっているという見方もあります。軍事支援ではなく、必要な場所へ必要な人道支援を行うべきでしょう。

私たちは、与えられる情報に偏ることなく、自分でさまざまな角度から情報を求めていく必要があるのではないでしょうか。

The Russian invasion of Ukraine that occurred in February 2022 has been widely reported in Japan through the media. For nine years prior to the invasion, an armed conflict had been raging in eastern Ukraine, and citizens had been living side by side with death, hearing the sounds of gunfire and warning sirens on a daily basis. The current large-scale military invasion is an extension of this situation.

If we rely only on one-sided information from the media, we might tend to think that the invasion is the only conflict in the world, but there are many others happening. The mass media focuses people's attention on a single point by reporting what they most want to tell us every day, but hidden in the shadows are humanitarian crises and social issues that are not reported but are, in fact, very important. This is called a "silent crisis." "Silent" means "*shizukana, mugon no*," and "crisis" means "*kiki, kiki-teki jōkyō.*"

There has been civil war in Myanmar for more than 70 years, with military security forces massacring civilians, more than 800,000 Rohingya refugees in a neighboring country without citizenship and a quarter of the population in need of assistance. The Syrian Civil War, which has been raging since 2010, has so far resulted in more than 13 million refugees from the conflict. The civil war in Yemen, which has been going on since 2015, is worsening the food crisis due to economic insecurity, with 2.2 million children suffering from hunger. In Venezuela, political turmoil and economic crisis have driven people into extreme poverty and forced more than 6 million to flee their homes, yet adequate assistance is not being provided because it is not caused by conflict.

In fact, a quarter of the world's population is involved in some form of conflict. Even at this very moment, there are many people living in unstable situations in countries and regions around the world. Some people believe that the huge amount of military aid to Ukraine from the US and other countries is a factor in prolonging the invasion. Instead of military aid, we should provide humanitarian aid where it is needed.

We need to seek information from various angles on our own, without being biased by the information we are given.

Answer ② silent crisis

Goal 16

腐敗認識指数

次の表は、さまざまな国の政治家と公務員の汚職・腐敗を数値化した「腐敗認識指数2021」（Corruption Perception Index：CPI）の上位と下位を表したものです。各空欄にあてはまる国を下から選んでください。

Rank	Country (CPI)	Rank	Country (CPI)
1	Denmark (88)	180	（ ③ ） (11)
1	（ ① ） (88)	178	Syria (13)
1	New Zealand (88)	178	Somalia (13)
4	Norway (85)	177	（ ④ ） (14)
4	（ ② ） (85)	174	Yemen (16)
4	Sweden (85)	174	（ ⑤ ） (16)

- Venezuela　　・Singapore　　・Finland
- North Korea　　・South Sudan

　「腐敗認識指数」（CPI）は、汚職や賄賂などの腐敗防止に取り組む国際的NGOのトランスペアレンシー・インターナショナルが、専門家やビジネス関係者への調査に基づいて、世界各国の政治家と公務員の腐敗関与に関する認識を数値化・ランキングしたものです。CPIが0に近いほど汚職度が高く、100に近いほど汚職度が低いことになります。2021年度には180の国・地域が調査対象となり、平均CPIは43でした。180のうち131の国・地域は、過去10年間で腐敗防止への取り組みに対する大幅な向上が見られず、3分の2の国がCPIスコアが50以下でした（日本はCPIスコアが73で18位）。

　ランキング上位の国ではデンマーク、フィンランド、ニュージーランドが最もクリーンで、次にノルウェー、シンガポール、スウェーデンが挙がっています。一方、ワースト1は南スーダン、2位がシリア、ソマリア、3位がベネズエラ、4

位がイエメンと北朝鮮と続きます。

　トランスペアレンシー・インターナショナルによると、腐敗と闘うためには人権を守ることが極めて重要で、CPI スコアが高い国ほど人権が守られている傾向にあり、新型コロナウイルスのパンデミックが基本的人権を奪って、権力の抑制と均衡の問題を避ける口実になっていたといいます。

　The Corruption Perceptions Index (CPI), developed by Transparency International, an international NGO working against corruption and bribery, quantifies and ranks perceptions regarding politicians and public officials around the world regarding their involvement in corruption. The closer the CPI is to 0, the higher the level of corruption, and the closer it is to 100, the lower the level of corruption. In 2021, 180 countries/regions were surveyed, and the average CPI was 43. Of the 180 countries/regions, 131 have not made significant improvements in their anti-corruption efforts over the past decade, and two-thirds of the countries had a CPI score of 50 or less. Japan ranked 18th with a CPI score of 73.

　Among the top-ranking countries, Denmark, Finland and New Zealand are the cleanest, followed by Norway, Singapore and Sweden. On the other hand, the worst country is South Sudan, followed by Syria and Somalia in second place, Venezuela in third, and Yemen and North Korea in fourth.

　According to Transparency International, protecting human rights is crucial to fighting corruption, and countries with higher CPI scores tend to have better human rights protection, and the COVID-19 pandemic was an excuse to deprive people of basic human rights and avoid the issue of curbing and balancing power.

Point

　「内部告発者」のことを whistleblower といいます。ホイッスル（警笛）を吹く人から転じて、組織の不正を内部から告発する人を表す言葉になりました。blow a whistle は「笛を吹く」、blow the whistle は「内部告発をする」です。

Answer　① Finland　② Singapore　③ South Sudan
④ Venezuela　⑤ North Korea

Goal 16

社会参加に対する意識

下のグラフは若者の「社会参加に対する6カ国の意識調査」(International Awareness Survey of Social Participation) をまとめたものです。次の①〜④の内容が正しければT、間違っていればFをつけてください。

	I think I am mature	I see myself as a responsible member of society	I believe that I can change my country and society through my actions	I want to do something useful for my country and society
Japan	27.3%	48.4%	26.9%	61.7%
United States	85.7%	77.1%	58.5%	73.0%
United Kingdom	85.9%	79.9%	50.6%	71.2%
China	71.0%	77.1%	70.9%	82.1%
South Korea	46.7%	65.7%	61.5%	75.2%
India	83.7%	82.8y%	78.9%	92.6%

① 日本には「国や社会に役立つことをしたいと思う」人が6割　　（　　　）
以上いる。

② インドでは「はい」と回答した人の割合がすべての項目で70　　（　　　）
パーセント以上である。

③ イギリスには「自分は大人だと思っている」人が6カ国中最　　（　　　）
も多くいる。

④ すべての国で「自分の行動で国や社会を変えられると思う」　　（　　　）
人の割合が50パーセント以上である。

　この意識調査は、日本財団が2022年に6カ国（日本、アメリカ、イギリス、中国、韓国、インド）の17～19歳の男女1,000人を対象に行ったものです。①は、「国や社会に役立つことをしたいと思う」という項目に、日本の若者の61.7パーセントがyesと回答しているので、Tです。6カ国中では最下位ですが、若者の半数以上が社会貢献したいという気持ちを持っているということはすばらしいのではないでしょうか。ただ、その方法がわからないということには、これまでの与えられたことだけをやる「受け身教育」の影響が表れているのかもしれません。

　②は、インドにおいてすべての項目でyesと回答している人の割合が70パーセント以上なので、Tです。

　③は、イギリスの85.9パーセントの若者が「自分は大人だと思っている」と回答しており、この比率は6カ国中で最も高いのでTです。アメリカ（85.7パーセント）やインド（83.7パーセント）も高い割合です。一方、日本は27.3パーセントと最下位で、この数値は「自分の行動で国や社会を変えられると思う」（26.9パーセント）とほぼ同じです。日本に「自分が大人だ」と思っていない若者が多いのは、自信がないからではないでしょうか。自信がないから自分の言動・行動に責任をもてない（もちたくない）、責任をもてないから国や社会を変えられるわけがないと思っているように感じます。何事においてもまずは「自信をもつこと」が重要でしょう。

　④は、日本以外の国では50パーセント以上なのでFです。興味深いのは、民主主義国家のイギリスが50.6パーセントに対して、社会主義国家の中国が70.9パーセントだということです。政治的には社会主義の中国ですが、経済的には資本主義が導入されているので、そう考える人が多いのかもしれません。

Answer　①T　②T　③T　④F

Goal 16

「平和と公正をすべての人に」
──そのためにあなたは何ができると思いますか？

What can you do to bring "peace, justice and strong institutions"?

　世界の紛争問題の解決に貢献する方法としてまず思いつくのは、寄付だと思います。しかし、各国の政治家や公務員の何らかの不正行為について知ってしまうと、寄付を送る場所の選択に慎重にならなければなりません。紛争当事国に送るのではなく、支援をしている第三国へ送るほうが賢明でしょう。

　そのほかに、学校や会社、地域社会など身近なところから関心をもってみることです。自分たちと関わりがあるところでどんな問題が起こっているのか、どんな制度があるのか、どんな解決策があるのかなどを考えてみます。そうすることで、さらに視点を広げれば、国の社会問題や国際問題にも興味がもてるようになるでしょう。今やインターネットで世界各国のさまざまな情報を得ることができます。新聞やテレビの情報だけに頼るのではなく、自分から積極的に調べて情報を集めてみると、これまで見えていなかったものが見えてくるはずです。

　The first thing that comes to mind as a way to contribute to solving the world's conflict problems is donations. However, having learned about the corruption of politicians and public officials in various countries, we must be careful in choosing where to send our donations. It would be wiser to send them to a third country that is providing assistance, rather than to a country involved in the conflict.

　In addition, we should start by taking an interest in places close to us, such as schools, companies and local communities. Think about what kind of problems are happening in the places you are involved with, what kind of systems are in place, what kind of solutions are available, etc. This will further broaden your perspective. By doing so, we can become interested in national social issues and international issues. Nowadays, you can obtain a variety of information about countries around the world via the internet. If you actively research and gather information on your own, rather than relying solely on newspapers and TV, you will be able to see things that you have not been able to see before.

Goal 17

パートナーシップで目標を達成しよう
Partnership for the Goals

持続可能な開発のための実施手段を強化し、
グローバル・パートナーシップを活性化する。

**Strengthen the means of implementation and revitalize
the global partnership for sustainable development.**

　SDGs目標の達成には地球と私たちの未来のために解決すべき複雑で難しい問題がたくさんあります。それはひとつの国では到底解決できることではありません。各国が資金や技術を出し合って解決していくのが理想です。しかし、経済面・技術面に乏しい途上国はどうでしょうか。2030年のSDGs達成には途上国だけで年間約284兆円のお金が必要だといわれています。お金の問題だけでなく、途上国では技術や教育の遅れもあります。逆にいえば、途上国の発展なくしてSDGsは達成されないということです。国を超えたパートナーシップを強化するとともに、私たちも身近なところからパートナーシップについて学び、国際援助の必要性について考えてみましょう。

参照：UNCTAD: World Investment Report 2014

支援組織に関する用語

次の単語とその意味を線で結んでください。

① cooperation　　　・　　　　　・　　非営利組織

② NGO　　　　　　・　　　　　・　　協力

③ development　　 ・　　　　　・　　非政府組織

④ NPO　　　　　　・　　　　　・　　援助

⑤ assistance　　　 ・　　　　　・　　発展

Point

　①のcooperationは、広い意味での「協力、協調、連携」を言う場合に用いられます。同じような意味の語にcollaborationがあります。collaborationは、一つの目的達成のために複数の人々や組織が一丸となることです。coordinationも似たような意味の語ですが、これには上に立って複数の人々や意見を取りまとめる、調整するというニュアンスがあります。

　②のNGOはnon-governmental organizationの略称です。外務省は、「貧困、飢餓、環境など、世界的な問題に対して取り組む市民団体」をNGOと定めています。

　④のNPOはnon-profit organizationの略称です。営利を目的としない市民団体のことで、利益があってもそれを団体の活動目的達成のための費用にあてています。日本では、海外の問題に取り組む団体をNGO、国内の問題に対して活動する団体をNPOと呼ぶ傾向があります。

　⑤のassistanceは、「支援、補助」という意味をもつsupportと同様に、「金銭的・財政的に支える」ことを表して使われます。aidにも同じ意味がありますが、こちらは命を助けるような深刻な「援助」を指して用いられます。helpも「援助、支援、助け」という意味ですが、ややカジュアルな響きがあります。

Answer　　① cooperation = 協力　② NGO = 非政府組織
③ development = 発展　④ NPO = 非営利組織
⑤ assistance = 援助

政府開発援助

「政府開発援助」をアルファベット3文字で何と言いますか？

① ODA
② AED
③ DNA

　「政府開発援助」は略してODAと言います。ODAは主に途上国への、開発を目的とする政府・政府関係機関による国際協力活動のための経済的・技術的援助のことです。一般的に経済協力には、公的資金（OF）、民間資金（PF）、非営利団体による贈与金（Grants by NPO）の3つがあり、公的資金の中に政府開発援助（ODA）とその他の公的資金（OOF）があります。政府や政府関係機関は途上国のさまざまな発展のために途上国や国際機関に対して資金や技術を提供し、開発協力します。

　ODAの日本での例には、農業技術をタンザニアの技術者へ指導することで稲作技術を向上させたり、バングラデシュの川に全長5キロの橋を架ける費用を貸し付けたり、全世界でのポリオ撲滅のためのワクチンや機材を提供したり、などがあります。

　"Official Development Assistance" is abbreviated as ODA. ODA is economic and technical assistance for international cooperation activities by governments and government-affiliated organizations for the purpose of development, mainly to developing countries. In general, there are three types of economic cooperation: Official Funds (OF), Private Funds (PF), and grants by Non-Profit Organizations (NPOs). Within Official Funds, there is Official Development Assistance (ODA) and Other Official Flows (OOF). Governments and government-related organizations cooperate by providing funds and technology to developing countries and international organizations for various projects in developing countries.

　Examples of ODA in Japan include improving rice farming techniques

Goal 17

371

by teaching agricultural technology to Tanzanian technicians, lending money to build a 5-kilometer-long bridge over a river in Bangladesh and providing vaccines and equipment for polio eradication worldwide.

Answer ① ODA

政府開発援助

政府開発援助（ODA）は大きく2種類の援助に分けられます。下の図を参考にして、それぞれの援助の名称を日本語で答えてください。

援助国を日本として説明すると、日本が発展途上国と資金や技術を提供する約束を交わし、その結果、2国間で直接実施される援助のことを二国間援助と言います。援助には、無償資金協力、技術協力、有償資金協力の3種類があります。

多国間援助は、日本とほかの複数の先進国が、UNICEFなどの国際機関に資金を提供して、国際機関が複数の途上国に状況に応じて援助活動を行うものです。多国間援助では国際機関が援助活動を行うので、各国の政治情勢の影響を受けにくく安定した長期的な援助ができたり、難民問題や環境問題など世界規模の問題に取り組めたり、小さな国にも援助が行き渡ったりするなどのメリットがあります。

A **donor country** like Japan often makes a promise to provide funds and technology to a developing country, and aid that is implemented directly between the two countries as a result is called **bilateral aid**. There are three types of aid: grant aid, technical cooperation and paid aid.

In **multilateral aid**, Japan and other developed countries provide funds to international organizations, such as UNICEF, which in turn provide aid to developing countries according to their circumstances. Multilateral aid has the

Goal 17

advantages of being less susceptible to the political situation in each country, allowing for stable, long-term aid, addressing global issues, such as refugees and environmental problems, and allowing the distribution of aid to even the smallest countries.

Point

二国間援助は、bilateral assistance または aidを使って、bilateral aid も通じます。bilateral の bi- は「two = 2」を意味する接頭辞で、lateral（側面の）につけることで「2つの側面の」という意味になります。

多国間援助も同様に multilateral assistance または multilateral aid と言えます。multi- は「many = 多い」を意味するので、multilateral で「多国間の」という意味になります。

Answer ① 二国間援助　② 多国間援助

三角協力

下の図は先進国と途上国との多様なパートナーシップの関係を表した「三角協力」(triangle cooperation) の流れです。①と②に当てはまる協力の名称を下の語群から選んでください。

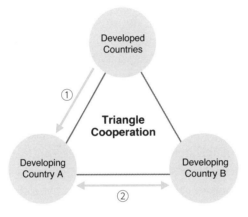

The Flow of Triangle Cooperation

· north-south cooperation　　· south-east cooperation

· south-south cooperation　　· north-west cooperation

· east-west cooperation

途上国間の協力に先進国が参加する協力関係のことを「三角協力」と言います。一般的に、先進国は北半球に多く、途上国は南半球に集中していることから、先進国と途上国の経済的格差問題は南北格差（問題）と呼ばれています。この格差をなくすために、先進国から途上国へ資金や技術、能力開発のノウハウなどの支援を提供することを、①の南北協力と呼びます。

一方、途上国間で、開発が進んだ分野の技術などをもつ国が、開発が進んでい

ない国にそのノウハウなどを支援することを、②の南南協力と言います。途上国同士が技術面や経済面で協力し合うことで、国としての自立や持続的な発展、途上国同士のパートナーシップの強化と活性化などにつながると考えられています。しかし、南南協力のデメリットは、どちらも途上国であるため、資金不足だということです。そこで先進国が途上国に資金や能力の不足を補うことで途上国同士の協力関係を維持させることができます。

Cases in which developed countries participate in cooperation among developing countries are called "triangular cooperation." Generally, developed countries are located in the northern hemisphere, while developing countries are concentrated in the southern hemisphere; thus the problem of economic disparity between developed and developing countries is called the "North-South divide." In order to eliminate this disparity, the provision of assistance from developed countries to developing countries in the form of funds, technology and capacity-building know-how is referred to as North-South cooperation in ① above.

On the other hand, South-South cooperation ② is when a developing country that possesses technology in a field provides that know-how to another developing country. It is believed that cooperation among developing countries in terms of technology and economics will lead to national self-reliance, sustainable development and the strengthening and revitalization of partnerships among developing nations. However, the disadvantage of South-South cooperation is lack of funds, since both are developing nations. Therefore, developed countries can make up for the lack of funds and capacity in developing countries to maintain the cooperative relationship between developing countries.

> **Point**
>
> 三角協力は、triangle cooperation の他に、trilateral cooperation とも言えます。

Answer ① north-south cooperation
② south-south cooperation

日本の国際協力団体

次のうち日本の国際協力関連団体はどれだと思いますか？

① NORAD
② UNDP
③ JICA
④ USAID

　JICA（独立行政法人 国際協力機構）はJapan International Cooperation Agencyの略で「ジャイカ」と呼びます。外務省の管轄で、政府開発援助（ODA）を実施する機関の一つでもあります。自然環境を守りながら、誰もが平等に安心して健康に暮らせる経済・社会を目指し、国内外のパートナーと協力してさまざまな取り組みを行っています。一般によく知られている協力活動は、技術協力プロジェクトです。途上国へ技術協力の専門家を派遣したり、海外協力隊などの海外ボランティアを派遣したり、途上国の技術者や研究者を研修員として受け入れて、知識や技術の研修を行ったりしています。現在、国内の拠点は15カ所、海外の拠点は96カ所で、これまでに5万人以上が海外ボランティア活動に参加しています。

　JICA stands for Japan International Cooperation Agency. Under the jurisdiction of the Ministry of Foreign Affairs, it is also one of the agencies that implement Official Development Assistance (ODA). It works with partners in Japan and abroad to implement a variety of initiatives aimed at creating an economy and society in which everyone can live equally, safely and healthily while protecting the natural environment. The most commonly known cooperative activities are technical cooperation projects. It dispatches technical cooperation experts to developing countries, dispatches overseas volunteers such as Japan Overseas Cooperation Volunteers, and accepts engineers and researchers from developing countries as trainees to provide them with knowledge and technology training. Currently, there are 15 offices

Goal 17

in Japan and 96 offices overseas, and more than 50,000 participated in overseas volunteer activities to date.

Point

その他の略称は海外にある国際協力機関のもので、①の NORAD はノルウェー開発協力庁（Norwegian Agency for Development Cooperation）の略、②の UNDP は国連開発計画（United Nations Development Programme）の略、④の USAID はアメリカ国際開発庁（United States Agency for International Development）の略です。

Answer ③ JICA

民間企業の取り組み

民間企業が長期的な成長のために重視する取り組みの対象として、環境（environment）、社会（social）、企業統治（governance）の3つの分野があります。それぞれの取り組み例として適切なものを線で結んでください。

① Environment
環境

ⓐ
・Customer service performance
・Employee sexual harassment prevention

② Social
社会

ⓑ
・Transparency of shareholder communications
・Diversity of the board and management team

③ Governance
企業統治

ⓒ
・Renewable energy usage
・Recycling and disposal practices

*prevention 防止　　transparency 透明性　　shareholder 株主　　board 役員会
disposal 廃棄　　practices 慣行

　環境、社会、企業統治は、民間企業が長期的に成長するために重要とされている分野で、それぞれの頭文字をとってESGと呼ばれています。ESGは2006年に国連が投資家や金融機関の投資判断の基準を変えるために提唱した言葉で、投資家のお金を動かすことで企業の財政改革を促し、環境問題や社会問題を解決しようとする試みでした。近年では、投資家がESGを考慮して投資するESG投資や、ESGに積極的に取り組む経営スタイルを取り入れる企業が増えています。

　環境への具体的な取り組みとして企業が配慮していることに、再生エネルギーの使用やリサイクル・廃棄物の管理、温室効果ガス排出量削減などが挙げられます。

Goal 17

社会への配慮としては、従業員のカスタマーサービスに関する対応、従業員へのセクハラ防止、商品の安全性向上などの取り組みがあります。

企業統治またはガバナンスとは、企業が健全に経営していくために企業自身が管理体制を整えることです。取り組みの例としては、株主との間での情報の透明性の確保、役員と経営陣の多様性の確保、取締役とCEO（最高経営責任者）の分離などが挙げられます。

The environment, society and corporate governance are areas that are considered important for the long-term growth of private companies, and are collectively referred to as ESG (Environment, Social and Governance). It is a term proposed by the United Nations in 2006 to change the criteria for investment decisions by investors and financial institutions. Shifting where investors put their money encourages corporate financial reforms and solves environmental and social problems. In recent years, an increasing number of companies have embraced ESG investing, in which investors take ESG considerations into account and management styles actively address ESG issues.

Specific environmental considerations that companies are taking into account include the use of renewable energy, recycling and waste management, and reduction of greenhouse gas emissions.

Social considerations include initiatives such as responding to problems with customer service, preventing sexual harassment of employees and improving product safety.

Corporate governance is the management system that a company has put in place to ensure that it operates in a sound manner. Examples of initiatives include ensuring transparency of information with shareholders, ensuring diversity among board members and management, and separating directors from the CEO (chief executive officer).

Answer ▶ ① = ⓒ ② = ⓐ ③ = ⓑ

エシカル消費

個人が実践できるパートナーシップに、エシカル消費 (ethical consumption) があります。エシカル消費の行動として正しいものはどれだと思いますか？

① 伝統工芸品を購入する。
② 再生可能エネルギーを扱っている電力会社を選ぶ。
③ 地元の生産品を買ったり、地元で買い物をしたりする。
④ 自然災害などで被災した地域の生産品を購入する。

エシカルとは「倫理的、道徳的な」という意味で、人・社会・地域・環境に配慮した消費行動のことを「エシカル消費」と言います。自分のことだけでなく、自分以外の人・社会・環境を包括的に考えて商品やサービスを購入することで、地域の活性化や雇用の促進、社会的課題の解決に取り組む生産者や企業の支援ができます。

①と③は地域にやさしいエシカル消費の例です。伝統工芸品を購入すれば人手不足の産業に雇用が生まれ、伝統技術や技法の継承に貢献することができるでしょう。また、地元の生産品を買ったり、地元で買い物したりすることは、地産地消や地域の活性化につながります。

②は環境に配慮した例です。太陽光や風力、バイオマスなど再生可能エネルギーを積極的に扱う電力会社があり、そのような会社のサービスに乗り換えることもエシカル消費になります。

④は人や社会に配慮した例です。災害で被災した地域では生産者や事業者が思うように活動できないため、生産物などを積極的に購入することで生産や事業を支援することができます。

消費するだけでなく、マイボトルやエコバッグを持ち歩くこと、食べ残しを無くすこと、3Rを意識することなど、日常の暮らしの中でできるちょっとした行動も、環境や社会問題などへの貢献につながります。

Goal 17

Ethical consumption refers to consumption behavior that is considerate of people, society, the community and the environment. By purchasing products and services that are inclusive of people, society and the environment, and not just yourself, you can help revitalize local communities, promote employment, and support producers and companies that are working to solve social issues.

① and ③ are examples of community-friendly ethical consumption. Buying traditional crafts will create employment and make sure traditional skills and techniques are passed on. In addition, buying locally produced goods and shopping locally will lead to local production for local consumption and local revitalization.

② is an environmentally friendly example. There are electric power companies that actively deal with renewable energy sources, such as solar, wind and biomass, and switching to the services of such companies is also an example of ethical consumption.

④ is an example of consideration for people and society. In areas affected by disasters, producers and businesses are not able to operate as efficiently as they would like, so by actively purchasing their products and other goods, we can support their production and business.

In addition to consumption, small actions that we can take in our daily lives, such as carrying our own bottles and eco-bags, eliminating leftover food and being aware of the 3Rs, can also contribute to solving environmental and social issues.

Answer ▶ すべて正しい。

SDGs レポート

国連では毎年、「持続可能な開発レポート」（Sustainable Development Report）で、国別の SDGs の目標達成度に関する順位を発表しています。2022 年のレポートで、日本は何位だったと思いますか？

① 19 位　　② 38 位　　③ 62 位　　④ 120 位

　「持続可能な開発レポート」では、各 Goal の達成状況を 4 段階——目標達成、課題あり、重要課題あり、主要課題ありで評価しています。日本は Goal 4（質の高い教育をみんなに）、Goal 9（産業と技術革新の基盤をつくろう）、Goal 16（平和と公正をすべての人に）の 3 つでは目標を達成しましたが、「課題がある」が 5 つ、「重要な課題がある」が 3 つ、「深刻な課題がある」が 6 つでした。

　The Sustainable Development Report evaluates the achievement of each Goal on four levels: SDG Achieved, Challenges Remain, Significant Challenges Remain, and Major Challenges Remain. Japan achieved Goal 4 (Quality Education), Goal 9 (Industry and Innovation and Infrastructure), and Goal 16 (Peace, Justice and Strong Institutions), but five of the goals were rated as "Challenges Remain," three as "Significant Challenges Remain," and six as "Major Challenges Remain."

Point

　国連に加盟している 193 の国・地域の中で、日本は 19 位でした。20 位以内に入ってはいるものの、2017 年の 11 位をピークに順位が下降しているため、地道な取り組みが必要です。順位を見ると、1 位がフィンランド、2 位がデンマーク、3 位がスウェーデン、4 位がノルウェー、5 位がオーストリア、6 位がドイツ、7 位がフランス、8 位がスイスで、圧倒的にヨーロッパ諸国が積極的に取り組んでいることがわかります。

Answer　　① 19 位

グローバルに行動する人々

地球のさまざまな問題解決のために、地球的視点で行動する人々が必要とされています。その人々のことを英語で何と呼びますか？

① global citizen
② worldwide citizen
③ global communities
④ people of the world

人間は誰もが特定のコミュニティーに属していて、その中で行動していますが、広い視野に立って見てみると、世界の国々は良い意味でも悪い意味でも影響し合って成り立っています。それは経済・政治・社会・文化・技術・環境など、さまざまな分野にわたる世界の問題となって現れます。そうした地球規模の問題を知り、地球規模で考え、その場で行動を起こす人々が今、必要とされています。年齢・性別・人種・民族・宗教・経済的状況・障がいの有無などにかかわらず、「地球の一員」として責任をもち、変化を起こせる人材です。そのような人々のことを英語でglobal citizensと呼び、日本語では「地球市民」や「グローバル市民」と呼んでいます。

各国で、地球市民育成のための「地球市民教育／グローバルシチズンシップ教育」（GCED）が推進され、平和で持続可能な世界に向けて、国際的な諸問題に向き合い解決するために必要な知識やスキル、価値感、態度を育成しようとしています。日本にも、グローバルシチズンシップ教育を行う中学校や、地球市民学科を設けた大学などがあります。

地球市民になるということは、正義と闘うヒーローのような存在になるのではなく、地球の一員としてのつながりを意識し、自分以外の人・社会・文化などに理解を示す人になるということです。環境問題を考えるときによく聞かれる「地球規模で考えて、地域で行動しよう」という言葉があります。これは見方を変えると、地域で行動したことが、地球全体の問題に変化をもたらすことができると

いうこと。まさに地球市民的思考・行動と言えます。

Every human being belongs to and acts within a particular community, but when viewed from a broader perspective, the nations of the world are made up of influences that affect one another in both positive and negative ways. This is manifested in global issues in various fields such as economics, politics, society, culture, technology and the environment. People who are aware of these global issues, think on a global scale, and take action on the spot are needed today. These are people who can take responsibility as "citizens of the earth" and make a difference regardless of age, gender, race, ethnicity, religion, economic status, disability, etc. Such people are called "global citizens" in English and "*chikyū shimin*" or "*gurōbaru shimin*" in Japanese.

Global Citizenship Education (GCED) is being promoted in many countries to foster global citizenship and to develop the knowledge, skills, values and attitudes necessary to face and solve international problems for a peaceful and sustainable world. In Japan, there are junior high schools that offer global citizenship education and universities that have established global citizenship departments.

Becoming a global citizen does not mean becoming a hero who fights for justice, but rather becoming a person who is aware of their connections as a citizen of the earth and shows understanding of people, societies and cultures other than their own. "Think globally, act locally" is a phrase often heard when considering environmental issues. From a different perspective, this means that actions taken locally can bring about changes to the problems of the entire planet. It is truly a global citizen's way of thinking and acting.

Answer ① global citizen

Goal 17

「パートナーシップで目標を達成しよう」
──そのためにあなたは何ができると思いますか？
What can you do to support the "partnership for the goals"?

　Goal 17「パートナーシップで目標を達成しよう」は、SDGsのすべてのGoal達成に向けてパートナーシップをもって取り組もう、ということです。そのためにはまず自分を取り巻く環境で何が起きているか知り、考え、できることがあればやってみることです。そこから、関連する事柄についてさらに調べ、視野を広げてみてください。自分の地域以外、国やアジアという大きなくくり、さらには世界全体にまで目を向けて、自分に何ができるのかを考えてみます。募金やエシカル消費のように、1人で行動を起こせることもありますが、もちろん難しいこともあるでしょう。国内外で企業や団体がSDGsに関連したイベントやキャンペーンを行っているので、そういったものに参加すれば自分もパートナーシップを築いていることになります。小さなことから行動に移せば、それが未来につながることを信じて、地道に取り組んでいきましょう。

　Goal 17 "Partnership for the goals" is about working together to achieve all the SDGs. To do this, first learn about what is happening in your environment. Then, think about it and do what you can to help. From there, do further research on related issues and broaden your horizons. Think about what you can do outside of your own community, in the larger context of your country, in Asia and even the world as a whole. There are things you can do alone, such as fundraising and ethical consumption, but, of course, there are also things that may be difficult. Companies and organizations in Japan and abroad are holding events and campaigns related to the SDGs, and if you participate in such things, you are building your own partnership. Believe that if you take action, starting with small steps, it will lead to the future, so let's work steadily to make a difference.

SDGs Glossary

用語集

1.5 degrees	1.5度（目標）	The Paris Agreement calls for countries to achieve the goal of limiting global warming to a rise of **1.5 degrees** by 2030.
4Rs	4R（Refuse, Reduce, Reuse, Recycle）	Environmentalists are encouraging people worldwide to practice the **4Rs** all the time.
absolute poverty	絶対的貧困	Many people in India live in **absolute poverty**, with no access to healthcare, potable water or proper education.
relative poverty	相対的貧困	Many Americans are experiencing **relative poverty**, as they people rely on monthly government assistance.
abuse	酷使	The manager's treatment of his employees was a clear example of **abuse** of power.
accountable	責任がある	We are **accountable** for all the environmental problems we are experiencing now.
active learning	アクティブラーニング（能動的学習）	The education ministry is encouraging teachers to use **active learning**, in which students discuss and solve problems related to current environmental issues.
adaptable	順応できる、適応できる	Birds can survive in many different habitats because they are **adaptable** in their eating habits.
advanced country	先進国	**Advanced countries** in Asia, like Japan, Singapore and Korea, implement strict waste disposal guidelines.
affordable	（困難などが）十分に乗り越えられる	Electric cars are good for our environment but are only **affordable** to some.
afforestation	植林、造林	NGOs encourage schools, companies and the local community to join their **afforestation** activities.
aged	高齢	Homes for the **aged** are common in countries with a significant aging population.
aging	高齢化	The **aging** population of Japan significantly affects its workforce.
super-aged	超高齢化	Many people in Japan and Germany are **super-aged**.
aging of society	高齢化社会	The **aging of society** is a problem that countries like Japan, China and Korea are all experiencing.
AI, Artificial Intelligence	AI（人工知能）	**AI**, or **artificial intelligence**, is gaining popularity due to Japan's lack of labor force.
alternative	［名］代替策、代替手段 ［形］別の、代わりの	**Alternative** energy sources are being developed to lessen the use of fossil fuels.

assistance	援助、支援	About one-fifth of the population receives **assistance** from the government.
basic living standards	基本的生活水準	None of the buildings in the slum area are even close to meeting **basic living standards**.
biocapacity	バイオキャパシティ(ある地域、あるいは地球全体の生態系が供給できる資源の量)	Some experts worry that humans have already exceeded the world's **biocapacity**.
biodegradable non-biodegradable	生(物)分解性の、生(物)分解可能な 生(物)分解不可能な、微生物で分解できない	Japan and Korea have implemented the separation of **biodegradable** and **non-biodegradable** wastes.
biodiversity	生物多様性	The local and international sectors aim to tackle **biodiversity** loss.
biomass	バイオマス(代替エネルギーの供給源としての植物)	Experts are also looking into **biomass** fuels as another energy source.
black water	(工場やトイレなどから出る)汚水、下水	Water from the toilet, kitchen sink and dishwashers is categorized as **black water**.
grey water	(風呂や洗濯機など)家庭から出る排水	Some building owners in Tokyo installed individual recycling or rainwater harvesting systems using **grey water**.
bluewashing	ブルーウォッシング(企業や政府組織が広報・経済的利益目的で見せかけの人道支援を行うこと)	Many people see the company's new ads about its environmental commitment as an example of **bluewashing**.
greenwashing	グリーンウォッシング(環境配慮をしているように見せかけること)	The company's donations to the environmental group are generally seen as **greenwashing**.
bribery	[名] 贈収賄	It is hoped that the new law will reduce **bribery** by increasing the penalties for who are caught doing it.
bribe	[動] 賄賂を贈る	Some corrupt government officials receive **bribes** from companies committing environmental offenses.
BYO	Bring Your Own (各自持参のこと)の略	Companies and cafes have **BYO** (bring your own) programs to encourage people to help lessen plastic waste.
carbon credit	炭素クレジット、カーボンクレジット(先進国間で温暖化ガスの排出削減量を排出枠として売買可能にする仕組み)	It is hoped that the use of **carbon credits** will help to reduce carbon dioxide emissions.
carbon offset	炭素オフセット、カーボンオフセット(炭素クレジットを購入することで排出量の一部を相殺すること)	Using advanced technology to turn carbon dioxide emissions into a usable product is an example of a **carbon offset**.

carbon footprint	カーボンフットプリント（商品やサービスのライフサイクル全体で排出される温室効果ガスの排出量をCO_2排出量に換算して表示したもの）	To reduce one's **carbon footprint**, driving electric cars is a great choice.
carbon-neutral [neutrality]	[形] カーボンニュートラルな（二酸化炭素の排出量と吸収量のバランスが取れている）	Some company buildings are attempting to become **carbon-neutral** by using solar-powered energy sources.
	[名] カーボンニュートラル（二酸化炭素プラスマイナスゼロ）	
child mortality	小児死亡率	Globally infectious diseases are still some countries' most significant causes of **child mortality**.
circular economy	循環型経済、サーキュラー・エコノミー（廃棄物の発生を最小限にする経済システム）	E-cycling of used and dead batteries is an example of the **circular economy**.
class	階級	The social **class** division in society gives unequal access to rights and resources to those at the top.
climate action	気候変動に関する行動	Environmental activists have been staging protests to encourage people to support **climate action**.
climate change adaptation	気候変動適応策	**Climate change adaptation** already exists as people are now more conscious and are using sustainable and renewable resources.
climate change disasters	気候変動災害	**Climate change disasters** are more common these days.
climate change mitigation	気候変動緩和策	**Climate change mitigation** is essential for the prevention of severe catastrophes.
cohousing	共同住宅地（住居者が共同で施設を所有・管理する助け合いの住み方）	There are many seniors in the **cohousing** community.
combat	（犯罪、問題など）〜と闘う、（〜の治療に）効く	Various medications have been used and tested to help **combat** COVID-19.
Compact City	コンパクトシティ（生活に必要な諸機能が近接した効率的で持続可能な都市・都市政策）	Hong Kong is an ultra-**compact city** with a mix of trees and an urban area co-existing simultaneously.
composting	[名] 堆肥化	To get started with **composting**, you first need a container to keep the waste in.
compostable	[形] 堆肥化可能な	**Compostable** waste, such as food leftovers from the kitchen, is good for your garden.

conflicts	紛争	**Conflicts** among countries worldwide have become more visible because of the internet.
conserve	[動] 保護する、保全する	Driving more slowly helps to **conserve** fuel.
conservation	[名] 保護、保存	NGOs joined forces with the government to improve **conservation** efforts.
consumption	[名] 消費(量[高])	The **consumption** of fossil fuels is contributing to climate change.
consume	[動] 消費する	We must **consume** less so future generations can enjoy a clean environment.
coral bleaching	サンゴ白化現象	Climate change is the primary cause of **coral bleaching**.
corruption	汚職、不正行為	**Corruption** is still a problem experienced by all countries.
cruelty-free	動物実験を行っていない	**Cruelty-free** products are emerging to discourage people from buying products from companies that use live animals for product testing.
cultural heritage	文化遺産	Italy is known for its long **cultural heritage**.
decent work	ディーセントワーク(働きがいのある人間らしい仕事)	The NGO is working to increase opportunities for **decent work** among people with disabilities.
deforestation	森林伐採	**Deforestation** is the primary cause of the country's flash floods and landslides.
reforestation	森林再生	NGOs and the government are working hand-in-hand to promote **reforestation** and solve this problem.
development	発達、開発	The **development** of advanced technology is a significant contributor to pollution.
digital divide	デジタル格差	One way to overcome the **digital divide** is to provide computers to poor families.
dignity	尊厳	The former president was known to be a man of **dignity** with a strong persona.
disadvantage	[名] 不利な状況、デメリット	One **disadvantage** of electric cars is that they do not have as much range as gasoline-powered vehicles.
disadvantaged	[形] (経済的・社会的に)恵まれない	The city has launched a program to help people who are **disadvantaged** due to lack of education.
discrimination	差別	Racial **discrimination** gave birth to the Black Lives Matter (BLM) movement.
digital transformation	デジタル変革、デジタル・トランスフォーメーション(最新のデジタル技術の活用によってさまざまな分野でより便利に進化すること)	Improvements in internet technology have led to **digital transformation** in many industries.

e-cycling	電子機器のリサイクル	These days, many batteries undergo **e-cycling** after they die.
ecolabel	エコラベル	**Ecolabels** are placed on products to inform consumers about how eco-friendly they are.
ecological [nature] restoration	生態[自然]回復	**Ecological restoration** programs encourage farmers to use natural fertilizers to control pests.
ecological devastation	生態[環境]破壊	The global economy is impacted by the **ecological devastation** caused by global warming.
ecosystems	生態系、エコシステム	Marine **ecosystems** must be preserved and restored.
education gap	教育格差	The **education gap** between men and women in the country has declined by 20 percent over the past two decades.
elimination	排除	It is hoped that improvements in electric vehicles will someday lead to the **elimination** of gasoline-powered ones.
emissions	(複数形で)排出物	Electric cars produce fewer carbon **emissions** than ordinary vehicles do.
empowerment	[名](女性の)社会的地位の向上	The government believes very strongly in the **empowerment** of women.
empower	[動]権限・力を与える	It is hoped that the new policies will help to **empower** women and minorities.
endangered [threatened] species	絶滅危惧種	Many animals that are common today may become **endangered species** if the effects of global warming are not reduced.
energy conservation	省エネ、エネルギー保存	We can create new appliances that promote **energy conservation** using new technology.
energy efficient	エネルギー効率の良い	More and more companies are creating **energy-efficient** products to help lessen the effects of global warming.
equitable	[形]公平な、公正な	**Equitable** wages will never become a reality as long as divisions between social classes exist.
equity	[名]公平、公正	The NGO hopes that its work will help women to achieve **equity** in the workplace.
ESG	environmental, social and governanceの略、企業が長期的成長のために重視する3つの観点、環境・社会・ガバナンス(企業統治)のこと	**ESG** (environmental, social and governance) investing is often criticized because it confuses investors.
ethical consumption	エシカル消費(人・社会・地域・環境などに配慮した消費行動)	Environmentalists are encouraging everyone to practice **ethical consumption**.

ethical fashion	エシカル・ファッション（環境などに配慮した衣料品）	Many brands are introducing **ethical fashion** collections to support the fight against climate change.
fast fashion	ファスト・ファッション（安価で大量生産された衣料品）	**Fast fashion** companies are often accused of contributing to environmental problems.
slow fashion	スローファッション（人権・環境・動物などに配慮した衣料品）	The use of linen and organic cotton by **slow fashion** retailers helps to keep the environmental impact low.
exploitation	搾取、利己的な目的での利用	Child **exploitation** is still common worldwide.
extreme weather	異常気象	**Extreme weather**, such as massive typhoons and hurricanes, is becoming more common.
fair trade	フェアトレード、公正貿易	More and more supermarkets are selling **fair trade** products.
food mileage	フードマイレージ（食料の輸送距離のこと。食料の輸送に伴い排出される二酸化炭素が地球環境に与える負荷を輸入重量×輸送距離で表したもの）	Some groups are advocating that **food mileage,** or food mile labels, should be placed on products so consumers will know how far their food has traveled and how it affects the environment.
food shortage	食糧不足	There are still many places in Africa experiencing water and **food shortages**.
free trade	自由貿易	The government is confident that the new **free trade** agreement will help to reduce prices for consumers.
gender bias	性差別、性差に関する偏見	Unfortunately, there is still a lot of **gender bias** that makes it difficult for women to get promoted.
gender disparities	ジェンダー格差、男女間格差	Companies need to do more to reduce **gender disparities** in worker pay.
gender diversity	ジェンダーの多様性	To promote **gender diversity**, the firm has been trying to recruit more female employees.
gender equality	男女平等、ジェンダーの平等	Many women feel that the government needs to do more to promote **gender equality**.
gender inequality	男女不平等、女性蔑視	**Gender inequality** is still common in many societies due to old-fashioned attitudes.
gender pay gap	性別による賃金格差	The **gender pay gap** was a common problem in the past, as women were thought to be less talented than men.
geothermal	地熱の	**Geothermal** energy sources are an option experts are looking into because the amount of heat generated by the Earth's core is unlimited.

global partnership	グローバル・パートナーシップ、世界的提携	**Global partnership** is needed because we all know that "no man is an island."
global warming	地球温暖化	**Global warming** exists because humans use and abuse the earth's natural resources.
governance	企業統治、ガバナンス	The company has promised to improve its **governance**, especially in terms of environmental responsibility.
green infrastructure	グリーンインフラ（自然の多機能を活用した生活空間の整備や土地利用の考え方）	Governments are making efforts to create **green infrastructure** within the cities.
habitat	生息地、居住環境	Many marine animals' **habitats** have been damaged by illegal fishing.
hate crime	ヘイトクライム、憎悪犯罪	The number of **hate crimes** against Asians increased during the pandemic.
health care	医療の、健康管理の	The COVID-19 pandemic was a huge strain on **health care** systems around the world.
human rights	人権	People are angry because the government has violated many people's **human rights**.
human trafficking	人身売買	**Human trafficking** is still common in some parts of the world.
hunger	飢え、飢餓	Poverty is one of the many causes of **hunger** worldwide.
hygiene	衛生状態	The lack of water in African countries prevents many from being able to have proper **hygiene**.
ICT, information and communication technology	情報通信技術	**ICT**, or **information and communication technology**, students are growing in number as the demand for jobs in the industry increases.
ICT education	ICT教育（パソコンやタブレット端末、インターネットなどの情報通信技術を用いた教育手法）	Elementary students are now taught **ICT education** because of the advancement of technology.
illicit financial flows	違法な資金の流れ	Africa loses billions of dollars every year due to **illicit financial flows**.
illiterate	読み書きのできない	The number of **illiterate** people is still growing, even with the development of technology.
inadequate	不十分な、不適切な	**Inadequate** education on contraception is a major cause of teenage pregnancy.
inclusion	[名] インクルージョン、多様性の受け入れ	The company has updated its **inclusion** policy to make sure that all employees are treated fairly.
inclusive	[形] 包括的な、包摂的な	Many shops or restaurants have gender-**inclusive** restrooms to cater to all sexes.

Industrial Revolution	産業革命	Steam power and the **Industrial Revolution** transformed the world in the late 1700s.
infected	感染した	People **infected** with COVID-19 are kept isolated until their test comes out negative.
infectious	感染性の、感染力のある	COVID-19 is the most recent **infectious** disease and has killed millions worldwide.
infrastructure	社会の基盤、インフラ	A huge amount of **infrastructure** was damaged because of the recent torrential rains and heavy floods.
internally displaced people	国内(避)難民	Many **internally displaced people** have been spread throughout the country.
international aid	国際協力	**International aid** came to the country after it was hit with one of the strongest typhoons in its history.
labor	労働	Because of the aging society in some countries, their **labor** force is decreasing.
forced labor	強制労働	Human trafficking poses a lot of risks which include **forced labor**.
leading cause	主要因	The **leading cause** of death worldwide is cardiovascular disease.
LGBTQ+	性的マイノリティ(レズビアンLesbian, ゲイGay, バイセクシャルBisexual, トランスジェンダー Transgender, クイアQueer[クエスチョニングQuestioning], その他plus)	Although their rights were once ignored, members of the **LGBTQ+** community have worked hard to gain acceptance in society.
life expectancy	平均寿命	The **life expectancy** of a man in North America is between 75 and 78 years of age, depending on where he lives.
lifelong learning	生涯学習	To encourage **lifelong learning**, the university has added more classes that are open to members of the local community.
literacy	識字能力	English **literacy** is essential in this generation since the world is becoming globalized.
low-carbon	低炭素	Electric vehicles are an important part of the **low-carbon** economy.
malnourished	栄養失調の、栄養不良の	One in every three children under the age of five is **malnourished**.
marine ecology	海洋生態学	One of the most important principles of **marine ecology** is to maintain a balance in the ecosystem.
microorganism	微生物	Due to the COVID-19 pandemic, people are now more cautious about any **microorganisms** that they might come into contact with.

Glossary

microfibers microplastics	マイクロファイバー マイクロプラスチック	**Microfibers** are one example of **microplastics** that, once inhaled by humans, may affect one's health.
migrants	移住者、移民	A large number of **migrants** have arrived in the city to look for work.
migration	移住	International **migration** is popular nowadays as people search for better opportunities abroad.
modern slavery	現代版奴隷（強制労働や人身売買など）	Forcing people to work in factories for little or no pay is a form of **modern slavery**.
nature-based solutions	自然を基盤とした解決策	Land conservation and restoration are some examples of **nature-based solutions** to decrease the effects of climate change.
non-binary	ノンバイナリー（男性・女性の二者択一におさまらないジェンダー）	People who are **non-binary** often prefer not to be referred to as "he" or "she."
non-discrimination	差別のないこと、無差別	The right to equal treatment before the law is the main principle of equality and **non-discrimination**.
numeracy	基本的な計算能力	**Numeracy** is essential nowadays due to the growing advancement of technology.
nutritious	栄養のある、栄養になる	Fruits and vegetables are far more **nutritious** when they are fresh.
ocean acidification	海洋の酸性化	**Ocean acidification** is an increasing problem for the marine ecosystem.
organ harvesting	臓器摘出	**Organ harvesting** is another example of why human trafficking is happening.
organic	オーガニックな、有機栽培の	**Organic** produce is often much more expensive than foods that are grown using chemicals.
overfishing	魚の乱獲	**Overfishing** is a common practice when people want to consume more protein every day.
overpopulation	人口増加、過密居住	One of the world's biggest problems is still **overpopulation**, as the data show there are already over eight billion people on Earth.
pandemic	パンデミック、（病気が）世界的に流行している	The COVID-19 **pandemic** shut down borders worldwide in March 2020.
permaculture	持続型農業、パーマカルチャー	The **permaculture** movement is still criticized even though it has introduced energy-saving green initiatives.
polluted	［形］汚染された	**Polluted** sea waters have caused various marine organisms to die.
pollution	［名］汚染	In some cities, people have to stay indoors because the air **pollution** is so bad.

preserve	[動] 保護する、保存する	Many environmentalists aim to **preserve** nature for future generations.
preservation	[名] 保護、保存	The **preservation** of this forest will greatly benefit the plants and animals that live there.
prevent	～を防ぐ、抑える	All employees were asked to wear masks in order to **prevent** the spread of COVID-19.
productive	[形] 生産性の高い、多くの利益を生む	Thanks to computers, most workers have become far more **productive** in recent years.
productivity	[名] 生産性、生産力	Working from home during the pandemic caused a rise in employees' **productivity**.
QOL, Quality of Life	生活の質	To enjoy a good **quality of life**, you need health and friends as well as money.
race	人種	**Race** should never be considered when making decisions about hiring.
redistribution of wealth	富の再分配	Taxes are one of the most effective ways of achieving **redistribution of wealth**.
refugees	難民	Ukrainian **refugees** have escaped to various countries for safety.
renewable energy	再生可能エネルギー	Consumers these days are looking for more **renewable energy** sources.
resilience	[名] 回復力、復元力	The local people showed great **resilience** after the terrible earthquake.
resilient	[形] 回復力のある、立ち直りが早い	Some species are more **resilient** than others when their habitats are polluted.
resources	資源、天然資源	Experts are looking for more-efficient energy **resources** to help fight global warming.
responsible	責任のある	Everyone is **responsible** for protecting the environment.
rural depopulation	農村部の人口減少	Some areas in Japan are experiencing **rural depopulation** because most people have moved to bigger cities and the birth rate has dropped.
sanitation	公衆衛生	Proper handwashing and **sanitation** would greatly help us lessen the spread of COVID-19.
save	節約する、蓄える	The government is trying to **save** the environment by encouraging people to recycle.
sexual exploitation	性的搾取	**Sexual exploitation** is an ongoing problem that affects women in many countries.

sharing economy	シェアリングエコノミー、共有型経済(個人が保有する物やスキル、サービスをインターネットを介して提供したり共有したりする仕組み)	The popularity of Airbnb is a great example of the benefits of the **sharing economy**.
social protection	社会的保護	Pensions are an important **social protection** that help people to have financial security after they retire.
social good	社会を良くするもの、ソーシャルグッドなもの	Healthcare, literacy and sustainable energy are all examples of **social goods**.
starve	飢えに苦しむ	Many people were left to **starve** for days when help could not reach the remote area.
struggle	もがく、悪戦苦闘する	Many refugees **struggle** with their new country's language.
suffer from	〜に苦しむ、〜に見舞われる	Patients who **suffered from** COVID-19 shared what it felt like to have the sickness.
sufficient	十分な、足りる	Recent research suggests that the COVID-19 vaccine has the potential to provide **sufficient** protection after a single dose.
sustainable industrialization	持続可能な産業化	Renewable energy sources, like solar, will help us to achieve **sustainable industrialization**.
sustainable	[形] 持続可能な、環境を壊さず利用可能な	Solar energy is one of the few familiar **sustainable** energy sources.
sustainability	[名] 持続可能性	Environmental **sustainability** practices aim to reduce emissions, prevent pollution and waste, and reduce energy use.
technological innovation	技術革新	**Technological innovation** is essential for building a strong economy.
throw away	捨てる、浪費する	Many people **throw away** their used masks carelessly.
transparency	透明性	**Transparency** is what people always want from government officials.
triangular cooperation	三角協力(開発支援において途上国間の協力に先進国が加わること)	The Philippines is the beneficiary of **triangular cooperation** in agriculture with Indonesia and Japan.
universal health coverage	国民保険制度	Having **universal health coverage** lessens people's problems when they become ill.
urban congestion	都市過密化	With more people living in urban areas, **urban congestion** is becoming more serious.
urbanization	都市化(現象)	**Urbanization** has led to shrinking population in the countryside.
vegan	ヴィーガン、完全菜食主義者	**Vegan** diets are becoming more popular these days.

virtual water	バーチャルウォーター、仮想水（輸入した食料を自国で生産した場合に必要となる水の量を推定した数値）	Many items we use every day, such as jeans, smartphones, electricity and even hamburgers, use **virtual water**.
vocational training	職業教育	The Department of Education emphasizes the importance of giving **vocational training** to students.
vulnerable	弱い、脆弱な	Young children and senior citizens are the most **vulnerable** to COVID-19.
water security	水の安全保障（その国の水資源量や水資源管理において安全な状態を保障すること）	Climate change and drastic environmental changes are causing panic over **water security**.
water shortage	水不足	**Water shortages** are a common problem following typhoons and other disasters.
water stress	水ストレス（水に関して日常生活に不便を感じる状態）	**Water stress** is a significant effect of global warming.
well-being	福祉、満足できる生活状態	Parents are responsible for their children's **well-being**.
work-life balance	仕事と生活の調和、ワーク・ライフ・バランス	Having a good **work-life balance** lessens a person's stress.
zero-waste	廃棄物ゼロの、ごみゼロの	Many governments are looking for ways to become **zero-waste** countries.

Glossary

E-CATとは…
英語が話せるようになるための
テストです。インターネット
ベースで、30分であなたの発
話力をチェックします。

www.ecatexam.com

iTEP®とは…
世界各国の企業、政府機関、アメリカの大学
300校以上が、英語能力判定テストとして採用。
オンラインによる90分のテストで文法、リー
ディング、リスニング、ライティング、スピー
キングの5技能をスコア化。iTEP®は、留学、就
職、海外赴任などに必要な、世界に通用する英
語力を総合的に評価する画期的なテストです。

www.itepexamjapan.com

日英対訳
英語で話す SDGs

2023年 2 月 1 日　第 1 刷発行

著　者　　山口晴代

発行者　　浦　　晋亮

発行所　　IBCパブリッシング株式会社
　　　　　〒162-0804 東京都新宿区中里町29番3号 菱秀神楽坂ビル
　　　　　Tel. 03-3513-4511　Fax. 03-3513-4512
　　　　　www.ibcpub.co.jp

印刷所　　株式会社シナノパブリッシングプレス

ISBN978-4-7946-0746-1